OXFORD WORLD'S CLASSICS

GEORGE SAVILE, MARQUESS OF HALIFAX

The Character of a Trimmer and Other Writings

Edited with an Introduction and Notes by
BRIAN R. CLACK AND WILLIAM GIBSON

W0114019

OXFORD
UNIVERSITY PRESS

OXFORD

UNIVERSITY PRESS

Great Clarendon Street, Oxford, OX2 6DP,
United Kingdom

Oxford University Press is a department of the University of Oxford.
It furthers the University's objective of excellence in research, scholarship,
and education by publishing worldwide. Oxford is a registered trade mark of
Oxford University Press in the UK and in certain other countries

Editorial material © Brian R. Clack and William Gibson 2025

The moral rights of the authors have been asserted

Published in the United States of America by Oxford University Press
198 Madison Avenue, New York, NY 10016, United States of America

British Library Cataloguing in Publication Data

Data available

Library of Congress Control Number: 2024943681

ISBN 9780198879527

Printed and bound in the UK by
Clays Ltd, Elcograf S.p.A.

The manufacturer's authorised representative in the EU for product safety is
Oxford University Press España S.A. of El Parque Empresarial San Fernando de Henares,
Avenida de Castilla, 2 – 28830 Madrid (www.oup.es/en or product.safety@oup.com).
OUP España S.A. also acts as importer into Spain of products made by the manufacturer.

OXFORD WORLD'S CLASSICS

THE CHARACTER OF A TRIMMER
AND OTHER WRITINGS

GEORGE SAVILE, 1st Marquess of Halifax, was born in 1633, the eldest son of the wealthy landowner Sir William Savile and Anne Coventry, daughter of Lord Keeper Thomas Coventry. The English Civil War had a dramatic impact on Savile's early life, his father dying from wounds inflicted during the siege of Sheffield Castle in 1644. He received much of his education in Europe, but returned to England in 1652 and was elected as Member of Parliament for Pontefract in the Convention Parliament of 1660. Created Viscount Halifax in 1668, he became a vocal supporter in the House of Lords of King Charles II and his brother James, Duke of York, and rose to the position of Lord Privy Seal in 1682, the year in which he was made Marquess of Halifax. His reservations about Charles II's rule were pushed to their limits when James II ascended to the throne in 1685, and he was dismissed from office, spending the next three years in opposition and writing some of his most important political pamphlets. When William of Orange invaded England in November 1688, Halifax ultimately sided with William. Elected speaker of the Lords in the Convention, he formally offered the crown to William and Mary at their coronation and was appointed Lord Privy Seal in the new administration. His enemies in both the Whig and the Tory parties, ever distrustful of Halifax's shifting, moderating position as a 'Trimmer', forced him to resign in February 1690. He spent the remaining five years of his life in an embittered condition, though one in which he could further add to his literary output. Halifax's writings, published anonymously in his lifetime, range widely across subjects. They came to be admired after his death for their distinctive style and for their insights into both the particularities of late seventeenth-century British life and the more abiding problems of political activity. His major political works, such as *The Character of a Trimmer* and *Rough Draught of a New Model at Sea*, present the case for moderation and are rooted in the experiences of a man who spent his life at the heart of politics. Halifax died on 5 April 1695, as the result of eating an undercooked chicken.

BRIAN R. CLACK is Professor of Philosophy at the University of San Diego. He is the author of two books on the philosophy of Wittgenstein—*Wittgenstein, Frazer and Religion* (1999) and *An Introduction to Wittgenstein's Philosophy of Religion* (1999)—and of *Love, Drugs, Art, Religion: The Pains and Consolations of Existence* (2014), and co-author of *The Philosophy of Religion: A Critical Introduction* (3rd edn., 2019). He has edited Edmund Burke's *Reflections on the Revolution in France* for the Broadview Editions series (2022).

WILLIAM GIBSON is Professor Emeritus at Oxford Brookes University and an associate member of the Faculty of Theology and Religion at the University of Oxford. He has written widely on religion and politics in the period 1660–1800, including *James II and the Trial of the Seven Bishops* (2009) and *Samuel Wesley and the Crisis of Tory Piety, 1685–1720* (2021). He is editor of the *Journal of Religious History, Literature and Culture* and is a fellow of the Society of Antiquaries.

OXFORD WORLD'S CLASSICS

*For over 100 years Oxford World's Classics have brought
readers closer to the world's great literature. Now with over 700
titles—from the 4,000-year-old myths of Mesopotamia to the
twentieth century's greatest novels—the series makes available
lesser-known as well as celebrated writing.*

*The pocket-sized hardbacks of the early years contained
introductions by Virginia Woolf, T. S. Eliot, Graham Greene,
and other literary figures which enriched the experience of reading.
Today the series is recognized for its fine scholarship and
reliability in texts that span world literature, drama and poetry,
religion, philosophy, and politics. Each edition includes perceptive
commentary and essential background information to meet the
changing needs of readers.*

CONTENTS

INTRODUCTION

*A man's industry is kept up by the mistake of thinking most
things of more importance than they are.*

Halifax, *Miscellanys*

HALIFAX is an enigma. For it was no cloistered philosopher or loun-
ging flâneur who wearily proclaimed that 'There are very few things
in the world that can in truth excuse men's being busy about them'
(p. 217), but a man at the very heart of English political life during
one of its most tumultuous periods. He was a statesman in whom
vigorous engagement in political life and high-minded detachment
sat side by side; one who left the very stamp of his character on the
Glorious Revolution of 1688, but could nonetheless write that 'The
first mistake belonging to business [i.e., politics] is the going into it'
(p. 190). To his contemporaries, he was almost inexplicable: a royalist
suspected of republican sympathies; a man of profoundly anti-papist
sentiments but who served under the Catholic King James II ('I could
never understand his politics', James said);[1] and a political intriguer
whose shifting positions made him hard to predict and—for some—
impossible to trust. It is for this protean quality that Halifax is perhaps best known. His neutrality and frequent positional adjustments
between raging political parties earned him the nickname of the
'Trimmer'. Though intended as an insult, Macaulay declared that
Halifax 'assumed it as a title of honour, and vindicated, with great
vivacity, the dignity of the appellation' (Appendix, p. 229).

Halifax's literary achievements add another curious quality to his
life. It was as a statesman and not as a writer that he was known in his
lifetime; his political pamphlets were often circulated anonymously,
and it was only after his death that the extent and character of his
literary work became known. Halifax's works exhibit a lofty view of
things, as though written from an eminence, and range across a wide
variety of subjects. The reader encounters within them an uneasy balance of gentle humanity and caustic, biting observation, born of the

---

[1] *Historic Manuscripts Commission, Report. XI, Pt. V (Earl of Dartmouth MSS)*,
pp. 40–1.

experience of a man who has not merely thought about human life but has seen it and dealt with it in the raw. His major political works have the rare quality of being written, not by a mere theorist, but a practitioner. In this regard, Halifax bears comparison with Bolingbroke and Burke; like them, his writings rest upon an extensive experience of government. This judgement applies also to those pieces of his writing which illuminate that period of British history from the Restoration to the reign of William and Mary, principally his *Character of King Charles II* and the celebrated *Letter to a Dissenter*, one of the pamphlets published as the reign of James II barrelled towards its dramatic conclusion. Much can be learned about Restoration manners and the role of women in late seventeenth-century Britain from the warm and affectionate *Advice to a Daughter*, in which another side of Halifax appears: the loving and solicitous father.

The richness of Halifax's mind, and his quality of detachment, made him capable of drawing more generalizable truths from his observations of events. This is on full display in the remarkable sets of various *Thoughts and Reflections* included here, in which Halifax incisively explores philosophical matters such as ambition, motivation, the passions, the sense of time, and death. He stands here among the other great moral psychologists of the early modern period and has with reason been called 'the English La Rochefoucauld'.[2] His mind was large, but it was also cautious and moderate, 'instinct with the spirit of sweet reasonableness'.[3] Halifax's writings are of perennial value, perhaps most especially to those living in extreme and polarized times; and as Macaulay held, these works 'well deserve to be studied for their literary merit, and fully entitle him to a place among English classics' (Appendix, p. 229).

The span of Halifax's life coincided with some of the most convulsing events in England's history. Within his lifetime there occurred civil war, regicide, the establishment of a commonwealth and a short-lived experiment with republicanism, the restoration of the monarchy, and the accession to the throne of James II, whose Catholic identity and absolutist tendencies led to the revolution of 1688 and the crown passing jointly to James's Dutch son-in-law,

---

[2] H. R. Trevor-Roper, 'The Marquis of Halifax', in *Historical Essays* (London: Macmillan, 1957), 254.

[3] F. J. C. Hearnshaw, *Conservatism in England* (London: Macmillan, 1933), 45.

William of Orange, and his daughter Mary. England in the seventeenth century was, indeed, so unstable and unpredictable that
neighbouring nations could reasonably view it as 'a failed state'.[4]
A full appreciation of Halifax's thought requires an understanding
of both his written works and the dramatic political times in which
he lived and acted.

Halifax's Life and Career

George Savile, 1st Marquess of Halifax, was born in November 1633
at Thornhill Hall in Yorkshire, eldest son of Sir William Savile,
3rd Baronet, a wealthy landowner. Halifax's youth was disrupted by
the Civil War which erupted in 1642, and even for such uncertain
times he was dramatically buffeted by political and military forces
beyond his control. His father was a royalist who took arms with the
King in 1642, and who died from wounds inflicted during the siege of
Sheffield Castle in 1644. As a minor aged 13, Halifax's wardship was
important and lucrative for Lord Wharton who obtained it in 1645.
To avoid Wharton's clutches Halifax was taken abroad to France,
Italy, and the Netherlands, in which countries he received a remark-
ably diverse education. In 1652 he returned to England, marrying
Lady Dorothy Spencer in 1656. In the 1660s Halifax and his wife had
five children, of whom four survived. Dorothy died in 1670, and two
years later, Halifax married Gertrude Pierrepont of Thorsby.

Like many royalists in 1660, Halifax had high hopes for the repair
of his fortunes at the Restoration. But he only briefly held a seat in the
House of Commons and held no significant office other than deputy
lieutenant and colonel of the Yorkshire militia. He was friendly with
James, Duke of York, but even such an elevated influence was insufficient to secure Halifax a peerage, since Charles II's leading minister,
Lord Clarendon, suspected he was an atheist. The origins of this suspicion lie in Halifax's wit and humour regarding religion. This led
some to suspect he did not take it seriously. Though Halifax repeat-
edly denied that he was an atheist, he stated (to Gilbert Burnet) that
'he could not digest iron, as an ostrich did, nor take into his belief
things that burst him' (Appendix, p. 227), and it seems that he was by

[4] Clare Jackson, *Devil-Land: England Under Siege 1588–1688* (London: Allen Lane, 2021), 1.

no means an orthodox member of the Church of England. Halifax's writings were inflected with religious concerns, and he realized that religion was one of the most powerful human motivators. But he viewed institutional religion dispassionately and this was sufficient for Clarendon to condemn him. The fall of Clarendon, precipitated by the naval failure of 1667 in which the Dutch sailed up the River Medway and captured the Royal Navy's flagship, the *Royal Charles*, from Chatham Docks, brought Halifax's allies the Duke of Buckingham and Sir William Coventry to power. Appointed to the Commission on Naval Expenditure, Halifax was created Baron Savile of Eland and Viscount Halifax. To some, it seemed like an advancement for supporting the King's policies on naval expenditure. Others, it may also be noted, felt that Halifax's coveting of titles was at odds with his philosophical contempt for worldly follies. His response, later voiced to Burnet, was that titles were indeed silly 'rattles', but 'since the world were such fools as to value those matters, a man must be a fool for company' (Appendix, p. 228).

From 1667, Halifax became a government supporter and was a vocal royalist in the House of Lords, promoting the interests of both Charles II and his brother James, Duke of York. Gradually he became a trusted courtier, admitted to the Privy Council in 1672. As is evident in the posthumously published *Character of King Charles II*, Halifax had misgivings about the nature of Charles's rule, about the moral deficiencies of his character, and especially about his pro-French policies. News that James had converted to Catholicism concerned Halifax, and he said in the House of Lords that he hoped the King would live forever—suggesting that he feared the succession of a Catholic ruler. He also supported the first Test Act in 1673, a move not calculated to win the King's favour; nor was his confiscation of arms from Catholics in Yorkshire in 1674. Halifax's hopes that, with Coventry, he might be offered a ministerial post were dashed with the King's advancement of the Earl of Danby who accommodated Charles II's pro-French policies. He also proposed a test that would require pledges of non-resistance to the Crown, which seemed to Halifax to smack of royal absolutism. Halifax publicly refused to consider voting for such a measure. In the weeks that followed, Halifax's relations with the Duke of York and Lord Danby collapsed, and in January 1676 he was dismissed from the Privy Council. He did not, however, fall into the trap of switching support to the Shaftesbury and the emerging Whig faction,[5] with whom his relations were similarly strained. In this, Halifax's perennial distaste for factional party politics showed itself.

In opposition, Halifax saw that the Popish Plot, the imaginary claim that there was a conspiracy to kill the King, was an important moment. Together with Shaftesbury, Essex, and Buckingham, Halifax led the investigation into the plot by the House of Lords. While Halifax was not taken in by the plot, and did not believe that people should be condemned by uncorroborated informers, he nevertheless saw it as an opportunity to remove Danby. By the end of 1678, discredited by his handling of the plot and universally unpopular, Danby was dismissed. When it was known that Danby had been pardoned and granted a pension, Halifax in the Lords attacked it as an act of ingratitude by the King to his people. Charles was furious.

In early 1679 the King attempted to draw some of the opposition over to his side by expanding the Privy Council. Essex and Sunderland were appointed to it, and they persuaded the reluctant King to include Halifax. Halifax began to play an important role in the direction of policy, yet it was not without ambivalence. In May 1679 Halifax wrote to his brother in France that politics in England had led him to be 'engaged in an active and angry world' and that though he felt obliged to play a part, he did so 'with grief'.[6] Halifax was pragmatic and sought to satisfy both extremes of politics: he advocated execution of Catholic priests; but at the same time advised the King to dissolve Parliament when the Commons refused to accept limited restrictions on the powers of a Catholic successor to the throne. It was a position that satisfied few, and the King in particular found such 'trimming' unacceptable. Nevertheless, on the dissolution of Parliament in 1679 he was advanced to an earldom.

Despite concerns about the King's duplicity, and an episode of depression, Halifax's role in 1680 can be seen as the high point of his part in government. At the opening of the new Parliament in October 1680 the King pledged himself to protect the Protestant religion and Halifax introduced a bill to penalize Catholics further. But those

---

[5] The Whigs were the loose grouping of politicians who were inclined to resist royal absolutism and preferred parliamentary authority; to be distinguished from the Tories, who were associated with the landed classes and inclined to support the Church and hereditary monarchy.

[6] Letter to Henry Savile, 1 May 1679, in *Savile Correspondence: Letters to and from Henry Savile, Esq.*, ed. W. D. Cooper (London: Camden Society, 1858).

determined to try to exclude James, Duke of York from the throne
brought in a bill to change the succession. It passed the Commons but
was rejected in the Lords, with Halifax opposing it. Halifax's role, as
both a natural moderate and an inspired orator, was seen as central to the
defeat of the Exclusion Bill. He would later hold the King to a promise
of the post of Lord Privy Seal and was in 1682 elevated to a Marquessate.

The revelation of the Rye House Plot in the summer of 1683,
a conspiracy to kill Charles and James and make Charles's illegitimate
son the Duke of Monmouth king, shocked the country. The government took the opportunity to round up and put on trial particularly
troublesome Whigs. Halifax seems to have been doubtful of the guilt
of Lord William Russell and Algernon Sidney and tried to intercede
for them with the King. But the Tory revenge was too strong and both
were executed, with eight others. Halifax was now a moderate in
a government packed with hard-line Tories, but Charles was unwilling
to throw his hand in entirely with them and kept Halifax in office.
Halifax brokered a reconciliation between the King and Monmouth,
which enabled the Duke to return to court despite being implicated in
the Rye House Plot. Nevertheless, Charles did not find Halifax easy to
accommodate; he annoyed the King by reminding him that he was vio-
lating the Triennial Act by not holding elections for a parliament in
1684. He also stubbornly refused to permit the release of those Catholics
who had been imprisoned during the Popish Plot, insisted on denying
Irish army commissions to Catholics, and ensured that the charter for
Massachusetts should include provision for a representative assembly.
All these drew Tory criticisms to Halifax, and an alliance of the Duke of
York, the Duchess of Portsmouth, and Lord Sunderland began to agi-
tate Charles for his dismissal from office, but even on the eve of the
King's collapse, Charles and Halifax seemed on friendly terms.

Before Charles's death, Halifax's *Character of a Trimmer* was circulated in manuscript, and William Sancroft, Archbishop of Canterbury
showed it to the King.[7] This pamphlet was initially printed under the

---

[7] It was much more widely circulated than people at the time realized. D. Wykes and
B. D. Greenslade, ' "The Trimmer's Character": a Further Reply to Halifax', *Huntington
Library Quarterly*, 35/2 (1972), 207. Tracing manuscript copies has become something of
an academic pastime: R. Gathorne-Hardy, 'Halifax's *Character of a Trimmer*: Some
Observations in the Light of the Manuscript from Ickworth', *The Library*, 5th ser., 14/2
(1959), 117–23; Mark N. Brown, 'Sir William Trumbull and the Marquis of Halifax',
British Library Journal, 19/2 (1993), 142–7.

name of Sir William Coventry, Halifax's uncle, and it was only after his death that Halifax was revealed as its author. It captured exactly the problems that Halifax had encountered as a moderate in a government which was veering increasingly to a hard-line royalist position. It argued that the government did best when it followed the rule of law, and that moderation was preferable to sectarian extremism; such a policy was the best security for the King and the people. Halifax applied this moderation to the Church as well, advocating toleration of Protestant Dissent rather than persecution. The context of its composition should briefly be noted.

The meaning that the word 'Trimmer' had acquired by 1684 was largely pejorative. For the Tory propagandists Roger L'Estrange and John Dryden, a Trimmer was an unprincipled political operator whose proclaimed moderation was merely a cloak for ulterior motives, timidity, and fundamentally Whiggish attitudes. Between 1682 and 1687, the pages of L'Estrange's newspaper *The Observator* were festooned with the most colourful and savage denunciations of 'The Trimmer', who had come to replace the Whig as the focus of the Tory's ire. The flexibility of the Trimmer meant that he could be characterized as 'a Hundred Thousand Things; A Trimmer I tell ye, is a man of Latitude, as well in Politiques as in Divinity', but this rather sober assessment—the Trimmer as general latitudinarian—sat alongside more imaginatively worded depictions of this worryingly protean and unscrupulous type of politician: the Trimmer was 'an inexhaustible fountain of varieties of mischiefs', 'an arrant, juggling hocus', and 'a kind of state-otter, neither fish, nor flesh, and yet he smells of both' ('a state hermaphrodite . . . two natures joined' was how another satirist of the period similarly characterized the Trimmer's mutable disposition). For L'Estrange, this type of political monster was even worse than the Whig: at least the Whig (awful though he was) had a discernible and stable set of principles: 'Your downright stark-staring-Whig is much more tolerable in a state, than your temporizing, fleering, and glozing Trimmer.'[8]

---

[8] The quotations in this paragraph are drawn from D. R. Benson, 'Halifax and the Trimmers', *Huntington Library Quarterly*, 27/2 (Feb. 1964), 115–34, and T. C. Faulkner, 'Halifax's "The Character of a Trimmer" and L'Estrange's Attack on Trimmers in "The Observator" ', *Huntington Library Quarterly*, 37/1 (Nov. 1973), 71–81.

It was the vehemence of such insulting words that in part provoked Halifax to write *The Character of a Trimmer*.[9] Clearly alluding to the imagery in *The Observator* and elsewhere, Halifax expressed astonishment as to how such a moderate thing as a Trimmer, properly understood, could be depicted as 'a strange kind of monster, whose deformity is so exposed, that . . . it would be enough to fright children, and make women miscarry at the sight of it' (p. 4). Against such horrors, Halifax returned to the original nautical meaning of the term, seeing in this a desirable image of responsible statesmanship, particularly in a time of political turbulence:

This innocent word 'Trimmer' signifies no more than this, that if men are together in a boat, and one part of the company would weigh it down on one side, another would make it lean as much to the contrary, it happens there is a third opinion, of those who conceive it would do as well, if the boat went even, without endangering the passengers. (p. 4)

Such a conception of steadying political activity had a distinguished pedigree,[10] and even L'Estrange, in a more measured moment, could with fairness have the figure of the Trimmer in *The Observator* declare that the term 'had an allusion to the language of the River. When a vessel does not row even, they'll cry trimm the boat: And so when one side is lower than t'other, 'tis our way to lean to the upper side: and still make the best of things'.[11] The ideal of trimming was so vital for Halifax that it indicated not merely prudent guidance for the pressing problems of his time (specific matters of foreign policy, for example, or the question of religious toleration), but became enlarged into a near-rapturous vision of all good things existing between extremes, encompassing matters ecclesiastical, moral, and divine, and extending even to England's healthy climate ('a Trimmer between

---

[9] We will not here survey the controversies regarding to what extent L'Estrange was targeting Halifax or how closely Halifax was identified with anything like 'a Trimmer party'. For this, see Benson, 'Halifax and the Trimmers'; M. N. Brown, 'Trimmers and Moderates in the Reign of Charles II', *Huntington Library Quarterly*, 37/4 (Aug. 1974), 311–36; and Faulkner, 'Halifax's "The Character of a Trimmer"'.

[10] Plutarch, for example, described Pericles as acting 'like the pilot of a ship, who, when a gale blows up at sea, makes everything tight, trims his sails, and exerts his seaman's arts to the utmost, disregarding the tears and entreaties of seasick and terrified passengers' (Plutarch, *Selected Lives and Essays* (Roslyn, NY: Walter J. Black, Inc., 1951), 160).

[11] *The Observator* (13 Nov. 1682), quoted in Faulkner, 'Halifax's "The Character of a Trimmer"', 71.

that part of the world where men are roasted, and the other where they are frozen', p. 49).[12]

Charles's death in February 1685 was a turning point for Halifax. To his surprise, the newly crowned James II did not dismiss him, though he was demoted to Lord President of the Council. Halifax could not be accommodated for long, however, and he made clear that he opposed repeal of the Test and the Habeas Corpus Acts.[13] In October 1685 James dismissed Halifax from office, saying that only unreserved commitment to his policies could be tolerated in his ministers.

Halifax retired to Rufford and spent some time reflecting on government and his part in it. Among the works that can be attributed to this time of relative seclusion is *Advice to a Daughter*, Halifax's runaway bestseller, reaching its fifteenth edition by 1765 in addition to numerous pirated copies. Some later editions even titled it *The Lady's Chesterfield*, twinning it accordingly with the celebrated *Letters to his Son*, written by Halifax's grandson, Philip Stanhope, 4th Earl of Chesterfield. The purpose of *Advice to a Daughter* was to address matters of family, marriage, friendship, and conversation, and it stands as an illuminating account of the social expectations informing women's lives in the late seventeenth century. The range of challenges posed by living with a difficult husband is both memorable and unsettling, with recommendations as to how to deal with a man who is sullen, or choleric, or a 'close-handed wretch', or who perhaps 'may love wine more than is convenient' (pp. 80, 76), to name but a few of the types enumerated. It is telling that religion was given a central role in this picture, and Halifax's own refined attitude towards the subject can be found in the *Advice*'s pages. Though to be embraced in some sense as 'the only thing necessary', 'the reality and the pretence' are carefully to be distinguished (p. 69). Importantly, credulousness and 'violent raptures' (p. 72) are strongly advised against: 'our faith, like our stomach, is capable of being overcharged; and that as the last is destroyed by taking in more than it can digest, so our reason may be

[12] It can be noted that the Trimmer's search for the mean is also present in Halifax's recommendations concerning household expenditure in *Advice to a Daughter* (see p. 87).

[13] The Test Act made a person's eligibility for public office depend upon receipt of Holy Communion in the Church of England; repealing it would have constituted a significant advance for Catholics.

extinguished by oppressing it with the weight of too many strange things' (p. 70).

Religious matters, meanwhile, dominated the political scene, and not in the quiet and 'cheerful' form that Halifax recommended to his daughter. In the face of James II's policies of both relieving Catholics of the Test Act and extending religious toleration to Protestant Dissenters as a Trojan horse for wider toleration of Catholics, Halifax despaired. In correspondence with William of Orange, he simply hoped that James would not find a sufficient majority in Parliament for either measure. But it was clear that James was determined to fix elections which would give him a majority. At the same time, James clearly wanted to transform Oxford into a Catholic seminary. He took the opportunity of a vacancy in the presidency of Magdalen College to install a Catholic, and he ejected all the fellows when they refused to vote him into office. As worrying was his investigation into the right of the university to publish books. Louis XIV's Revocation of the Edict of Nantes, which had guaranteed freedom of worship to French Protestants, also caused great concern. While few thought that James would go to such an extreme, might he be inspired by the actions of the French king to check the powers of the English national Church? The stage was set for the power struggles that would result in England's Glorious Revolution of 1688.

Halifax saw James's absolutist tendencies clearly in 1687 when the King wanted to install Andrew Popham, a Catholic, as a brother in Charterhouse,[14] of which Halifax was a governor. The governors rejected Popham's appointment since he refused to take the oaths of allegiance and supremacy. James tried to install Popham using his claim to the prerogative to dispense with laws, but Halifax and the other governors again rejected him. Halifax had stared into the face of James's absolutism, something that ran entirely counter to his own trenchant support for the rule of law: 'The reason of any law is, that no man's will should be a law' (p. 182).

Halifax feared that James's tactic of driving a wedge between the Anglicans and Dissenters could work. If the latter could be brought

---

[14] A charitable almshouse for poor men in London, established by Thomas Sutton in 1611. Religious requirements are no longer required for admittance to the Charterhouse, which since 2017 has also welcomed women into its community (they too are called 'brothers').

to support religious toleration it could bring sufficient votes in boroughs to win James a majority in the Commons. Halifax's *Letter to a Dissenter*, published in September 1687, was a major intervention in these circumstances.[15] He asserted that James's Declaration of Indulgence of May 1687 (like his claim to the dispensing power) was illegal and that the Dissenters were being duped into supporting a policy which would result in the legalization of Catholicism, but afterwards the persecution of Dissenters. Halifax's genius in framing the situation was summed up in his phrase: 'You are therefore to be hugged now, only that you may be the better squeezed at another time' (p. 107). 'This', he added, 'is a violent change, and it will be fit for you to pause upon it, before you believe it' (p. 107)—it was as close as Halifax came to calling James a liar. Halifax argued that all Protestants should unite to fight off a Catholic absolutist threat, which would bear fruit in greater tolerance from Anglicans. The *Letter to a Dissenter* went through six editions (with more than twenty-four replies) and had a cumulative printing of 20,000 copies; it was circulated so widely that few could not have heard of it.[16] The *Letter* prevented many Dissenters from throwing their lot in with James. Most Dissenters held back, waiting to see whether Halifax's *Letter* would have an effect.[17] The Anglican clergy in London, especially Latitudinarians, were alert to Halifax's signal and held a series of meetings with leading Dissenting ministers which suggested that the Church was willing to embrace toleration of Protestant Dissent as the price of avoiding Catholic tyranny.[18]

By 1688, Halifax was an open opponent of James. Though he was not one of the conspirators who plotted William of Orange's invasion, he had some contact with William's envoy, Everaard Van Weede. Halifax drafted a possible defence of the seven bishops whom James prosecuted for refusal to order the second Declaration of Indulgence

[15] Sir James Mackintosh called it 'the most perfect example of a political tract' (H. C. Foxcroft, 'New Light on George Savile, First Marquis of Halifax, "The Trimmer"', *History*, NS 26 (1941), 181).

[16] See Jackson, *Devil-Land*, 473.

[17] E. Calamy, *An Abridgment of Mr Baxter's History of his Life and Times* (London: S. Bridge, 1702), 624.

[18] William Gibson, *James II and the Trial of the Seven Bishops* (Basingstoke: Palgrave Macmillan, 2009).

in May 1688;[19] his role in the trial of the bishops a month later was so significant that, when a verdict of not guilty was returned, his shout of joy was recorded by witnesses. The birth of a son to James II in June 1688 meant that his Catholic reign could no longer be regarded as a temporary state before Mary of Orange, James's Protestant daughter, succeeded to the throne. Halifax's criticisms, accordingly, became more pointed. *The Anatomy of an Equivalent*, a 'sharp and biting'[20] work published in the summer of 1688, derided James's claim that he would offer equivalent security to the Church of England if the Test Act and oaths were removed.

Events developed rapidly once William of Orange's invasion fleet set sail. William declared that he had been invited by 'a great many lords both spiritual and temporal', not to take the throne, but simply to ensure that a free and lawful parliament should be assembled. It was at this point that James began to reverse course. The fellows of Magdalen College were restored and all sorts of sackings and ejections were rescinded. It also seems that James contemplated restoring Halifax to office, but he refused to sign a document abhorring William's invasion. With an easterly 'Protestant wind' speeding his fleet, William landed on English soil on 5 November, the anniversary of the thwarting of a previous Catholic conspiracy, the Gunpowder Plot of 1605. Despite moving to Salisbury Plain to engage with William's army, James's confidence collapsed. Halifax, Godolphin, and Nottingham—none of whom had signed the invitation to William— were sent to William's camp to negotiate a settlement. When they returned to the King he had temporarily fled. Now Halifax finally abandoned James and committed himself to William's cause. Halifax's standing as a senior peer, a moderate, and one who had only reluctantly

---

[19] The Declaration of Indulgence—also called the Declaration for Liberty of Conscience—suspended the penal laws enforcing conformity to the Church of England and thereby advanced James's Catholic agenda. It should be noted that for some historians James might genuinely have been making an attempt to establish religious toleration in England, a goal that was thwarted by the 1688 Revolution (see John Miller, *James II* (New Haven: Yale University Press, 2000), esp. 126, 128, 145, 155–6, 169). In this context, Halifax's strident anti-Catholic views, as expressed in *The Character of a Trimmer*, should also not be ignored: 'If a man would speak maliciously of this religion, one might say it is like those diseases, where as long as one drop of the infection remains, there is still a danger of having the whole mass of blood corrupted by it' (p. 27).

[20] M. N. Brown, in *Works of George Savile, Marquis of Halifax* (Oxford: Clarendon Press, 1989), ed. Brown, i. 111.

abandoned James, meant that he was the obvious candidate to chair a meeting of peers on 13 December. On 22 December James fled to France and Halifax chaired the meeting of peers which invited William to assume the duties of government.

Halifax's role in the Convention Parliament, which was called in January 1689 to settle the issue of the throne, was one of the clearest and least equivocal. So central, indeed, were Halifax's actions during this time that the 1688 Revolution has been described as 'a victory of moderation, a victory not of Whig or Tory passions, but of the spirit and mentality of Halifax the Trimmer'.[21] He was chosen as speaker of the House of Lords in the knowledge that during the Exclusion Crisis he had favoured the idea of a regency during James's reign. But times had changed. In the Convention meetings, Clarendon said Halifax 'drove furiously' for William, arguing that, after an exception of an elected monarch in 1689, the throne could become hereditary again.[22] In the fraught debates between Lords and Commons, Tories and Whigs, Halifax was clear that William should be offered the throne. In the end, the Convention offered the throne to William and Mary jointly. At their coronation, Halifax formally invited them to take the crowns. Halifax was restored to the office of Lord Privy Seal by William and easily fought off attempts to impeach him by Whigs in Parliament. Nevertheless, in the autumn of 1689 there were continued attempts by hard-line Whigs to investigate Halifax's role as a minister under Charles II. He gave up the speakership of the Lords and by the end of the year, feeling unwell, he decided to give up the privy seal. When he finally resigned in February 1690, William only reluctantly accepted the seals of office and insisted that Halifax return to government when he felt able to. William kept the post of Lord Privy Seal vacant for two years.[23]

It was during these final years of retirement that Halifax wrote some of his most important works, including *Some Cautions Offered to the Consideration of those who are to Choose Members to Serve in the Next Parliament* and *A Rough Draught of a New Model at Sea*. In March 1695, he ate an undercooked chicken, which led to food poisoning

---

[21] G. M. Trevelyan, *The English Revolution 1688–1689* (London: Oxford University Press, 1938), 241.

[22] *The State Letters of Henry Earl of Clarendon* (Oxford: Clarendon Press, 1763), ii. 164.

[23] William's admiration for Halifax is seen in his compliment that he did not hesitate in calling himself a 'trimmer', Foxcroft, 'New Light on George Savile', 182.

and an oesophageal rupture. As Halifax lay dying, he took the sacrament from an Anglican priest and apologized for talking loosely about religion. He died on 5 April 1695.

The Elements and Ambiguities of Halifax's Political Thought

Halifax's writings occupy a central place in the development of the British conservative tradition, the ideal of trimming informing the conservative's inclination to lean 'against the prevailing fashion'.[24] Sir Ian Gilmour, a minister in the governments of both Edward Heath and Margaret Thatcher, described Halifax as a thinker whose writings 'provide almost a grammar of Conservatism'.[25] Even the comparatively slender quantity of his works is consistent with this claim, since conservatism derides the production of lengthy political treatises based on theoretical abstractions. This is true even of the most eminent and loquacious of conservative thinkers, Edmund Burke, whose works, like those of Halifax, were written largely in response to some undesirable development (the French Revolution, most notably, in Burke's case). Conservatives, accordingly, find themselves provoked, rather than inclined, to write; and that reluctant spirit is uppermost in the very opening line of *The Character of a Trimmer*: 'It must be more than an ordinary provocation that can tempt a man to write in an age overrun with scribblers' (p. 3). The act of political writing is justified, then, only when an unnecessary innovation disrupts a tolerable and long-standing situation, when 'the simple habit of living more or less unconsciously'[26] needs deliberate and conscious support in the face of radical change. In Halifax one also finds the characteristically conservative distinction between the concrete realities of real political life and the unrealities of pristine theory: 'The government of the world is a great thing; but it is a very coarse one too, compared with the fineness of speculative knowledge' (p. 190).

---

[24] Ian Gilmour, *Inside Right: A Study of Conservatism* (London: Hutchinson, 1977), 44. The 'conservative tradition' is characterized by a cautious attitude to change, preferring custom and continuity to radical, theory-driven innovation; with a capital 'C', it gave its name to the political party which emerged in Britain in the 1830s.

[25] Gilmour, *Inside Right*, 44.

[26] Karl Mannheim, 'Conservative Thought', in K. H. Wolff (ed.), *From Karl Mannheim* (New York: Oxford University Press, 1971), 173.

The conservative disdain for abstraction is uppermost in Halifax's critique of the notion of a 'Fundamental', some solid principle that should ground policy. No such thing is to be found, and what is regarded as 'a peg of iron' is just 'a wisp of straw', any fundamental going the way of everything else in this fleeting world: 'Everything that is created is mortal, *ergo* all Fundamentals of human creation will die' (p. 172). In place of anything so neat and immoveable as a fundamental, Halifax emphasizes contingency and circumstance, things which are always to be taken into account and which will inevitably undermine the politics of theory and dogma: 'Circumstances must come in, and are to be made a part of the matter of which we are to judge; positive [i.e. theoretical] decisions are always dangerous, and more especially in politics' (p. 142). Halifax warns of those who are tempted to 'mend' things (words directed, presumably, at the type of politician who, as Burke would later put it, is 'habitually meddling'),[27] noting that the desire to alter is frequently not matched by any skill in doing so; the result being that the menders 'pull the faults down upon their heads' (p. 217). Halifax's alternative to dangerous projects of alteration is to accept a situation and make the best of it.[28] 'Desiring to have anything mended,' he writes in full conservative tone, 'is venturing to have it spoiled: to know when to let things alone is a high pitch of good sense' (p. 201).

A preference for what is present and customary, as opposed to what is innovative is, of course, a largely constant theme in the conservative tradition, and Halifax roots this preference in the nature of human beings themselves, this nature defined as 'not that which is born with them, but that which they are used to' (p. 217).[29] Custom is a vital guide, too, because the faculty of reason in humans is very slight; contrary to the pretensions of the rational theorist, it cannot be relied

---

[27] Edmund Burke, *Reflections on the Revolution in France* (London: J. Dodsley, 1790), 62.

[28] 'Halifax perhaps came nearer than any man in the seventeenth century to making this frame of mind [i.e., making the best of things] a working political hypothesis' (G. H. Sabine, *A History of Political Theory* (New York: Henry Holt & Company, 1937), 518). It was also something akin to a philosophy, not just of politics, but of life for Halifax: 'There is a scurvy side of every kind of life to which a man can apply himself. We must take all together, and make the best of it' (p. 223).

[29] See here also Lord Hugh Cecil, *Conservatism* (London: Williams & Norgate, 1912), 9: 'Natural conservatism is a tendency of the human mind', springing 'partly from a faculty in men to adapt themselves to their surroundings so that what is familiar merely because of its familiarity becomes more acceptable or more tolerable than what is unfamiliar.'

upon to shape the social and political order. In words which would be echoed by Burke a century later, Halifax expressed great reticence to set his 'slender stock of reason' against 'the supreme wisdom of the nation' (p. 149).[30] Uppermost here are the important conservative themes of prescription and presumption, and of how the individual reason, however impressive, should bow to the collective wisdom of a tradition existing time out of mind. A further reason for scepticism concerning the power of reason is its subservience to passion. Halifax notes, for example, how most people 'put their reason out to service to their will' (p. 212), and—even more strikingly—how reasons

are less necessary than is generally thought; they are oftener mustered to make a show, than for anything else. Men's resolutions are generally formed by their appetite or their interest. Reason is afterwards called in for company, but it has no vote. (p. 221)

Here it can be seen how Halifax's political stance is, in part, informed by a distinctive view of the limitations and infirmities of human nature.

Halifax's thought is infused with a deep pessimism about this 'scurvy' world ('To understand the world,' he writes, 'and to like it, are two things not easily to be reconciled', p. 189), and this pessimism extends to people and their capabilities. It applies both to their intellectual qualities ('they understand nothing', p. 219), and to their moral ones. Never satisfied, and with their true motives generally hidden from themselves, even a person's most seemingly virtuous of acts is rarely unmixed with some degree of vice: compassion towards a person's suffering is not infrequently a disguise for one's hatred of the oppressing agent; commiserating with another is more often than not accompanied by feelings of superiority; pity may be more to do with imagining ourselves in the same sad situation as the sufferer; and it is fear of public shame rather than any inner moral sense that generally motivates a person (see pp. 221–2). There are here clear echoes of both Hobbes and La Rochefoucauld. Halifax's emphasis on the imperfectability of human beings is yet another part of the grammar of conservatism, the incurably frail nature of humankind rendering futile and quixotic any ambitious schemes for social transformation.

[30] Compare Burke: 'We are afraid to put men to live and trade each on his private stock of reason; because we suspect that this stock in each man is small, and that the individuals would do better to avail themselves of the general bank and capital of nations, and of ages' (*Reflections on the Revolution in France*, 129).

Worse than this, however, and more harrowing than a stress on intellectual and moral imperfectibility, is the human propensity to violence, which is something that any government ignores at its peril. The process of civilization, which Halifax—anticipating Freud—felt was hardly worth the expense of energy required, has only superficially altered the violent nature of people, the least thing unleashing 'the original beast again' (p. 218): 'Man is still a beast of prey: he is only brought out of the woods, and ranges in towns' (p. 218). Violent propensities intensify when individuals are aggregated, there being 'an accumulative cruelty in a number of men' (p. 180), and the mass of people, once roused from a dead water to a rough sea, become terrible. 'The angry buzz of a multitude,' he says, 'is one of the bloodiest noises in the world' (p. 180). Hence Halifax's dread of popular discontent; and hence also his articulation of the importance of government and law. The Trimmer, he writes, venerates laws as 'the chains that tie up our unruly passions, which else, like wild beasts let loose, would reduce the world into its first state of barbarism and hostility' (p. 4). The existence and extent of laws are an indictment of the minacious human nature that requires them. Halifax was no authoritarian, but he was unsympathetic to any complaints that the people merited better government ('it is hard for them to be worse governed than they deserve', p. 218); and his answer to the question why nations have generally been so ill-governed rests on the unflattering judgement that the world is itself 'a great blockhead' composed of self-confessed idiots (p. 170).

Halifax's wariness towards groups of people ('herds') manifested itself also in his dislike of political parties. This had been a characteristic feature of Halifax's own political career, of course, and had resulted in his often mistrusted and isolated position. It was also the focus of a sustained polemic contained in his final published pamphlet, *Some Cautions Offered*. While it is entirely understandable that people should lean towards those who hold similar political views and principles, the further cementing of loose affinities into organized and disciplined parties brings with it notable hazards. The uniformity of party does not conduce to the flourishing of politicians of independent spirit, fostering instead the rise of 'low and insignificant men' (p. 163), cyphers whose talents do not exceed the mastery of a party's line. This reduction of talent would be bad enough if accompanied by nothing else, but a party system also tends to undermine both the liberty and the tranquillity of a nation. As Halifax writes, 'when a man is drowned in a party, plunged in it beyond his depth, he . . . can hardly be called a free agent, and for that reason is very unfit to be trusted with the people's liberty, after he has given up his own' (p. 162). As for the nation's tranquillity, rivalry between parties introduces animosities within the state, the heated eagerness of competition eclipsing the threats from more important enemies (namely, from hostile foreign powers), and dividing the nation against itself. The resulting spectacle is likely to be more akin to a spiteful and destructive game than to the cool and steady deliberation required to steer the ship of state: 'it is pretty sure that whilst these opposite sets of angry men are playing at football, they will break all the windows, and do more hurt than their pretended zeal for the nation will ever make amends for' (p. 164).

A contempt for the rigidity of party allegiance is, of course, a feature of the Trimmer's political stance (and a reason why there was no 'party' of Trimmers, with Halifax at its head); it goes some way, too, in accounting for his political isolation.[31] Halifax's advocacy of limited (or mixed) monarchy as the most suitable form of government for England serves as a further illustration of his trimming mentality. The dispute as to whether an absolute monarchy or a commonwealth is the best form of government is dismissed by Halifax as an unhelpfully immoderate one, each side taking the words 'in the utmost extent' (p. 7). Monarchy, in its absolute form, 'leaves men no liberty', while a commonwealth 'allows them no quiet' (p. 7). An absolute monarchy does not suit England, since despotic power destroys individual liberties and accordingly extinguishes the initiative upon which England's success in trade depends; as for a pure commonwealth, it requires the population having more virtue than they in fact possess (it is 'too hard for the bulk of mankind to come up to', p. 8), and is also disliked for its lack of 'the bells and the tinsel' that draw the English people to the spectacle of monarchy. Dismissing both extreme positions, Halifax isolates the 'wise mean' (p. 7) of a mixed or 'bounded' monarchy, in

[31] Halifax's isolation is uppermost in the anecdote about a Court wit who, upon observing him entering Whitehall alone, remarked 'yonder goes the Marquess of Halifax with all his friends' (Brown, 'General Introduction' to *The Works of George Savile*, ed. Brown, vol. i, p. xx). He certainly did 'plough a rather lonely and delicately trimmed furrow of [his] own' (Keith Feiling, *A History of the Tory Party: 1640–1714* (Oxford: Clarendon Press, 1924), 179).

which monarchical power is tempered and restrained by parliaments and by the rule of law, and 'in which dominion and liberty are so happily reconciled' (p. 15). One can see here that what L'Estrange condemned as a temporizing lack of principle is in fact an amalgamation of several strands of thinking. Trimming is not simply a search for a mean between extremes but the attempt to attain a healthy balance rooted in practicalities. This is achieved by balancing, compensating, and weighing competing factors; by paying attention to the particularities of any given state of affairs ('Our situation, our humour, our trade', p. 143); and by attaining an intimate grasp of what Halifax rather obscurely calls 'natural reason of state' (p. 13), some 'undefinable thing' neither theoretical nor eternally valid, but rather a historically conditioned understanding of the ongoing tradition and political life of a community.

Halifax's ideas have not enjoyed the same level of attention as has been given to those other leading British seventeenth-century political thinkers, Hobbes and Locke, but the ideal of political activity described in *The Character of a Trimmer* has nonetheless exerted a quiet influence in the work of subsequent theorists, and predictably on those of a conservative disposition. While Halifax is not mentioned by name in *Reflections on the Revolution in France*, it is the spirit—and the very language—of the Trimmer that animates the book's closing peroration, in which Burke defends his own consistency. It is a consistency, he says, which is preserved 'by varying his means to secure the unity of his end; and, when the equipoise of the vessel in which he sails may be endangered by overloading it upon one side, is desirous of carrying the small weight of his reasons to that which may preserve its equipoise'.[32] This barely requires commentary, though one may note how a Trimmer's actions, which can appear shifting and even irresolute, will in fact be informed and motivated by a consistent goal, namely the balance and equipoise of the state, particularly in a time when enthusiasms of one kind or another threaten to unleash destabilization.

In the more recent work of Michael Oakeshott, however, there is a more studied—and an acknowledged—influence. Echoes of Halifax's ideas can be discerned in Oakeshott's account of political activity, an

---

[32] Burke, *Reflections on the Revolution in France*, 356. Like Halifax before him, Burke was derided by his contemporaries for his perceived changes of position.

activity in which 'men sail a boundless and bottomless sea', the enterprise being 'to keep afloat on an even keel; the sea is both friend and enemy; and the seamanship consists in using the resources of a traditional manner of behaviour in order to make a friend of every hostile occasion'.[33] Something akin to a Halifaxian weariness is also exhibited in Oakeshott's depiction of the perennially 'unpleasing spectacle' of politics, its intrigue and meddlesomeness and futility ('Like an old horse in a pound').[34] The influence emerges most directly in Oakeshott's posthumous *The Politics of Faith and the Politics of Scepticism*, in which he presents for examination the two poles of European thought about the purpose of government: a 'politics of faith', in which the power of government is utilized in the service of the perfection or improvement of humankind; and a 'politics of scepticism' which eschews grand and all-encompassing schemes, pursuing the more pragmatic and judicial task of lessening the severity of conflicts generated by the inherent complexity of human affairs. In this context, Halifax is described as 'a political sceptic', whose method of trimming constitutes 'the mean in action', seen as 'a middle region of movement, not a central point of repose'. Oakeshott's description is worth quoting at length:

The 'trimmer' is one who disposes his weight so as to keep the ship upon an even keel. . . . Being concerned to prevent politics from running to extremes, he believes that there is a time for everything and that everything has its time—not providentially, but empirically. He will be found facing in whatever direction the occasion seems to require if the boat is to go even. Nevertheless, his changes of direction will neither be frequent, sudden nor great; for the changes his movement is designed to counter-balance are not, for the most part, either frequent or sudden. Further, he will recognize the necessity of others facing in a different direction from himself: the mean in action is never to be achieved by a general surge this way or that; indeed, such surges are precisely what it is designed to exclude.[35]

Oakeshott's account details the rationale for the Trimmer's changes of direction (those shifts that so vexed Halifax's contemporaries),

---

[33] Michael Oakeshott, *Rationalism in Politics and Other Essays* (London: Methuen, 1962), 127.
[34] Michael Oakeshott, *The Politics of Faith and the Politics of Scepticism* (New Haven: Yale University Press, 1996), 19.
[35] Oakeshott, *Politics of Faith*, 123.

stressing the non-dogmatic flexibility required to respond to developments and challenges, and it also brings out an aspect of Halifax's thinking that is strikingly modern, namely a recognition of the value of difference, of others facing in a range of directions and pursuing an irreducible plurality of aims.[36]

This modern—and profoundly liberal—dimension of Halifax's thought is worth emphasizing, particularly in a time in which conservatism has itself hardened into something of a rigid position, far from the flexible, moderating force promoted by such a centrist politician as Ian Gilmour. In this context, Halifax might best be twinned with a thinker like Sir Isaiah Berlin, whose version of liberalism stresses the variety and incommensurability of human goals, and whose depiction of the middle ground as 'a notoriously exposed, dangerous, and ungrateful position'[37] aptly captures Halifax's predicament. Berlin and Halifax are foregrounded, indeed, in Aurelian Craiutu's recent work on the virtue of political moderation, where they emerge as two exemplary voices in the pursuit of compromise and the avoidance of violence.[38] A further complicating of Halifax's conservative identity occurs in an essay by the British novelist Zadie Smith. Its focus is on President Barack Obama, whose characteristic as 'a genuinely many-voiced man' was seen by many merely as his suspiciously 'doubling ways'.[39] Smith finds support for the integrity of Obama precisely in the figure of Halifax the Trimmer, the type of figure averse to the dangerous allure of 'ideological heroism'[40] and pursuing instead the political equivalent of Keats's 'negative capability': a treasuring of diverse voices and of 'being in uncertainties'.[41]

Across the centuries, therefore, Halifax still speaks to us, not with the glamour of the visionary or the ideologue, but with a voice alert to

---

[36] G. P. Gooch attributes Halifax's isolation to the modernity of his thought as much as to his detestation of party (*Political Thought in England from Bacon to Halifax* (London: Thornton Butterworth, 1914), 199).

[37] Isaiah Berlin, *Russian Thinkers* (London: The Hogarth Press, 1978), 297.

[38] See Aurelian Craiutu, *Faces of Moderation* (Philadelphia: University of Pennsylvania Press, 2017).

[39] Zadie Smith, 'Speaking in Tongues', in *Changing My Mind: Occasional Essays* (New York: Penguin, 2009), 136, 139. Smith's essay was first published in the *New York Review of Books* (26 Feb. 2009).

[40] Smith, 'Speaking in Tongues', 144.

[41] John Keats, quoted in Smith, 'Speaking in Tongues', 144.

pluralities and compromise, rooted in experience (which 'makes more prophets than revelation', p. 206), and always keen to divert human beings from their worst impulses and excesses. Much still is to be learned from the works of 'the eminently sane and moderate George Savile, successively viscount, earl, and marquis of Halifax'.[42]

---

[42] Hearnshaw, *Conservatism in England*, 103.

NOTE ON THE TEXT

THE selections included in this volume have been drawn from the three-volume *Works of George Savile, Marquis of Halifax*, edited by Mark N. Brown and published by the Clarendon Press, an imprint of Oxford University Press, in 1989. Spellings have been modernized, and the use of capital letters has been modified. Halifax's punctuation has been altered where the original form is an impediment to understanding. Other published editions of Halifax's works, as detailed in the Select Bibliography, have also been consulted.

SELECT BIBLIOGRAPHY

Works by Halifax

THE first collection of Halifax's pamphlets was published in London in 1700 under the title *Miscellanies by the Right Noble Lord the Late Lord Marquess of Halifax*. It gathered together *Advice to a Daughter*, *The Character of a Trimmer*, *The Anatomy of an Equivalent*, *A Letter to a Dissenter*, *Some Cautions Offered to the Consideration of those who are to Choose Members to Serve in the Ensuing Parliament*, *A Rough Draught of a New Model at Sea*, and *Maxims of State* (in the present edition called by its alternative title, *Maxims of the Great Almansor*), together with a letter sent by Halifax to Charles Cotton concerning the latter's new translation of Montaigne's *Essays*, and a 'Funeral Poem' composed in Halifax's honour by Elkanah Settle. Second and third editions of the *Miscellanies* appeared in 1704 and 1717, with that third edition adding a brief 'Character of the Late Bishop Burnet'. A second volume of Halifax's works was published in London in 1750, and contained *A Character of King Charles II* and the *Political, Moral and Miscellaneous Thoughts and Reflections*.

It was not until 1898 that all the pieces of those two books (minus the letter to Cotton) were published together, when they were collected in the second volume of H. C. Foxcroft's *Life and Letters of Sir George Savile First Marquis of Halifax* (London: Longmans, Green). Foxcroft also included some additional items attributed to Halifax. This was shortly followed by Walter Raleigh's *Complete Works of George Savile First Marquess of Halifax* (Oxford: Clarendon Press, 1912; republished New York: Augustus M. Kelley, 1970). A Penguin edition of Halifax's *Complete Works*, edited by J. P. Kenyon, was published in 1969, and this also included a selection of Halifax's letters. The definitive edition is the three-volume *Works of George Savile Marquis of Halifax*, edited by Mark N. Brown and published by the Clarendon Press in 1989. In addition to the major works, the Brown edition includes *Observations Upon a Late Libel* (the authorship of which is contested) and many previously unpublished works, some of which are in fragmentary form.

Biography

The two major biographical studies of Halifax are both by H. C. Foxcroft: *The Life and Letters of Sir George Savile First Marquis of Halifax* (London: Longmans, Green, 1898) and *A Character of the Trimmer: Being a Short Life of the First Marquis of Halifax* (Cambridge: Cambridge University Press, 1946).

Halifax's Political Thought

Historical accounts of the 1688 Revolution can be consulted for analyses of Halifax's political activity during that time: the classic text, and the one which most emphasizes Halifax's influence, is Thomas Babington Macaulay's *History of England from the Accession of James II*, first published in 1848 (many editions); see also W. A. Speck, *Reluctant Revolutionaries: Englishmen and the Revolution of 1688* (Oxford: Oxford University Press, 1989), and G. M. Trevelyan, *The English Revolution 1688–1689* (London: Oxford University Press, 1938).

The following provide briefer, though worthy, discussions of the distinctive character of Halifax's political thought:

Brown, Mark N., 'Sir William Trumbull and the Marquis of Halifax', *British Library Journal*, 19/2 (1993), 142–7.

Fletcher, J. S., 'The Marquis of Halifax', in *Yorkshiremen of the Restoration* (London: G. Allen & Unwin Ltd, 1921), 151–67.

Foxcroft, H. C., 'New Light on George Savile first Marquis of Halifax, "The Trimmer"', *History*, 26 (1941), 176–87.

Gilmour, Ian, *Inside Right: A Study of Conservatism* (London: Hutchinson, 1977), 43–7.

Mitchell, David, 'Politics without Party: The Marquis of Halifax's Dream', *History Today*, 14/1 (January 1964), 52–9.

Paul, Herbert, 'The Great Tractarian', in *Men and Letters* (London: John Lane, 1901), 209–40.

Quinton, Anthony, *The Politics of Imperfection* (London: Faber & Faber, 1978), 35–8.

Reed, A. W., 'George Savile, Marquis of Halifax', in F. J. C. Hearnshaw (ed.), *The Social and Political Ideas of Some English Thinkers of the Augustan Age* (London: George G. Harrap, 1928), 47–68.

Trevor-Roper, Hugh, 'The Marquis of Halifax', in *Historical Essays* (London: Macmillan, 1957), 254–9.

Walpole, Sir Spencer, 'George Savile, Lord Halifax', in *Essays Political and Biographical* (London: T. F. Unwin, 1908), 1–35.

Further Reading in Oxford World's Classics

Hobbes, Thomas, *Leviathan*, ed. Noel Malcolm.

Hyde, Edward, Earl of Clarendon, *The History of the Rebellion*, ed. Paul Seaward.

La Rochefoucauld, *Collected Maxims*, trans. E. H. Blackmore, A. M. Blackmore, and Francine Giguère.

Machiavelli, Niccolò, *The Prince*, trans. Peter Bondanella, ed. Maurizio Viroli.

Restoration Literature: An Anthology, ed. Paul Hammond.

A CHRONOLOGY OF THE
MARQUESS OF HALIFAX

1633 (11 November) George Savile born at Thornhill Hall, Yorkshire, son of Sir William Savile and of Anne Coventry, who was daughter of Lord Keeper Thomas Coventry, 1st Baron Coventry.

1641 Enters the private school of Charles Croke DD in Amersham, Buckinghamshire.

1642 (22 August) English Civil War begins.

1643 (February–May) Moves to Shrewsbury School.

1644 William Savile dies from wounds inflicted during the siege of Sheffield Castle; upon his father's death George Savile becomes 4th Baronet.

1645 Savile's wardship is granted to Lord Wharton.

1646 Sent abroad to school in France under a Scottish Presbyterian tutor and later at a Huguenot academy in Paris; subsequently spends time in Italy and the Netherlands.

1649 (30 January) Execution of Charles I; (19 May) England declared a Commonwealth.

1652 Returns to England to live with his mother in Worcestershire; is tutored by the royalist cleric Henry Hammond.

1654 Attaining full legal age, Savile establishes his home at Rufford Abbey in Nottinghamshire.

1655 The Savile family is implicated in an attempted uprising for the royalist cause.

1656 Marries Lady Dorothy Spencer, daughter of the Earl of Sunderland; together they have five children.

1660 (29 May) Restoration of the monarchy and accession of Charles II to the throne; Halifax is elected MP for Pontefract, but does not stand in the 1661 election.

1660 Appointed deputy lieutenant and colonel in the Yorkshire militia.

1668 Created Baron Savile of Eland and Viscount Halifax.

1670 Halifax's wife Dorothy dies.

1672 Appointed to the Privy Council; with Buckingham and Arlington he negotiates a peace treaty with France. Marries Gertrude Pierrepoint, a Presbyterian and a niece of the Earl of Kingston.

1674 Advocates confiscation of firearms from Catholics.

1676 Dismissed from the Privy Council.

1678 Halifax, Shaftesbury, Buckingham, and Essex lead the House of Lords investigation into the Popish Plot; advocates that the Duke of York should retire from the King's presence.

1679 Halifax is readmitted to the Privy Council; argues a middle path between popular concern over the Popish Plot and the King's refusal to exclude the Duke of York from the succession. Created Earl of Halifax. Affected by depression.

1681 The Whig House of Commons declares Halifax, Worcester, and Clarendon enemies of the King.

1682 Created Marquess of Halifax and appointed Lord Privy Seal.

1683 Organizes a reconciliation of the King and Duke of Monmouth after the Rye House Plot.

1684 Warns the King that failure to call a parliament is illegal.

1685 Manuscript copies of *The Character of a Trimmer*, attributed originally to the authorship of Sir William Coventry, begin to be circulated, including to William Sancroft, Archbishop of Canterbury. (6 February) Death of Charles II; accession of James II to the throne. Continues in office as Lord President of the Council until October, when Halifax refuses to agree to suspending the Test Act.

1686 Begins a private correspondence with William of Orange.

1687 Leads the governors of Charterhouse in refusing to admit a Catholic member. Publishes anonymously *A Letter to a Dissenter*; 20,000 copies circulated.

1688 *Anatomy of an Equivalent* written after the birth of the Prince of Wales. (5 November) William of Orange's forces land at Brixham. (13 December) Chairs the meeting of peers which issued the 'Guildhall Declaration', which declared that in James's absence they would assist the Prince of Orange in the stated aim of his invasion, namely, to summon a free parliament.

1689 Halifax elected speaker of the Lords in the Convention Parliament; formally offers the crowns to William and Mary at their coronation; is appointed Lord Privy Seal.

1690 Resigns as Lord Privy Seal.

1692 Dismissed from the Privy Council.

1693 *Maxims of the Great Almansor* published.

1694 *Rough Draught of a New Model at Sea* published anonymously.

1695 (5 April) Halifax dies after eating an undercooked chicken, causing
       an oesophageal rupture; he leaves an estate worth £350,000. *Some
       Cautions Offered to the Consideration of those who are to choose
       Members to serve in the next Parliament* is circulated.

1700 *Miscellanies by the Right Noble Lord the Late Lord Marquess of
       Halifax* published.

1750 *A Character of King Charles II* published, along with the *Political,
       Moral and Miscellaneous Thoughts and Reflections.*

THE CHARACTER OF
A TRIMMER AND OTHER
WRITINGS

THE CHARACTER OF A TRIMMER

It must be more than an ordinary provocation that can tempt a man to write in an age overrun with scribblers, as Egypt was with flies and locusts.* That worst vermin of small authors has given the world such a surfeit that instead of desiring to write, a man would be more inclined to wish, for his own ease, that he could not read. But there are some things which do so raise our passions, that our reason can make no resistance; and when madmen in the two extremes shall agree to make common sense treason, and join to fix an ill character upon the only men in the nation who deserve a good one, I am no longer master of my better resolution to let the world alone, and must break loose from my more reasonable thoughts to expose these false coiners, who would make their copper words pass upon us for good payment.

Amongst all the engines of dissension there has been none more powerful in all times than the fixing names upon one another of contumely and reproach: and the reason is plain in respect of the people, who though generally they are incapable of making a syllogism or forming an argument, yet they can pronounce a word, and that serves their turn, to throw it with their dull malice at the head of those they do not like; such things ever begin in jest and end in blood, and the same word which at first makes the company merry, grows in time to a military signal to cut one another's throats.

These mistakes are to be lamented, though not easily to be cured, being suitable enough to the corrupted nature of mankind: but it is hard that men will not only invent ill names, but they will wrest and misinterpret good ones; so afraid some are even of a reconciling sound, that they raise another noise to keep it from being heard, lest it should set up and encourage a dangerous sort of men, who prefer peace and agreement before violence and confusion.

Were it not for this, why, after we have played the fool with throwing 'Whig' and 'Tory' at one another, as boys do snowballs, do we grow angry at a new name, which by its true signification might do as much to put us into our wits, as the others have done to put us out of them?

This innocent word 'Trimmer' signifies no more than this, that if men are together in a boat, and one part of the company would weigh it down on one side, another would make it lean as much to the contrary, it happens there is a third opinion, of those who conceive it would do as well, if the boat went even, without endangering the passengers. Now it is hard to imagine, by what figure in language, or by what rule in sense, this comes to be a fault, and it is much more a wonder that it should be thought a heresy.

But so it happens that the poor Trimmer has now all the powder spent upon him alone, whilst the Whig is a forgotten, or at least a neglected enemy: there is no danger now to the state, if some men may be believed, but from the beast called a Trimmer; take heed of him, he is the instrument that must destroy Church and state; a strange kind of monster, whose deformity is so exposed, that were it a true picture that is made of him, it would be enough to fright children, and make women miscarry at the sight of it.

But it may be worth examining whether he is such a beast as he is painted. I am not of that opinion, and am so far from thinking him an infidel either in Church or state, that I am neither afraid to expose the articles of his faith in relation to government, nor to say that I prefer them before any other political creed that either our angry divines or our refined statesmen would impose upon us.

I have therefore in the following discourse endeavoured to explain the Trimmer's principles and opinions, and then leave it to all discerning and impartial judges, whether he can with justice be so arraigned, and whether those who deliberately pervert a good name, do not very justly deserve the worst that can be put upon them.

THE TRIMMER'S OPINION ABOUT LAWS AND GOVERNMENT IN GENERAL, WITH SOME REFLECTIONS RELATING TO OUR OWN

Our Trimmer has a great veneration for laws in general, as he has more particularly for our own. He looks upon them as the chains that tie up our unruly passions, which else, like wild beasts let loose, would reduce the world into its first state of barbarism and hostility. All the good things we enjoy we owe to them, and all the ill things we avoid is by their protection.

God himself thought it not enough to be a creator without being a lawgiver, and his goodness had been defective towards mankind in making them, if he had not prescribed rules to make them happy too. All laws flow from that of Nature, and where that is not the foundation, they may be legally imposed, but they will be lamely obeyed. By this Nature is not meant, that which fools and libertines would misquote to justify their excesses: it is innocent and uncorrupted Nature, that which disposes men to choose virtue without its being prescribed, and which is so far from inspiring ill thoughts into us, that we take pains to suppress the good ones it infuses.

The civilized world has ever paid a willing subjection to laws: even conquerors have done homage to them, as the Romans, who took patterns of good laws even from those they had subdued, and at the same time that they triumphed over an enslaved people, the laws of that very place did not only remain safe, but became victorious: their new masters instead of suppressing them paid them more respect, than they had from those who first made them; and by this wise method they arrived to such an admirable constitution of laws, that to this day they reign by them. The excellency of them triumphs still, and the world now pays an acknowledgement of their obedience to that mighty Empire, though so many ages after it is dissolved. And by a later instance the Kings of France, who in practice use the laws pretty familiarly, yet they think their picture is drawn with most advantage upon their seals when they are placed in their seat of justice, and though the hieroglyphic is not of so much use to the people there as they might wish, yet it shows that no prince is so great, as not to think fit for his own credit to give at least an outward, when he refuses a real worship to the laws.

They are to mankind that which the sun is to plants, as it cherishes and preserves them. Where they have their force, and are not clouded or suppressed, everything smiles and flourishes; but where they are darkened and not suffered to shine out, it makes everything wither and decay. They secure men not only against one another, but against themselves too. They are a sanctuary to which the Crown has occasion to resort, as often as the people, so that it has an interest as well as a duty to preserve them.

There would be no end of making a panegyric of laws; let it be enough to add that without laws, the world would become a wilderness and men little less than beasts. But with all this the best things may come to be the worst if they are not in good hands; and if it is true that the wisest men generally make the laws, it is as true that the strongest do too often interpret them; and as rivers belong as much to the channel where they run, as to the spring from whence they first arise, so the laws depend as much upon the pipes through which they are to pass, as upon the fountain from whence they flow. The authority of a king who is head of the law, as well as the dignity of public justice, is debased when the clear stream of the law is puddled and disturbed by bunglers, or conveyed by unclean instruments to the people.

Our Trimmer would have them appear in their full lustre, and would be grieved to see the day, when instead of their speaking with authority from the seats of justice, they should speak out of a grate with a lamenting voice, like prisoners that desire to be rescued.

He wishes that the Bench may ever have a natural as well as a legal superiority to the Bar.* He thinks men's abilities very much misplaced, when the reason of those who plead is visibly too strong for those who are to judge and give sentence. When those from the Bar seem to dictate to their superiors upon the Bench, their furs will look scurvily about them, and the respect of the world will leave the bare character of a judge to follow the essential knowledge of a lawyer, who may be greater in himself, than others can ever be with all their trappings. An uncontested superiority in any calling will have the better of any discountenance that authority can put upon it, and therefore if ever such an unnatural method should be introduced, it is then that Westminster Hall* might be said to stand upon its head, and though justice itself can never be so, yet the administration of it would be rendered ridiculous.

A judge has such a power lodged in him, that the king will never be thought to have chosen well, where the voice of mankind has not beforehand recommended the man to his station. When men are made judges of what they do not understand, the world censures such a choice, not out of ill will to the men, but fear for themselves. If the king had the sole power of choosing physicians, men would tremble to see bunglers preferred; and yet the necessity of taking physic from a doctor is generally not so great as that of receiving justice from a judge. The inferences will be very severe in such cases, for either it will be thought that such men bought what they knew not how to deserve, or which is as bad, that obedience shall be looked upon as a better qualification in a judge than skill or integrity. When such sacred things as the laws are not only touched but guided by profane hands, men will fear that out of the tree of the law, from whence we expect shade and shelter, such workmen will make cudgels to beat us with, or rather that they will turn the cannon upon our properties, that were entrusted with them for their defence.

To see the laws mangled, disguised, made speak quite another language than their own, to see them thrown from the dignity of protecting mankind, to the disgraceful office of destroying them, and notwithstanding their innocence in themselves, to be made the worst instruments that the most refined villainy can make use of, will raise men's anger above their power to lay it down again, and tempt them to follow the ill example given them of judging without hearing, when so provoked by their desire of revenge.*

Our Trimmer therefore, as he thinks the laws are jewels, so he believes they are nowhere better set than in the constitution of our English government, if rightly understood and carefully preserved. It would be too great partiality to say it is perfect, or liable to no objection; such things are not of this world: but if it has more excellencies and fewer faults than any other we know, it is enough to recommend it to our esteem.

The dispute, which is the greater beauty, a monarchy or a commonwealth,* has lasted long between their contending lovers; and they have behaved themselves so like lovers, who in good manners must be out of their wits, and who used such figures to exalt their own idol on either side, and such angry aggravations to reproach one another in the contest, that moderate men have in all times smiled upon this eagerness, and thought it differed very little from a downright frenzy.

We in England, by a happy use of this controversy, conclude them both in the wrong, and reject them from being our pattern, taking the words in the utmost extent; which is, that monarchy is a thing which leaves men no liberty, and a commonwealth such a one as allows them no quiet. We think that a wise mean between these barbarous extremes, is that which self-preservation ought to dictate to our wishes, and we may say, we have attained this mean in a greater measure than any nation now in being, and perhaps than any we read of, though never so much celebrated for the wisdom or the felicity of their constitution. We take from one the too great power of doing hurt, and yet leave enough to govern and protect us; we take from the other the confusion, the parity, the animosities, and the licence, and yet reserve a due care of such a liberty, as may consist with men's allegiance.

But it being hard if not impossible to be exactly even, our government has much the stronger bias towards monarchy, which by the more general consent and practice of mankind, seems to have the advantage in the dispute against a commonwealth. The rules of a commonwealth are too hard for the bulk of mankind to come up to; that form of government requires such a spirit to carry it on, as does not dwell in great numbers, but is restrained to so very few, especially in this age, that let the methods appear never so reasonable in paper, they must fail in practice, which will ever be suited more to men's nature as it is than as it should be.

Monarchy is liked by the people for the bells and the tinsel, the outward pomp and the gilding, and there must be milk for babes, since the greater part of mankind are, and ever will be included in that list; and it is approved by wiser and more thinking men, as the best when compared with others, all circumstances and objections impartially considered. Then it has so great an advantage above all other forms, when the administration of that power falls into a good hand, that all other governments look out of countenance, when they are set in competition with it.

Lycurgus* might have saved himself the trouble of making laws if either he had been immortal, or that he could have secured to posterity a succeeding race of princes like himself; his own example was a better law than he could with all his skill tell how to make. Such a prince is a living law that dictates to his subjects, whose thoughts in that case never rise above their obedience, the confidence they have in the knowledge and virtue of the master preventing the scruples and apprehensions to which men are naturally inclined, in relation to those that govern them. Such a magistrate is the life and soul of justice, whereas the law is but the body, and a dead one too, without his influence to give it warmth and vigour; and by the irresistible power of his virtue, does so reconcile dominion and allegiance, that all disputes between them are silenced and subdued.

And indeed, no monarchy can be perfect and absolute without exception, but where the prince is superior by his virtues, as well as by his character, and his power. So that to screw out precedents of unlimited power, is a plain diminution to a prince that Nature has made great, and who had better make himself a glorious example to posterity, than borrow an authority from dark records raised out of the grave, which besides their non-usage, have always in them matter of controversy and debate. And it may be affirmed that the instances are very rare of princes having the worst in the dispute with their people, if they were eminent either for justice in time of peace, or conduct in time of war; such advantage the Crown gives to those who adorn and confirm it by their own personal virtues.

But since for the greater honour of good and wise princes, and the better to set off their character by the comparison, Heaven has decreed there must be a mixture, and that such as are perverse and insufficient, or perhaps both, are at least to have their equal turns in the government of the world; and besides that, the will of a man is so various, and so unbounded a thing, and so fatal too, when joined with power misapplied; it is no wonder if those who are to be governed are unwilling to have so dangerous as well as so uncertain a standard of their obedience. There must be, therefore, rules and laws, for want of which, or at least the observation of them, it was as capital for a man to say Nero did not play well on the lute, as to commit treason or blaspheme the gods, and even Vespasian* himself had like to have lost his life for sleeping, whilst he should have attended and admired that Emperor's impertinence upon the stage.

There is a wantonness in too great power that men are generally apt to be corrupted with; and for that reason a wise prince, to prevent the temptations arising from common frailty, would choose to govern by rules for his own sake, as well as for his people's, since it only secures him from errors, and does not lessen the real authority that a good magistrate would care to be possessed of. For if the will of a prince is contrary either to reason itself, or to the universal opinion of his subjects, the law by a kind restraint rescues him from a disease that would undo him; if his will, on the other side, is reasonable and well directed, that will immediately becomes a law, and he is arbitrary by an easy and natural consequence, without taking pains or over-turning the world for it.

If princes consider laws as things imposed on them, they have the appearance of fetters of iron, but to such as would make them their choice as well as their practice, they are chains of gold, and in that respect an ornament, as in others they are a defence to them; and by a comparison not improper for God's vicegerents upon earth, as our maker never commands our obedience to anything that as reasonable creatures we ought not to make our own election, so a good and wise governor, though all laws were abolished, would by the voluntary direction of his own reason, do without constraint the very same things that they would have enjoined.

Our Trimmer thinks that a king and kingdom are to be one creature, not to be separated in their political capacity, and when either of them undertake to act apart, it is like the crawling of worms after they are cut in pieces, which cannot be a lasting motion, the whole creature not stirring at a time. If the body has the dead palsy, the head cannot make it move, and God has not yet delegated such a healing power to princes, as that they can in a moment say to a languishing people oppressed into despair, 'take up your bed and walk'.*

The figure of a king is so comprehensive and so exalted a thing, that it is a kind of degrading him to lodge that power separately in his own natural person, which can never be truly nor safely great, but where the people are so united to him, as to be flesh of his flesh, and bone of his bone;* for when he is reduced to the single definition of a man, he shrinks into so low a character, that it is a temptation upon men's allegiance, and an impairing of that veneration which is necessary to preserve their duty to him. Whereas a prince that is so joined to his people, that they seem to be his limbs rather than his subjects, clothed with mercy and justice rightly applied in their several places, his throne supported by love as well as by power, and the warm wishes of his devoted subjects like a never failing incense still ascending towards him, looks so like the best image we can frame to ourselves of God Almighty, that men would have much ado, not to fall down and worship him, and would be much more tempted to the sin of idolatry than to that of disobedience.

Our Trimmer is of opinion that there must be so much dignity inseparably annexed to the regal function as may be sufficient to secure it from insolence and contempt; and there must be condescensions too from the throne, like kind showers from Heaven, that the prince may look so much the more like God Almighty's deputy upon earth. For power without love has a terrifying aspect, and the worship that is paid to it, is like that which the Indians give out of fear to wild beasts and devils. He that fears God only because there is a Hell, must wish there were no God, and he who fears a king only because he can

punish, must wish there were no king; so that without a principle of
love there can be no true allegiance, and there must remain perpetual
seeds of resistance against a power which is built upon such an unnatural foundation as that of fear and terror.

All force is a kind of foul play, and whosoever owns it himself does
by implication allow it to those he plays with, so that there will ever be
matter prepared in the minds of the people, when they are so provoked; and the prince, to secure himself, must live in the midst of his
own subjects as if he were in a conquered country, raise armies as if
he were immediately to make or resist an invasion, and all this while
sleep as unquietly from the fear of the remedies, as he did before from
that of the disease: it being hard for him to forget, that more princes
have been destroyed by their guards than by their people, and that
even at the time when the rule was *quod principi placuit lex esto*.* The
armies and Praetorian bands* which were the instruments of that
unruly power were frequently the means made use of to destroy those
who had it.

There will ever be this difference between God and his vicegerents,
that God is always above the instruments he uses, and out of the danger of receiving hurt from them, but princes can never lodge power in
any hands, which may not at some time turn it back upon them. For
though it is possible for a king to have power enough to satisfy his
ambition, yet no kingdom has money enough to satisfy the avarice of
the under-workmen, who learn from that prince who will exact more
than belongs to him, to expect from him much more than they
deserve; and growing angry upon the first disappointment, they are
like devils which grow terrible to the conjurers themselves who
brought them up, but cannot send them down again. And besides that
there can be no lasting radical security, but where the governed are
satisfied with the governors; it must be a dominion very unpleasant to
a prince of an elevated mind, to impose an abject and a sordid servility, instead of receiving the willing sacrifice of duty and obedience.
The bravest princes in all times, who were incapable of any other kind
of fear, have feared to grieve their own people. Such a fear is a glory,
and in this sense, it is an infamy not to be a coward; so that the mistaken heroes who are void of this generous kind of fear, need no other
aggravation to complete their ill character.

When a despotic prince has bruised all his subjects into a slavish
obedience, all the force he can use cannot subdue his own fears, enemies

of his own creation, to which he can never be reconciled, it being impossible to do injustice and not to fear a revenge. There is no cure for this fear, but the not deserving to be hurt, and therefore a prince who does not allow his thoughts to stray beyond the rule of justice has always the blessing of an inward quiet and assurance, as a natural effect of his good meaning to his people; and though he will not neglect due precautions to secure himself in all events, yet he is incapable of entertaining vain and remote suspicions of those of whom he resolves never to deserve ill. It is very hard for a prince to fear a rebellion who neither does nor intends to do anything to provoke it; therefore too great a diligence in the governors to raise and improve fears and dangers from the people, is no very good symptom, and naturally begets an inference that they have thoughts of putting their subjects' allegiance to a trial, and therefore not without some reason fear beforehand, that the irregularities they intend may raise men to a resistance.

Our Trimmer thinks it no advantage to a government to endeavour the suppressing all kind of right which may remain in the body of the people, or to employ small authors in it, whose officiousness or want of money may encourage them to write, though it is not very easy to have abilities equal to such a subject. They forget that in their too high strained arguments for the rights of princes they very often plead against human nature, which will always give a bias to those reasons which seem to be of her side. It is the people that reads those books, and it is the people that must judge of them, and therefore no maxims should be laid down for the right of government, to which there can be any reasonable objection. For the world has an interest, and for that reason is more than ordinarily discerning, to find out the weak sides of such arguments as are intended to do them hurt; and it is a diminution to a government to promote or countenance such well-affected mistakes, which are turned upon it with disadvantage whenever they are detected and exposed. And naturally the too earnest endeavours to take from men the right they have, tempt them by the example, to claim that which they have not; and in power as in most other things, the way for princes to keep it, is not to grasp more than their arms can well hold. The nice and unnecessary enquiry into these things, or the licensing some books and suppressing others, without sufficient reason to justify the doing either, is so far from being an advantage to a government, that it exposes it to the censure of being partial, and to the suspicion of having some hidden designs, to be carried on by these unusual methods.

When all is said, there is a natural reason of state, an undefinable thing grounded upon the common good of mankind, which is immortal, and in all changes and revolutions still preserves its original right of saving a nation, when the letter of the law perhaps would destroy it; and by whatsoever means it moves carries a power with it that admits no opposition, being supported by Nature, which inspires an immediate consent at some critical times into every individual member, to that which visibly tends to the preservation of the whole; and this being so, a wise prince, instead of controverting the right of this reason of state, will by all means endeavour it may ever be of his side, and then he will be secure.

Our Trimmer cannot conceive that the power of any prince can be lasting, but where it is built upon the foundation of his own unborrowed virtue; he must not only be the first mover and the fountain from whence all the great acts of state originally flow, but he must be thought so by his people, that they may preserve their veneration to him; he must be jealous of his power, and not impart so much of it to any about him, as that he may suffer an eclipse by it. He cannot take too much care to keep himself up; for when a prince is thought to be led by those with whom he should only advise, and that the commands he gives are transmitted through him, and are not of his own growth, the world will look upon him as a bird adorned with feathers that are not his own, or consider him rather as an engine than a living creature. Besides, it would be a contradiction for a prince to fear a commonwealth, and at the same time to create one himself, by delegating such a power, to any number of men near him, as is inconsistent with the true figure of a monarch. It is the worst kind of coordination the Crown can submit to, for it is the exercise of power that draws the respect along with it, and when that is parted with, the bare character of a king is not sufficient to keep it up.

But though it is a diminution to a prince to parcel out his power so liberally amongst his favourites, it is yet worse to divide with any other man, and to bring himself in competition with a single rival; a partner in government is so unnatural a thing, that it is a squint-eyed allegiance which must be paid to such a double bottomed monarchy. The two Czars are an example that the more civilized part of the world will not be proud to follow;* and whatever gloss may be put upon this method, by those to whom it may be of some use, the prince will do well to remember and reflect upon the story of certain men who had set up a statue in honour of the sun, yet in a very little time they turned their backs to the sun, and their faces to the statue. These mystical unions are better placed in the other world than they are in this, and we shall have much ado to find that in a monarchy God's vicegerency is delegated to more heads than that which is anointed.

Princes may lend some of their light to make another shine, but they must still preserve the superiority of being the brighter planet: and when it happens that the reversion is in men's eyes, there is more care necessary to keep up the dignity of possession, that men may not forget who is king, either out of their hopes or their fears who shall be. If the sun should part with all its light to any of the stars, the Indians would not know where to find their god, after he had so deposed himself, and would make the light wherever it went the object of their worship. All usurpation is alike upon sovereignty, it is no matter from what hand it comes, and crowned heads are to be the more circumspect in respect that men's thoughts are naturally apt to ramble beyond what is present; they love to work at a distance, and in the greedy expectation which their minds may be filled with of a new master, the old one may be left to look a little out of countenance.*

Our Trimmer owns a passion for liberty, yet so restrained that it does not in the least impair or taint his allegiance; he thinks it is hard for a soul that does not love liberty ever to raise itself towards another world. He takes it to be the foundation of all virtue, and the only seasoning that gives a relish to life; and though the laziness of a slavish subjection has its charms for the more gross and earthy part of mankind, yet to men made of a better sort of clay, all that the world can give without liberty has no taste. It is true, nothing is sold so cheap by unthinking men, but that does no more lessen the real value of it, than a country fellow's ignorance does that of a diamond, in selling it for a pot of ale. Liberty is the mistress of mankind; she has powerful charms, which so dazzle us, that we find beauties in her which perhaps are not there, as we do in other mistresses. Yet if she was not a beauty the world would not run mad for her. Therefore, since the reasonable desire of it ought not to be restrained, and that even the unreasonable desire of it cannot be entirely suppressed, those who will take it away from a people possessed of it are likely either to fail in the attempting, or to be very unquiet in the keeping of it.

Our Trimmer admires our blessed constitution, in which dominion and liberty are so happily reconciled; it gives to the prince the
glorious power of commanding freemen, and to the subjects the satisfaction of seeing that power so lodged, as that their liberties are
secure. It does not allow the Crown such a ruining power, as that no
grass can grow wherever it treads, but a cherishing and protecting
power; such a one as has a grim aspect only to the offending subjects,
but is the joy and the pride of all the good ones, their own interest
being so bound up in it, as to engage them to defend and support it.
As the king is in some instances restrained, so nothing in the government can move without him. Our laws make a true distinction
between vassalage and obedience, between a devouring prerogative,
and a licentious ungovernable freedom. And as of all the orders of
building the composite is the best, so ours by a wise mixture and
a happy choice of what is best in others, is brought into a form, that is
our felicity who live under it, and the envy of our neighbours who
cannot imitate it.* The Crown has power sufficient to protect our liberties; the people have so much liberty as is necessary to make them
useful to the Crown. Our government is in a just proportion, no tym-
pany, no unnatural swelling either of power or liberty; and whereas in
all overgrown monarchies, reason, learning, and enquiry are banished
and hanged in effigy for mutineers, here they are encouraged and
cherished, as the surest friends to a government established upon the
foundation of law and justice.

When all is done, those who look for perfection in this world may
look as long as the Jews have done for their messiahs; and therefore
our Trimmer is not so unreasonably partial, as to free our government
from all objections. No doubt there have been fatal instances of its
sickness, and more than that, of its mortality for some time, though
by a miracle it has been revived again. But till we have another mankind, in all constitutions that are bounded, there will ever be some
matter of strife and contention, and rather than want pretences,
men's passions and interests will raise them from the most inconsiderable causes.

Our government is like our climate, there are winds which are
sometimes loud and unquiet; and yet with all the trouble they give us,
we owe a great part of our health to them: they cleanse the air, which
else would be like a standing pool, and instead of a refreshment would
be a disease to us. There may be fresh gales of asserted liberty without

turning into such storms or hurricanes, as that the state should run any hazard of being cast away by them. These strugglings which are natural to all mixed governments, whilst they are kept from growing into convulsions, do by a mutual agitation, from the several parts, rather support and strengthen, than weaken or maim the constitution; and the whole frame, instead of being torn or disjointed, comes to be the better and closer knit, by being thus exercised.

But whatever faults our government may have, or whatever spots a discerning critic may find in it, when he looks upon it alone, let any other be set against it, and then it shows its comparative beauty. Let us look upon the most glittering outside of unbounded authority, and upon a nearer enquiry we shall find nothing but poor and miserable deformity within. Let us imagine a prince living in his kingdom, as if he was in a great galley, his subjects tugging at the oar, laden with chains, and reduced to real rags, to gain him imaginary laurels. Let us represent him gazing amongst his flatterers, like a child never contradicted and therefore always cozened, or like a lady complimented only to be abused; condemned never to hear truth, and consequently never to do justice; wallowing in the soft bed of wanton and unbridled greatness, not less odious to the instruments, than to the objects of his tyranny; blown up into an ambitious dropsy, never to be satisfied by the conquest of other people, or by the oppression of his own. By aiming to be more than a man, he becomes a beast; a mistaken creature swelled with panegyrics, and flattered out of his senses; not only an encumbrance but a common nuisance to mankind; a hardened and unrelenting soul, and like some creatures that grow fat with poisons, he grows great by other men's miseries; an ambitious ape of the divine greatness; an unruly giant that would storm even Heaven itself, but that his scaling ladders are not long enough: in short, a wild beast in rich trappings, and with all his pride, no more than a whip in God Almighty's hand, to be thrown into the fire when the world has been sufficiently scourged with it. This picture laid in right colours would not invite men to wish for such a government, but rather to acknowledge the happiness of our own, under which we enjoy all the privileges reasonable men can desire, and avoid all the miseries many others are subject to; so that our Trimmer would fain keep it with all its faults, and does as little forgive those who give the occasion of breaking it, as he does those that take it.

Our Trimmer is a friend to parliaments, notwithstanding all their faults and excesses, which of late have given such matter of objection to them. He thinks that though they may at some times be troublesome to authority, yet they add the greatest strength to it under a wise administration. He believes no government is perfect except a kind of omnipotence reside in it, to be exerted upon great occasions. Now this cannot be attained by force upon the people, let it be never so great; there must be their consent too, or else a nation moves only by being driven, a sluggish and constrained motion, void of that life and vigour which is necessary to produce great things. Whereas the virtual consent of the whole being included in their representatives, and the king giving the sanction to the united sense of the people, every act done by such an authority seems to be an effect of their choice, as well as a part of their duty; and they do with an eagerness, of which men are incapable whilst under a force, execute whatever is so enjoined as their own will better explained by parliament, rather than from the terror of incurring the penalty of the law for omitting it. And by the means of this political omnipotence, whatever sap or juice there is in a nation, may be to the last drop produced whilst it rises naturally from the root; whereas all power exercised without consent is like giving wounds and gashes, and tapping a tree at unseasonable times for the present occasion, which in a very little time must needs destroy it.

Our Trimmer believes that by the advantage of our situation, there can hardly any such sudden disease come upon us, but that the king may have time enough left to consult with his physicians in parliament; pretences indeed may be made, but a real necessity so pressing, that no delay is to be admitted is hardly to be imagined, and it will neither be easy to give an instance of any such thing for the time past, or reasonable to presume it will ever happen for the time to come. But if that strange thing should fall out, our Trimmer is not so strait-laced as to let a nation die or be stifled, rather than it should be helped by any other than the proper officers. The cases themselves will bring the remedies along with them, and he is not afraid to allow, that in order to its preservation there is a hidden power in government, which would be lost if it was defined, a certain mystery, by virtue of which a nation may at some critical times be secured from ruin. But then it must be kept as a mystery; it is rendered useless when touched by unskilful hands, and no government ever had or deserved to have that power which was so unwary as to anticipate their claim to it.

Our Trimmer cannot help thinking, it had been better, if the Triennial Act* had been observed; first because it is the law, and he would not have the Crown by such an example teach the nation to break it. All irregularity is catching; it has contagion in it, especially in an age so much more inclined to follow ill patterns than good ones. He would have had a parliament because it is an essential part of the constitution, even without the law, it being the only provision in extraordinary cases, in which there would be otherwise no remedy. And there can be no greater solecism in government than a failure of justice. He would have had one, because nothing else can unite and heal us; all other means are mere shifts and projects, houses of cards blown down with the least breath, and that cannot resist the difficulties which are ever to be presumed in things of this kind. And he would have had one, because it might have done the King good, and could not possibly have done him hurt without his own consent, which in that case is not to be supposed. Therefore for him to fear it is so strange, and so little to be comprehended, that the reasons can never be presumed to grow in our soil, or to thrive in it, when transplanted from any other country.*

And no doubt there are such irresistible arguments for the calling a parliament, that though it might be denied to the unmannerly threatening petitions of men that are mutinous and disaffected, it will be granted to the soft and obsequious murmurs of his majesty's best subjects, and there will be such a rhetoric in their silent grief, that it will at last prevail against the artifices of those, who either out of guilt or interest, are afraid to throw themselves upon their country, knowing how scurvily they have used it. That day of judgement will come, though we know neither the day nor the hour, and our Trimmer would live so as to be prepared for it, with a full assurance in the meantime, that the lamenting voice of a nation cannot long be resisted, and that a prince who could so forgive his people when they had been in the wrong, cannot fail to hear them, when they are in the right.*

THE TRIMMER'S OPINION CONCERNING RELIGION, IN RELATION TO THE PRODUCING QUIET AMONGST OURSELVES

RELIGION has such a superiority above all other things, and that indispensable influence upon all mankind, that it is as necessary to our living happily in this world, as it is to our being saved in the next. Without it man is an abandoned creature, one of the worst beasts Nature has produced, and fit only for the society of wolves and bears. Therefore in all ages it has been the foundation of government, and though false gods have been imposed upon the credulity of the world, yet they were gods still in their opinion, and the awe and deference men had to them and their oracles, kept them within bounds towards one another, which the laws alone with all their authority could never have effected. Without the help of religion, the laws would not be able to subdue the perverseness of men's wills, which are wild beasts that require a double chain to keep them down. For this reason it is said, that it is not a sufficient ground to make war upon a neighbouring state because they are of another religion, let it be never so differing; yet if they worship and acknowledge no deity at all, they may be invaded as public enemies of mankind, because they reject the only thing that can bind men to live well with one another. The consideration of religion is so twisted with that of government that it is never to be separated, and though the foundations of it are to be unchangeable and eternal, yet the forms and circumstances of discipline are to be suited to the several climates and constitutions, so as they may keep men in a willing acquiescence to them without discomposing the world by nice disputes, which can never be of equal moment with the public peace.

Our religion here in England seems to be distinguished by a peculiar effect of God Almighty's goodness in permitting it to be introduced, or more properly restored, by a more regular method than the circumstances of most other Reformed Churches would allow them to do in relation to the government; and the dignity with which it has supported itself since, and the great men our Church has produced, ought to recommend it to the esteem of all Protestants at least. Our Trimmer is very partial to it for these reasons, and many more, and desirous that it may preserve its due jurisdiction and authority; so far he is from wishing it oppressed, by the malicious or unreasonable cavils of those who take pains to raise objections to it.

The question then will be, how and by what methods this Church shall best support itself, the present circumstances considered, in relation to Dissenters of all sorts. I will first lay it for a ground, that as there can be no true religion without charity, so there can be no human prudence without some bearing and condescension. This

principle does not extend to oblige the Church always to yield to
those who are disposed to contest with it: the expediency of doing it
is to be considered, and determined according to the occasion; and
this leads me to lay open the thoughts of our Trimmer in reference
first to the Protestant, and then to the Popish recusants.

What has lately happened amongst us makes an apology necessary
for saying anything that looks like favour towards a sort of men who
have brought themselves under such a disadvantage. The late conspiracy* has such broad symptoms of the disaffection of the whole
party, that upon the first reflection, whilst our thoughts are warm, it
would almost persuade us to put them out of the protection of our
good nature, and to think that the Christian indulgence which our
compassion for other men's sufferings cannot easily deny, seems not
only to be forfeited by the ill appearances that are against them, but
even becomes a crime when it is so misapplied.

Yet for all this, upon second and cooler thoughts, moderate men
will not be so ready to involve a whole party in the guilt of a few, or to
admit inferences and presumptions to be evidence in a case where the
sentence must be so heavy, as it ought to be against all those who have
a fixed resolution against the government established. Besides, men
who act by a principle grounded upon moral virtue, can never let it be
entirely extinguished by the most repeated provocations. If a right
thing agreeable to Nature and good sense takes root in the heart of
a man that is impartial and unbiased, no outward circumstances can
ever destroy it. It is true, the degrees of a man's zeal for the prosecution of it may be differing: the faults of other men, the consideration
of the public, and the seasonable prudence by which wise men will
ever be directed, may give great allays, they may lessen and perhaps
for a time suppress the exercise of that which in a general proposition
may be reasonable; but whatever is so will inevitably grow and spring
up again, having a foundation in Nature which is not to be destroyed.

Our Trimmer therefore endeavours to separate the detestation he
has of those who had either a hand or a thought in the late plot, from
the principle of prudential as well as Christian charity towards mankind, and for that reason would fain use the means of reclaiming such
of the Dissenters as are not incurable, and even of bearing to a degree
those that are, as far as may consist with the public interest and security. He is far from justifying an affected separation from the communion
of the Church, and even in those who mean well and are misled, he

looks upon it as a disease that has seized upon their minds, very
troublesome to themselves as well as dangerous by the consequences
it may produce. He does not go about to excuse their making it an
indispensable duty to meet in numbers to say their prayers; such
meetings may prove mischievous to the state: at least the laws, which
are the best judges, have determined that there is danger in them. He
has good nature enough to lament that the perverseness of a part should
have drawn rigorous laws upon the whole body of the Dissenters; but
when they are once made, no private opinion must stand in opposition
to them. If they are in themselves reasonable, they are in that respect
to be observed, even without being enjoined; if by the change of times
and circumstances they should become less reasonable than when
they were first made, even then they are to be obeyed too, because they
are laws, till they are mended or repealed by the same authority that
enacted them.

He has too much deference to the constitution of our government,
to wish any more prerogative declarations in favour of scrupulous
men, or to dispense with penal laws in such a manner or to such an
end,* that suspecting men might with some reason apprehend, that
so hated a thing as a persecution could never make way for itself with
any hopes of success, otherwise than by preparing the deluded world
with a false prospect of liberty and indulgence: the inward springs
and wheels by which that engine moved are now so fully laid open and
exposed, that it is not supposable such a baffled experiment should
ever be tried again; the effect it had at the time, and the spirit it raised
will not easily be forgotten, and it may be presumed that the remembrance of it may secure us from any more attempts of that kind for the
future. We must no more break a law to give men ease, than we are to
rob a house with the devout intention of giving the plunder to the
poor; in this case our compassion would be as ill directed, as our charity in the other. In short, the veneration due to the laws is never to be
thrown off, let the pretences be never so specious.

Yet with all this, he cannot bring himself to think, that an extraordinary diligence to take the utmost penalties of the law upon a poor
offending neighbour, is of itself such an all-sufficient virtue, that
without something else to recommend men, it should entitle them to
all kind of preferments and rewards. He would not detract from the
merit of those who execute the laws; yet he cannot think that such
a piece of service as this can entirely change the man, or either make

him a better divine, or a more knowing magistrate than he was before; especially if it be done with a partial and unequal hand, in reference to greater and more dangerous offenders.

Our Trimmer would have those mistaken men ready to throw themselves into the arms of the Church, and he would have those arms as ready to receive them. He would have no supercilious looks to fright these strayed sheep from coming into the fold again; no ill-natured maxims of eternal suspicion, or a belief that those who have been once in the wrong can never be in the right again, but a visible preparation of mind, to receive with joy all the proselytes that shall come to us, and a much greater earnestness to reclaim than to punish them. It is to be confessed, there is a great deal to forgive, a hard task enough for the charity of a Church so provoked, but that must not cut off all hopes of being reconciled. Yet if there must be some anger left still, let it break out into a Christian revenge, and by being kinder to those children of disobedience than they deserve, let the injured Church triumph by throwing shame and confusion of face upon them. There should not always be storms and thunder; a clearer sky sometimes would make the Church look more like Heaven, and would do more towards reclaiming those wanderers than a perpetual terror which seems to have no intermission.

For there is in many, and particularly in English men, a mistaken pleasure in resisting the dictates of rigorous authority, a stomach that rises against a hard imposition; nay in some even a lust in suffering from a wrong point of honour, which yet does not want the applause of the greater part of mankind, who have not learnt to distinguish. Constancy will be thought a virtue even when it is a mistake, and the ill-judging world will be apt to think that opinion most in the right, which produces the greater numbers of those who are willing to suffer for it. All this is prevented and falls to the ground by using well-timed indulgence, and the stubborn adversary who values himself upon his resistance whilst he is oppressed, yields insensibly to kinder methods, when they are applied to him; and the same man naturally melts into conformity, who perhaps would never have been beaten into it. We may be taught by the compassion that attends the most criminal men when they are condemned, that faults are much more natural things than punishments, and that even the most necessary acts of severity do some kind of violence to our nature, whose indulgence will not be confined within the strait bounds of inexorable justice; so that this should be an argument for gentleness, besides that it is the likeliest way to make these men ashamed of their separation, whilst the pressing them too hard tends rather to make them proud of it.

Our Trimmer would have the clergy supported in their lawful rights, and in all the power and dignity that belongs to them, and yet he thinks that possibly there may be in some of them a too great eagerness to extend the ecclesiastical jurisdiction, which though it may be well intended, yet the straining it too high has an appearance of ambition that raises men's objections to it, and is so very unlike the apostolical zeal, which was quite otherwise applied, that the world draws inferences from it which do the Church no service.

He is troubled to see men of all sides sick of a calenture* of mistaken devotion, and it seems to him that the devout fire of mutual charity with which the primitive Christians were inflamed, is long since extinguished, and instead of it a devouring fire of anger and persecution breaks out in the world. We wrangle with one another for religion till the blood comes, whilst the Ten Commandments have no more authority with us, than if they were so many obsolete laws, or proclamations out of date. He thinks that a nation will hardly be mended by principles of religion, where morality is made a heretic; and therefore, as he believes devotion to be misplaced when it gets into a conventicle, he concludes that loyalty is so too when it is lodged in a drunken club: those virtues deserve a better seat of empire, and they are degraded, when such men undertake their defence, as have too great need of an apology for themselves.

Our Trimmer wishes that some knowledge may go along with the zeal on the right side, and that those who are in possession of the pulpit would quote at least as often the authority of the scriptures as they do that of the state; there are many who borrow too often from the government arms to use against their adversaries, and neglect those that are more proper and would be more powerful. A divine grows less, and puts a diminution upon his own character, when he quotes any law but that of God Almighty to get the better of those that contest with him; and as it is a sign of a decayed constitution when Nature with good diet cannot expel noxious humours, without calling foreign drugs to her assistance, so it looks like want of health in a Church, when instead of depending upon the power of that truth which it holds, and the good example of those who teach it to support itself and to suppress errors, it should

have a perpetual recourse to the secular authority, and even upon
the slightest occasions.

Our Trimmer has his objections to the too busy diligence and the
overdoing of some of the Dissenting clergy, and he does as little
approve those of our Church who wear God Almighty's livery, as
some old warders in the Tower do the King's, who do nothing that
belongs to their place but receiving the wages for it. He thinks that
the liberty of the late times gave men so much light, and diffused it
so universally amongst the people, that they are not now to be dealt
with, as they might have been in an age of less inquiry; and therefore, though in some well-chosen and dearly beloved auditories,
good resolute nonsense backed with authority may prevail, yet generally men are become so good judges of what they hear, that the
clergy ought to be very wary before they go about to impose upon
their understandings, which are grown less humble than they were
in former times, when the men in black had made learning such
a sin for the laity, that for fear of offending they made a conscience
of being able to read; but now the world is grown saucy, and expects
reasons, and good ones too, before they give up their own opinions
to other men's dictates, though never so magisterially delivered
to them.

Our Trimmer is far from approving the hypocrisy which seems to
be the reigning vice among some of the Dissenting clergy; he thinks
it the most provoking sin men can be guilty of in relation to Heaven;
and yet (which may seem strange) that very sin which shall destroy
the soul of the man who preaches, may help to save those of the company that hear him, and even those who are cheated by the false ostentation of his strictness of life, may by that pattern be encouraged to
the real practice of those Christian virtues, which he does so deceit-
fully profess. So that the detestation of this fault may possibly be carried too far by our more orthodox divines, if they think it cannot be
enough expressed without bending the stick another way: a dangerous method, and a worse extreme for men of that character, who by
going to the utmost line of Christian liberty, will certainly encourage
others to go beyond it. No man does less approve the ill-bred methods
of some of the Dissenters in rebuking authority, who behave themselves as if they thought ill manners necessary to salvation; yet he
cannot but distinguish and desire a mean between the sauciness of
some of the Scotch apostles,* and the indecent courtship of some

silken divines, who one would think did practice to bow at the altar, only to learn to make the better legs at court.*

Our Trimmer approves the principle of our Church, that dominion is not founded in grace, and that our obedience is to be given to a Popish king in other things, at the same time that our compliance with him in his religion is to be denied; yet he cannot but think it a very extraordinary thing, if a Protestant Church should by a voluntary election, choose a Papist for their guardian, and receive directions for the supporting our religion from one who must believe it a mortal sin not to endeavour to destroy it. Such a refined piece of breeding would not seem to be very well placed in the clergy, who will hardly be able to find precedents to justify such an extravagant kind of courtship, and which is so unlike the primitive methods that ought to be our pattern. He has no such unreasonable tenderness for any sort of men, as to expect their faults should not be impartially laid open, as often as they give occasion for it; and yet he cannot but smile to see, that the same man who sets up all his sales of rhetoric to fall upon the Dissenters, when Popery is to be handled, he does it so gingerly, that he looks like an ass mumbling of a thistle, so afraid he is of letting himself loose upon a subject when he may be in danger of letting his duty get the better of his discretion.

Our Trimmer is far from relishing the impertinent wanderings of those who pour out long prayers upon the congregation, and all from their own stock, which God knows for the most part is a barren soil that produces weeds instead of flowers, and by this means they expose religion itself, rather than promote men's devotions. On the other side, there may be too great restraint put upon men whom God and Nature have distinguished from their fellow labourers, by blessing them with a happier talent, and by giving them not only good sense but a powerful utterance too, have enabled them to gush out upon the attentive auditory with a mighty stream of devout and unaffected eloquence. When a man so qualified, endued with learning too, and above all adorned with a good life, breaks out into a warm and well-delivered prayer before his sermon, it has the appearance of a divine rapture; he raises and leads the hearts of an assembly in another manner than the most studied or best composed form of set words can ever attain to. And the 'pray-wees', who serve up all their sermons with the same garnishing, would look like so many statues or men of straw in the pulpit, compared with those who speak with such a powerful zeal, that men are tempted at the moment to believe Heaven itself had dictated their words to them.

Our Trimmer is not so unreasonably indulgent to the Dissenters, as to excuse the irregularities of their complaints, or to approve their threatening style, which is so ill-suited to their circumstances as well as to their duty: he would have them show their grief, and not their anger to the government, and by such a submission to authority as becomes them; if they cannot inwardly acquiesce in what is imposed, let them deserve a legislative remedy to their sufferings, there being no other way to give them perfect redress; and either to seek it or pretend to give it by any other method, would not only be vain, but criminal too in those that go about it.

Yet with all this, there may be in the meantime a prudential latitude left, as to the manner of prosecuting the laws now in force against them. The government is in some degree answerable for such an administration of them, as may be free from the censure of impartial judges, and in order to that, it will be necessary that one of these methods be pursued: either to let loose the laws to their utmost extent, without any moderation or restraint, in which at least the equality of the government would be without objection, the penalties being exacted without remission from the Dissenters of all kinds. Or if that will not be done (as indeed there is no reason it should) there is a necessity of some connivance to the Protestant Dissenters, to excuse that which in humanity must be allowed to the Papists, even without any leaning towards them, which might be supposed in those who are or shall be in the administration of public business. And it will follow that according to our circumstances, the distribution of such connivance must be made in such a manner, that the greater part of it may fall on the Protestants' side, or else the objections will be so strong, and the inferences so clear, that the friends as well as the enemies of the Crown will be sure to take hold of them.

It will not be sufficient to say the Papists may be connived at because they are good subjects, but that the Protestant Dissenters must suffer because they are ill ones: these general maxims will not convince discerning men, neither will any late instances make them forget what has passed at other times in the world.* Both sides have had their turns in being good and ill subjects, and therefore it is easy to imagine what suspicions would arise, in the present conjuncture, if such a partial argument as this should be imposed upon us. The truth is, this matter speaks so much of itself, that it is not only unnecessary, but it may be unmannerly to say any more of it.

Our Trimmer therefore could wish that since, notwithstanding the laws which deny churches to say mass in, not only the exercise but even the ostentation of Popery is as well or better performed in the chapels of so many foreign ministers where the English openly resort, in spite of proclamations and orders of council, which are grown to be as harmless things to them as the Pope's bulls and excommunications are to heretics who are out of his reach; I say he could wish that by a seasonable as well as an equal piece of justice, there might be so much consideration had of the Protestant Dissenters, as that there might be at some times, and in some places, a veil thrown over an innocent and retired conventicle; and that such an indulgence might be practised with less prejudice to the Church, or diminution to the laws, it might be done so as to look rather like a kind omission to inquire too strictly, than an allowed toleration of that which is against the rule established.

Such a skilful hand as this, is very necessary in our circumstances, and the government, by making no sort of men entirely disparate, does not only secure itself from the danger of any wild or villainous attempt, but lays such a foundation for healing and uniting laws, whenever a parliament shall meet, that the seeds of difference and animosity between the several contending sides may (Heaven consenting) be for ever destroyed.

THE TRIMMER'S OPINION CONCERNING THE PAPISTS

To speak of Popery leads one into such a sea of matter, that it is not easy to forbear launching into it, being invited by such a fruitful theme, and by a variety never to be exhausted; but to confine it to the present subject, I will only say a short word of the religion itself, of its influence here at this time, and of our Trimmer's opinion in relation to our manner of living with it.

If a man would speak maliciously of this religion, one might say it is like those diseases, where as long as one drop of the infection remains, there is still a danger of having the whole mass of blood corrupted by it. In Sweden there was an absolute cure, and nothing of Popery heard of till Queen Christina (whether moved by arguments of this or the other world, would not be good manners to enquire) thought fit to change her religion, and her country, and to live at Rome, where she might find better judges of her virtues, and less ungentle censurers of those princely liberties she was sometimes disposed to,* than she left at Stockholm, where the good breeding of the climate is much inferior to that of Rome, as well as the civility of the religion; the cardinals having rescued the Church from those clownish methods the fishermen had first introduced, and mended that pattern so effectually, that a man of that age, if he should now come into the world, would not possibly know it.

In Denmark the Reformation was entire, in some states of Germany as well as in Geneva the cure was universal; but in the rest of the world where the Protestant religion took place, the popish humour was too tough to be totally expelled. And so it was in England, though the change was made with all the advantage imaginable to the Reformation, it being countenanced and introduced by legal authority, and by that means might perhaps have been as perfect as in any other place, if the short reign of Edward VI, and the succession of a popish Queen* had not given such an advantage to that religion, that it has subsisted ever since, under all the hardships that have been put upon it. It has been a close compact body, and made the more so by their sufferings; it was not strong enough to prevail, but it was still able with the help of foreign support to carry on an interest which gave the Crown trouble, and to make a considerable, not to say a dangerous, figure in the nation.

So much as this could not have been done without some hopes, nor these hopes kept up without some reasonable grounds. In Queen Elizabeth's time, the Spanish zeal for their religion and their revenge for '88,* gave warmth to the Papists here; and above all the right of the Queen of Scots* to succeed, was, whilst she lived, sufficient to give them a better prospect of their affairs. In King James's time, the Spanish match and his gentleness towards them kept them up, which they were ready to interpret more in their favour than was either reasonable, or became them; so little tenderness they have, even where it is most due, if the interest of their religion comes in competition with it.

As for the late King,* though he gave the most glorious evidence that ever man did of his being a Protestant, yet by the more than ordinary influence the Queen was thought to have over him, and it so happening, that the greater part of his anger was directed against the

Puritans, there was such an advantage given to men disposed to suspect, that they were ready to interpret it a leaning towards Popery, without which handle, it was morally impossible that the ill-affected part of the nation could ever have seduced the rest into a rebellion.

That which helped to confirm many well-meaning men in their misapprehensions of the King, was the long and unusual intermission of parliaments, so that every year which passed without one, made up a new argument to increase their suspicions, and made them presume that the Papists had a principal hand in keeping them off. This raised such heat in men's minds, to think that men who were obnoxious to the laws, instead of being punished, should have credit enough to secure themselves, even at the price of destroying the fundamental constitution, that it broke out into a flame, which before it could be quenched, had almost reduced the nation into ashes.

Amongst the miserable effects of that unnatural war, none has been more fatal to us than the forcing our princes to breathe in another air, and to receive the early impressions of a foreign education. The barbarity of the English towards the King and the royal family might very well tempt him to think the better of everything he found abroad, and might naturally produce more gentleness at least towards a religion, by which he was hospitably received, at the same time that he was thrown off and persecuted by the Protestants, though his own subjects too, to aggravate the offence. The Queen Mother,* as generally ladies do with age, grew more devout and earnest in her religion, and besides the temporal rewards of getting larger subsidies from the French clergy she had motives of another kind to persuade her to show her zeal; and since by the Roman dispensatory a soul converted to the Church is a sovereign remedy, and lays up a mighty stock of merit, she was solicitous to secure herself in all events, and therefore first set upon the Duke of Gloucester,* who depended so much upon her goodwill, that she might for that reason be induced to believe the conquest would not be difficult. But it so fell out, that he either from his own constancy, or that he had those near him, by whom he was otherwise advised, chose rather to run away from her importunity, than by staying to bear the continual weight of it. It is believed she had better success with another of her sons,* who if he was not quite brought off from our religion, at least such beginnings were made as made them very easy to be finished. His being of a generous and aspiring nature, and in that respect less patient of the drudgery of arguing, might probably help to recommend a Church to him, that exempts the laity from the vexation of enquiring. Perhaps he might, though by mistake, look upon that religion as more favourable to the enlarged power of kings, a consideration which might have its weight, with a young prince in his warm blood, and that was brought up in arms.

I cannot hinder myself from a small digression, to consider with admiration that this old lady of Rome, with all her wrinkles, should yet have charms able to subdue great princes: so far from handsome and yet so imperious, so painted and yet so pretending, after having abused, deposed, and murdered so many of her lovers, she still finds others glad and proud of their new chains; a thing so strange to indifferent judges, that those who will allow no other miracle in the Church of Rome, must needs grant that this is one, not to be contested. She sits in her shop and sells at dear rates her rattles and her hobby horses, whilst the deluded world still continues to furnish her with customers.

But whither am I carried by this contemplation? It is high time to return to my text, and to consider the wonderful manner of the King's coming home again, led by the hand of Heaven, and called by the voice of his own people, who received him, if possible, with a joy equal to the blessings of peace and union which his Restoration brought along with it. By this there was an end put to the hopes, some might have abroad, of making use of his less happy circumstances to throw him into foreign interests or opinions, which had been wholly inconsistent with our religion, our laws, and all other things that are dear to us. Yet with all this something of those tinctures and impressions might so far remain, as though they were very innocent in him, yet they might have ill effects here, by softening the animosity, which seems necessary to the defender of the Protestant faith, in opposition to such a powerful and irreconcilable enemy.

You may be sure that among all the sorts of men, who applied themselves to the King at his first coming, for his protection, the Papists were not the last, nor as they would fain have flattered themselves, the least welcome, having their past sufferings as well as their present professions to recommend them; and there was something that looked like a particular consideration of them, since it so happened that the indulgence promised to Dissenters at Breda* was carried on in such a manner, that the Papists were to divide with them. And though the Parliament, notwithstanding its resignation to the Crown in all other things, rejected with scorn and anger a declaration framed for this purpose, yet the birth and steps of it gave such an alarm, that men's suspicions once raised, were not easily laid asleep again.

To omit other things, the breach of the Triple League,* and the Dutch War with its appurtenances, raised jealousies to the highest pitch imaginable, and fed the hopes of one party and the fears of the other to such a degree, that some very critical revolutions were generally expected, when the ill success of that war, and the sacrifice France thought fit to make of the Papists here, to their own interests abroad, gave another check; and the act of enjoining the Test to all in office,* was thought no ill bargain to the nation, though bought at the price of £1,200,000 and the money applied to the continuance of the war against the Dutch, than which nothing could be more unpopular, or less approved. Notwithstanding these discouragements, Popery is a plant which may be mowed down, but the root will still remain, and in spite of the laws it will sprout up and grow again; especially if it should happen that there will ever be men in power, who instead of weeding it out of our garden, will take care to cherish and keep it alive; and though the law of excluding them from places was tolerably kept, as to the outward form, yet there were many circumstances, which being improved by the quick-sighted malice of ill-affected men, did help to keep up the world in their suspicions, and to blow up jealousies to such a height, both in and out of Parliament, that the remembrance of them is very unpleasant, and the example so extravagant, that it is to be hoped, in our age nothing like it will be reattempted.*

But to come closer to the case in question, in this condition we stand with the Papists; what shall now be done, according to our Trimmer's opinion, in order to the better bearing this grievance, since as I have said before, there is no hope of being entirely freed from it? Papists we must have amongst us, and if their religion keeps them from bringing honey to the hive, let the government try at least by gentle, and not by violent means, to take away the sting from them.

The first foundation to be laid is, that a distinct consideration is to be had of the Popish clergy, who have such an eternal interest against all accommodation, that it is a hopeless thing to propose anything to them, less than all, their stomachs having been set for it ever since the Reformation. They have pinned themselves to a principle that will admit no mean; they believe Protestants must be damned, and therefore by an extraordinary effect of Christian charity, they would destroy one half of England that the other might be saved. Then for this world they must be in possession for God Almighty, and receive his rents for him, not to account till the day of judgment, which is a good kind of tenure; and you cannot well blame the good men, that they stir up their laity to run any hazard, in order to the getting them restored. What is it to the priest if the deluded zealot undoes himself in the attempt? He sings mass as jollily and with as good a voice at Rome or St Omers* as ever he did; he is a single man, and can have no wants, but such as may be easily supplied; yet that he may not seem altogether insensible or ungrateful to those who are his martyrs, he is ready to assure their executors, and if they please will procure a grant *sub annulo Piscatoris*,* that the good man by being hanged, has got a great bargain, and saved a singeing of some hundreds of years, which he would else have had in Purgatory. There is no cure for this order of men, no expedient to be proposed; so that though the utmost severity of the laws against them may in some sort be mitigated, yet no treaty can be made with men who in this case have left themselves no free will, but are so muffled by zeal, tied by vows, and kept up by such unchangeable maxims of the priesthood, that they are to be left as desperate patients, and to be looked upon as men who will continue in an eternal state of hostility, till the nation is entirely subdued to them.

It is therefore only the lay Papist that is capable of being treated with, and we are to examine of what temper he is, what arguments are the most likely to prevail upon him, and how far it is advisable for the government to be indulgent to him. The lay Papists generally keep their religion rather because they will not break company with those of their party, than out of any settled zeal that has any root in them. Most of them do by the mediation of the priests marry amongst one another, and so keep up an ignorant opposition by hearing only one side. Others look upon it as the better escutcheon, the more ancient religion of the two, and as some men of a good pedigree will despise meaner men, though never so much superior to them by nature, so these undervalue the Reformation as an upstart, and think there is more honour in supporting an old error, than in embracing what seems to them to be a new truth. The laws have made them men of pleasure, by excluding them from public business, and it happens well that they are so, since they will be the more easily persuaded by arguments of ease and convenience to them. They have not put off the man in general, nor the English man in particular: those who in the late storm against them went into other countries, though they had all the advantages which might recommend them to a good reception, yet after a little time they chose to steal over again, and live here with hazard rather than abroad with security. There is a smell in our native earth, better than all the perfumes of the East: there is something in a mother, though never so angry, that the children will naturally trust sooner than the most studied civilities of strangers, let them be never so hospitable. Therefore it is not advisable, nor at all agreeing with the rules of governing prudence, to provoke men by hardships, to forget that nature, which else is sure to be of our side.

When these men by fair usage are put again into their right senses, they will have quite differing reflections, from those which rigour and persecution had raised in them. A lay Papist will first consider his abbey lands,* which notwithstanding whatever has been or can be alleged, must certainly sink considerably in the value, the moment that Popery prevails; and it being a disputable matter, whether zeal might not in a little time get the better of the law in that case, a considering man will admit that as an argument to persuade him to be content with things as they are, rather than run this and other hazards by a change in which perhaps he may have no other advantage, than that his now humble confessor may be raised to a bishopric, and from thence look down superciliously upon his patron; or which is worse, come to take possession for God Almighty of his abbey, in such a manner that the usurping landlord, as he will then be called, shall hardly be admitted to be so much as a tenant to his own land, lest his title might prejudice that of the Church, which will then be the landlord.

He will think what a disadvantage it is to be looked upon as a separate creature depending upon a foreign interest and authority, and for that reason exposed to the jealousy and suspicion of his countrymen. He will reflect what an encumbrance it is, to have his house a pasture for hungry priests to graze in, who have such a never-failing influence upon the foolish, which is the greatest part of every man's family, that a man's dominion, even over his own children, is mangled and divided, if not totally undermined by them. Then to be subject to what arbitrary taxes the popish convocation shall impose upon them, for the carrying on the common interest of that religion, under the penalty of being marked out for half a heretic by the rest of the party; to have no share in business, no opportunity of showing his own value to the world; to live at the best a useless, and by others to be thought a dangerous member of the nation, where he is born, is a burden to a generous mind that cannot be taken off by all the pleasures of an easy unmanly life, or by the nauseous enjoyment of a dull plenty that produces no food for the mind, which will ever be considered in the first place, by a man that has a soul. When he shall think, that if his religion should, after wading through a sea of blood, come at last to prevail, it would infinitely lessen, if not entirely destroy, the glory, riches, strength, and liberty of his own country; and what a sacrifice is this to make to Rome, where they are wise enough to wonder, there should be such fools in the world, as to venture, struggle and contend, nay even to die martyrs, for that which should it succeed, would prove a judgment instead of a blessing to them; he will conclude, that the advantages of throwing some of their children back again to God Almighty, when they have too many of them, are not equal to the inconveniences they may either feel or fear, by continuing their separation from the religion established.

Mortal things will have their weight in this world, and though zeal may prevail for a time, and get the better in a skirmish, yet the war ends generally on the side of flesh and blood, and will do so, till mankind is another thing than it is at present. And therefore a wise Papist in cool blood, considering these and many other circumstances, will believe it worth his pains to see if he can unmuffle himself from the mask of infallibility, will think it reasonable to set his imprisoned senses at liberty, and that he has a right to see with his own eyes, hear with his own ears, and judge by his own reason; the consequence of which might probably be, that weighing things in a right scale, and seeing them in their true colours, he would distinguish between the merit of suffering for a right cause, and the foolish ostentation of drawing inconveniences upon himself, and therefore would not be unwilling to be convinced that our Protestant creed may make him happy in the next world and easier in this. A few of such wise proselytes would by their example draw so many after them, that the party would insensibly melt away, and in a little time, without an angry word, we should come to a union, that all good men would have reason to rejoice at.

But we are not to presume upon these conversions, without preparing men for them, by kind and reconciling arguments. Nothing is so against our nature, as to believe those can be in the right, who are too hard upon us; there is a deformity in everything that does us hurt, it will look scurvily in our eye, whilst the smart continues; and a man must have an extraordinary measure of grace, to think well of a religion, that reduces him and his family to misery. In this respect our Trimmer would consent to a mitigation of such laws, as were made (as it is said Henry VIII got Queen Elizabeth) in a heat against Rome. It may be said that even states as well as private men are subject to passions: a just indignation of a villainous attempt, produces at the time such remedies, as perhaps are not without a mixture of some revenge, and therefore though time cannot repeal a law, it may by a natural effect soften the execution of it. There is less danger to rouse lions when they are at rest, than to awake laws that were intended to have their times of sleeping: nay more than that, in some cases their natural periods of life too, dying of themselves, without the solemnity of being revoked any otherwise, than by the common consent of mankind, who cease to execute, when the reasons in great measure fail, that first created and justified the rigour of unusual penalties.

Our Trimmer is not eager to pick out the sore places in history against this or any other party; quite contrary, is very solicitous to find out anything that may be healing, and tend to an agreement: but to prescribe the means of this gentleness, so as to make it effectual, must come from the only place that can furnish remedies for this cure, *viz.* a parliament. In the meantime it is to be wished there might be such a mutual calmness of mind, that the Protestants might not be so jealous, as still to smell the match, which was to have blown up the King and both Houses in the Gunpowder treason,* or to start at every appearance of Popery, as if it were just taking possession; on the other side, that the Papists may not suffer themselves to be led by any hopes, though never so flattering, to a confidence or ostentation, which must provoke men to be less kind to them; that they may use modesty on their side, and the Protestants indulgence on theirs. By this means there would be an overlooking of all venial faults, a tacit connivance at all things that did not carry scandal with them; and it would amount to a kind of natural dispensation with the severe laws, since there would be no more accusers found, were the occasions of anger and animosity once removed.

Let the Papists in the meantime remember, that there is a respect due from all lesser numbers to greater, a deference to be paid, by an opinion that is exploded, to one that is established; such a thought well digested, will have an influence upon their behaviour, and produce such a temper as must win their most eager adversaries out of their ill humour to them, and give them a title to all the favour that may be consistent with the public peace and security.

THE TRIMMER'S OPINION IN RELATION TO THINGS ABROAD

THE world is so composed, that it is hard if not impossible for a nation not to be a good deal involved in the fate of their neighbours: and though by the felicity of our situation, we are more independent than any other people, yet we have in all ages been concerned for our own sakes in the revolutions abroad. There was a time when England was the overbalancing power of Christendom, and that either by inheritance or conquest, the better part of France received laws from us. After that, we being reduced into our own limits, France and Spain became the rivals for the universal monarchy, and our third power, though in itself less than either of the other, happened to be superior to any one of them, by the choice we had of throwing the scales on that side to which we gave our friendship; and I do not know whether this figure did not make us as great as our former conquests. To be a perpetual umpire between the two great contending powers, who gave us all their courtship, and offered all their incense at our altar, whilst the fate of either prince seemed to depend upon the oracles we delivered; for a King of England to sit on his throne, as in a supreme court of justice with the last appeal, the two great monarchs pleading their cause and expecting the sentence; declaring which side was in the right, or at least (if we pleased) which side should have the better of it; was a piece of greatness which was peculiar to us, and no wonder, if we endeavoured to preserve it, as we did for a considerable time, it being our safety, as well as our glory to maintain it.

But by a fatality upon our counsels, or by the refined policy of this latter age, we have thought fit to use industry to destroy this mighty power which we had so long enjoyed, and that equality between the two monarchies, which we might for ever have preserved, has been chiefly broken by us, whose interest it was above all others to maintain it. When one of them, like an overflowing of the sea, had gained more upon the other than our convenience, or indeed our safety, would allow, instead of mending the banks or making new ones, we ourselves with our own hands, helped to cut them, to invite and make way for a further inundation. Spain and France have had their several turns of making use of our mistakes, and we have been formerly as deaf to the instances, of the then weaker part of the world, to help them against the house of Austria, as we can now be to the earnestness of Spain, that we would assist them against the power of France. Gondomar* was as saucy, and as powerful too in King James his court, as any French ambassador can have been in any time since; men talked as wrong then on the Spanish side, and made their court as well by it, as any can have done since, by talking as much for the French: so that from that time, instead of weighing in a wise balance the power of either Crown, it looks as if we had learnt only to weigh the pensions, and take the heaviest.

It would be tedious as well as unwelcome, to recapitulate all our wrong steps; so that I will go no further back, than the King's Restoration, at which time the balance was on the side of France, and that by the means of Cromwell,* who for a separate interest of his own, had sacrificed that of the nation by joining with the stronger side, to suppress the power of Spain, which he ought to have supported. Such a method was natural enough to an usurper, and showed he was not the lawful father of the people, by his having so little care of them; and the example coming from that hand, one would think, should for that reason be less likely to be followed. But to go on, home comes the King followed with courtships from all nations abroad, of which some did it, not only to make him forget how familiarly they had used him whilst he was in other circumstances, but to bespeak the friendship of a prince, who besides his other greatness was yet more considerable, by being re-established by the love of his people.

France had an interest, either to dispose us to so much goodwill, or at least to put us in such a condition that we might give no opposition to their designs. And Flanders being a perpetual object in their eye,* a lasting beauty for which they have an incurable passion, and not being kind enough to consent to them, they meditated to commit a rape upon her, which they thought would not be easy to do whilst England and Holland were agreed to rescue her, whenever they should hear her cry out for help to them. To this end they put in practice seasonable and artificial whispers to widen things between us and the states. Amboyna and the Fishery* must be talked of here; the freedom of the seas and the preservation of trade, insinuated there; and there being combustible matter on both sides, in a little time it took fire, which gave those that kindled it sufficient cause to smile and hug themselves, to see us both fall into the net they had laid for us. And it is observable and of good example to us, if we will take it, that their design being to set us together at cuffs, to weaken us, they kept themselves indifferent, and lookers on, till our victories began to break the balance; and then the King of France, like a wise prince, was resolved to support the beaten side, and would no more let the power of the sea, than we ought to suffer the monarchy of Europe, to fall into one hand. In pursuance to this he took part with the Dutch, and in a little time made himself umpire of the peace between us.

Some time after, upon a pretence of his Queen's title to part of Flanders, by right of devolution, he falls into it with a mighty force, for which the Spaniards were so little prepared, that he made a very swift progress; and had such a torrent of undisputed victory, that England and Holland, though the wounds they had given one another were yet green, being struck with the apprehension of so near a danger to them, thought it necessary for their own defence, to make up a sudden league, into which Sweden was taken, to interpose for a peace between the two Crowns.* This had so good an effect, that France was stopped in its career, and the peace of Aix-la-Chapelle was a little after concluded.* It was a forced put,* and though the French wisely dissembled their inward dissatisfaction, yet from the very moment, they resolved to untie the triple knot, whatever it cost them. For his Christian majesty after his conquering meals ever rises with a stomach, and he liked the pattern so well, that it gave him a longing to have the whole piece.

Amongst the other means used to attain this end, the sending over the Duchess of Orleans* was not the least powerful; she was a very welcome guest here, and her own charms and dexterity, joined with all other advantages which might help her persuasions, gave her such an ascendant, that she could hardly fail of success. One of the preliminaries of her treaty, though a trivial thing in itself, yet was considerable in the consequence; as very small circumstances often are, in relation to the government of the world. About that time a general humour in opposition to France had made us throw off their fashion, and put on vests, that we might look more like a distinct people, and not be under the servility of imitation, which ever pays a greater deference to the original, than is consistent with the equality all independent nations would pretend to. France did not like this small beginning of ill humour, or at least of emulation, and wisely considering that it is a natural introduction, first to make the world their apes, that they may be afterwards their slaves, it was thought that one of the instructions Madame brought along with her, was to laugh us out of these vests; which she performed so effectually, that in a moment, like so many footmen who had quitted their master's livery, we all took it again and returned to our service: so that the very time of doing it gave a critical advantage to France, since it looked like an evidence of our returning to their interests, as well as to their fashion, and would give such a distrust of us to our new allies that it might facilitate the dissolution of this knot, which tied them so within their bounds that they were very impatient till they were freed from the restraint. But this lady had a more extended commission than this, and no doubt laid the foundation of making a new strict alliance quite contrary to the other in which we had been so lately engaged; and of this there were such early appearances that the world began to look upon us as falling into apostasy from the common interest.

Notwithstanding all this, France did not neglect at the same time to give very good words to the Dutch, and even to feed them with hopes of supporting them against us, when on a sudden that never-to-be-forgotten declaration of war against them comes out, to vindicate his own glory and to revenge the injuries done to his brother of England, by which he became our second in this duel; so humble can this great prince be, when at the same time he does us more honour than we deserved, he lay a greater share of the blame upon our shoulders than did naturally belong to us. The particulars of that war, our part in it whilst we stayed in, and when we were out of breath our leaving the French to make an end of it, are things too well known to make it necessary, and too unwelcome in themselves, to invite me to repeat them. Only the wisdom of France is in this to be observed, that when we had made a separate peace which left them single to oppose the united force of the Confederates, they were so far from being angry, that they would not so much as show the least coldness; hoping to get as much by our mediation for a peace, as they could have expected from our assistance in the war, our circumstances at that time considered. This seasonable piece of indulgence in not reproaching

us, but rather allowing those necessities of state, which we gave for
our excuse, was such an engaging method, that it went a great way to
keep us still in his chains, when to the eye of the world we had absolutely broken loose from them. And by what passed afterwards at
Nijmegen,* though the King's neutrality gave him the outward figure
of a mediator, it appeared that his interposition was extremely suspected of partiality by the Confederates; who upon that ground did
both at and before the conclusion of the treaty, treat his ministers
there with a great deal of neglect.

In this peace, as well as in that of the Pyreneans and of Aix-la-
Chapelle, the King of France at the moment of making, had the
thought of breaking it; for a very little time after he broached his pretensions upon Alost,* etc. Things that if they had been offered by
a less formidable hand, would have been smiled at; but ill arguments
being seconded by good armies, carry such a power with them, that
naked sense is a very unequal adversary. It was thought that these airy
claims were chiefly raised with the prospect of getting Luxembourg
for the equivalent, and this opinion was confirmed by the blocking it
up after pretending to the county of Chimay, that it might be entirely
surrounded by the French dominions. It was so pressed that it must
have fallen in a little time, if the King of France had not sent orders
to his troops to retire; and his Christian generosity, which was assigned
for the reason of it, made the world smile, since it is seen how differ-
ently his devout zeal works in Hungary: that specious reason was in
many respects ill-timed, and France itself gave it so faintly, that at the
very time, it looked out of countenance.

The true ground of his retiring is worth our observation, for at the
instance of the Confederates offices were done, and memorials given,
but all ineffectual, till the word 'parliament' was put into them: that
powerful word had such an effect, that even at that distance it raised
the siege; which may convince us of what efficacy a King of England's
words are, when he will give them their full weight, and threaten with
his Parliament. It is then that he appears that great figure we ought to
represent him in our minds; the nation his body, he the head, and
joined with that harmony, that every word he pronounces, is the word
of a kingdom. Such words even by this example, are as effectual as
fleets or armies, because they can create them, and without this his
words sound abroad like a faint whisper, that is either not heard, or
(which is worse) not minded.

But though France had made this step of forced compliance, it did not mean to leave off the pursuit of their pretensions, and therefore immediately proposed the arbitration to the King; but it appeared that notwithstanding his merit towards the Confederates in saving Luxembourg, the remembrance of what passed before had left so ill a taste in their mouths, that they could not relish our being put into a condition to dispose of their interests, and therefore declined it, by insisting upon a general treaty, to which France has ever since continued to be averse. Our great earnestness to persuade the Confederates to consent to it, was so unusual and so suspicious a method, that it might naturally make them believe that France spoke to them by our mouth; and for that reason, if there had been no other, might hinder their accepting it. And so little care has been taken to cure this or other jealousies the Confederates may have entertained, that quite contrary, their ministers here take every day fresh alarms from what they observe, in small as well as in greater circumstances; and they being apt both to take and improve apprehensions of this kind, draw such inferences from them, as make them entirely despair of us. Thus we now stand, far from being innocent spectators of our neighbours' ruin, and by a fatal mistake, forgetting what a certain forerunner it is to our own.

And now it is time that our Trimmer should tell somewhat of his opinion upon this present state of things abroad. He first professes to have no bias either for or against France, and that his thoughts are wholly directed by the interest of his own country. He allows and has read that Spain used the same methods when it was in its height as France does now, and therefore it is not partiality that moves him, but the just fear which all reasonable men must be possessed with, of an overgrown power. Ambition is a devouring beast; when it has swallowed one province, instead of being cloyed, it has so much the greater stomach to another, and by being fed becomes still the more hungry. So that for the Confederates to expect a security from anything but from their own united strength, is a most miserable fallacy. And if they cannot resist the encroachments of France by their armies, it is in vain for them to dream of any other means of preservation; it would have better grace, besides the saving so much blood and ruin, to give up all at once, make a present of themselves to appease this haughty monarch, rather than be whispered, corrupted, flattered, or cozened out of their liberty.

Nothing is so soft as the first applications of a greater prince to engage a weaker, but that smiling countenance is but a vizard,* it is not the true face; for as soon as the turn is served, the courtship flies to some other prince or state, where the same part is to be acted, leaves the old mistaken friend to neglect and contempt, and like an insolent lover to a cast mistress, reproaches him even with that infamy of which he himself was the author. Sweden, Bavaria, Palatine, etc., may by their fresh example teach other princes what they are reasonably to expect, and what snakes are hidden under the flowers the court of France so liberally throws upon them, whilst they can be useful.

The various methods and the deep riddles, with the differing notes in several countries, do not only give suspicion, but assurance, that everything is put in practice, by which the universal monarchy may be obtained. Who can reconcile the withdrawing his troops from Luxembourg in consideration of the war in Hungary, which was not then declared, and presently after encouraging the Turk to take Vienna, and consequently to destroy the Empire? Or who can think that the persecution of the poor Protestants in France* will be accepted by God as an atonement for hazarding the loss of the whole Christian faith? Can he be thought in earnest when he would seem afraid of the Spaniards, and for that reason must have Luxembourg, and that he cannot be safe from Germany except he be in possession of Strasbourg? All injustice and violence must in itself be grievous, but the aggravation of supporting them by false arguments and insulting reasons has something in it yet more provoking than the injuries themselves; and the world has ground enough to apprehend from such a method of arguing, that even their senses are to be subdued as well as their liberties.

Then the variety of arguments used by France in several countries is very observable. In England and Denmark, nothing is instilled but the greatness and authority of the Crown; on the other side, the great men in Poland are commended who differ in opinion with the King, and they argue like kind friends to the privileges of the Diet, against the separate power of the Crown. In Sweden they are troubled that the King should have changed some things there of late by his single authority, from the ancient and settled constitution. At Ratisbon* his most Christian Majesty takes the liberties of all the electors and free states into his immediate protection, and tells them the Emperor is a dangerous man, an aspiring hero that would infallibly devour them, if he were not at hand to resist him in their behalf. But above all in Holland he has the most obliging tenderness for the commonwealth, and is in such disquiets, lest it should be invaded by the Prince of Orange, that they can do no less in gratitude than to undo themselves when he bids them, to show how sensible they are of his excessive good nature.

Yet in spite of all these contradictions, there are in the world such very refined statesmen, as will upon their credit affirm the following paradoxes to be real truths. First that France alone is sincere, and keeps its faith, and consequently that it is the only friend we can rely upon. That the King of France of all men living has the least mind to be a conqueror. That he is a sleepy tame creature, void of all ambition, a poor kind of man, that has no further thought than of being quiet. That he is so charmed by his friendship to us, that it is impossible he should ever do us hurt, and therefore though Flanders were lost, it would not in the least concern us. That he would fain help the Crown of England to be absolute, which would be to take pains to put us in a condition to oppose him, as it is, and must be our interest, as long as he continues in such an overbalancing greatness. Such a creed as this, if once received, might prepare our belief for greater things, and as he that taught men to eat a dagger, began first with a penknife, so if we can be prevailed with to digest these smaller mistakes, we may at last make our stomachs strong enough for that of transubstantiation.

Our Trimmer cannot easily be converted out of his senses by these state sophisters, and yet he has no such peevish obstinacy as to reject all correspondence with France, because we ought to be apprehensive of the too great power of it. He would not have the King's friendship to the Confederates extend to the involving him in any unreasonable or dangerous engagements, neither would he have him lay aside the consideration of his better establishment at home, out of an excessive zeal to secure his allies abroad; but sure there might be a mean between the two opposite extremes, and it may be wished that our friendship with France should at least be so bounded, that it may consist with the honour as well as with the interest of England. There is no woman but has her fears of contracting too near an intimacy with a much greater beauty, because it exposes her too often to a comparison that is not advantageous to her. And sure it may become a prince, to be as jealous of his dignity as a lady can be of her good looks, and to be as much out of countenance, to be thought an humble companion to so much a greater power. To be always seen in such an ill light, to be so darkened by the brightness of a greater star, is somewhat mortifying; and when England might ride admiral at the head of the Confederates, to look like the kitchen yacht* to the Grand Louis, is but a scurvy figure for us to make in the map of Christendom.

It would rise upon our Trimmer's stomach, if ever (which God forbid) the power of calling and intermitting parliaments here should be transferred to the Crown of France, and that all the opportunities of our own settlements at home should give way to their designs and projects abroad, and that our interest should be so far sacrificed to our compliance that all the omnipotence of France can never make us full amends for it. In the meantime, he shrinks at the dismal prospect he can by no means drive away from his thoughts, that when France has gathered all the fruit arising from our mistakes, and that we can bear no more for them, they will cut down the tree and throw it into the fire. All this while some superfine statesmen, to comfort us, would fain persuade the world, that this or that accident may save us, and for all which is or ought to be dear to us, would have us rely merely upon chance, not considering that fortune is wisdom's creature, and that God Almighty loves to be on the wisest as well as on the strongest side; therefore this is such a miserable shift, such a shameful evasion, that they would be laughed to death for it, if the ruining consequence of this mistake did not more dispose men to rage, and detestation of it.

Our Trimmer is far from idolatry in other things, in one thing only he comes somewhat near it; his country is in some degree his idol: he does not worship the sun, because it is not peculiar to us, it rambles about the world and is less kind to us than it is to other countries; but for the earth of England, though perhaps inferior to that of many places abroad, to him there is divinity in it, and he had rather die than see a spire of English grass trampled upon by a foreign trespasser. He thinks there are a great many of his mind; for all plants are apt to taste of the soil in which they grow, and we that grow here have a root that produces in us a stalk of English juice, which is not to be changed by grafting, or foreign infusion; and I do not know whether anything less will prevail, than the modern experiment, by which the blood of one creature is transmitted into another, according to which, before the French blood can be let into our bodies, every drop of our own must be drawn out of them.

Our Trimmer cannot but lament, that by a sacrifice too great for one nation to make to another, we should lie like a rich mine, made useless for want only of being wrought; and that the life and vigour, which should move us against our enemies, is miserably applied to tear our own bowels; that being made by our happy situation, not only safer, but if we please greater too, than countries which far exceed us in extent; that having courage by nature, learning by industry, riches by trade, we should corrupt all these advantages, so as to make them insignificant, and by a fatality which seems peculiar to us, misplace our active rage against one another, whilst we are turned into statues on that side, where lies our greatest danger: to be unconcerned not only at our neighbour's ruin, but our own, and let our island lie like a great hulk in the sea, without rudder or sails, all the men cast away in her; or as if we were all children in a great cradle, and rocked asleep to a foreign tune.

I say, when our Trimmer represents to his mind our roses blasted and discoloured, whilst the lilies triumph and grow insolent upon the comparison; when he considers our once flourishing laurels, now withered and dying, and nothing left us but the remembrance of a better part in history than we shall make for the next age, which will now be no more to us than an escutcheon hung upon our door when we are dead; when he foresees from hence growing infamy from abroad, confusion at home, and all this without the possibility of a cure, in respect of the voluntary fetters good men put upon themselves by their allegiance; without a good measure of preventing grace, he would be tempted to go out of the world like a Roman philosopher,* rather than endure the burden of life, under such a discouraging prospect. But mistakes as all other things have their periods, and many times the nearest way to cure is not to oppose them, but stay till they are crushed with their own weight. For Nature will not allow anything to continue long that is violent; violence is a wound, and a wound must be curable in a little time, or else it is mortal: but a nation comes near being immortal, therefore the wound will one time or other be cured, though perhaps by such rough methods, if too long forborne, as may make even the best remedies we can propose to be at the same time a melancholy contemplation to us.

There is but one thing, God's providence excepted, to support a man from sinking under these afflicting thoughts, and that is the hopes we draw singly from the King himself, without the mixture of any other consideration. Though the nation was lavish of their kindness to him at his first coming, yet there remains still a stock of warmth in men's hearts for him. Besides, the good influences of his happy planet are not yet all spent, and though the stars of men past their youth are generally declining, and have less force, like the eyes of decaying beauties, yet by a blessing peculiar to himself, we may yet hope to be saved, even by his autumnal fortune. He has something about him that will draw down a healing miracle for his and our deliverance: a Prince who seems fitted for such an offending age, in which men's crimes have been so general, that the not forgiving his people had been the destroying them, whose gentleness gives him a natural dominion that has no bounds; with such a noble mixture of greatness and condescension, an engaging look that disarms men of their ill humour and their resentments; something in him that wants a name, and can no more be defined than it can be resisted; a gift of Heaven, of its last finishing, where it will be peculiarly kind; the only prince in the world that dares be familiar, or that has right to triumph over those forms, which were first invented to give awe to those that could not judge, and to hide defects from those that could; a Prince that has exhausted himself by his liberality, and endangered himself by his mercy, who outshines by his own light, and by his natural virtues, all the varnish of studied acquisitions. His faults are like shades to a good picture, or like alloy to gold to make it more useful; he may have some, but for any man to see them through so many reconciling virtues, is a sacrilegious piece of ill nature, of which no generous mind can be guilty. A Prince that deserves to be loved for his own sake, even without the help of a comparison. Our love, our duty, and our danger all join to cement our obedience to him. In short, whatever he can do, it is no more possible for us to be angry with him, than with the bank that secures us from the raging sea, the kind shade that hides us from the scorching sun, the welcome hand that reaches us a reprieve, or with the guardian angel that rescues our soul from the devouring jaws of wretched eternity.

CONCLUSION

To conclude, our Trimmer is so fully satisfied of the truth of those principles, by which he is directed in reference to the public, that he will neither be bawled, threatened, laughed, nor drunk out of them; and instead of being converted by the arguments of his adversaries to their opinion, he is very much confirmed in his own by them.

He professes solemnly, that were it in his power to choose, he had rather have his ambition bounded, by the commands of a wise and great master, than let it range with a popular license, though crowned with success. Yet he cannot commit such a sin against that glorious thing called liberty, or let his soul stoop so much below itself, as to be content, without repining, to have his reason entirely subdued, or the privilege of acting like a sensible creature torn from him, by the imperious dictates of unlimited authority, in what hand so ever it happens to be placed.

What is there in this, that is so criminal as to deserve the penalty, of that most singular apothegm, 'A Trimmer is worse than a rebel'?* What do angry men ail to rail so against moderation? Does it not look as if they were going to some very scurvy extreme, that is too strong to be digested by the more considering part of mankind? These arbitrary methods, besides the injustice of them, are (God be thanked) very unskilful too, for they fright the birds, by talking so loud, from coming into the net that is laid for them. When men agree to rifle a house, they seldom give warning or blow a trumpet: but there are some small statesmen, who are so full charged with their own expectations that they cannot contain; and kind Heaven, by sending such a seasonable curse upon their understandings, has made their ignorance an antidote against their malice.

Some of these cannot treat peaceably; yielding will not satisfy them, they will have men by storm. There are others who must have plots, to make their service necessary, and have an interest to keep them alive, since they are to live upon them. These men would persuade the King to retrench his own greatness, so as to shrink into the head of a party, which is a betraying him into such an unprincely mistake, and into such a wilful diminution of himself, that they are the last enemies he ought to allow himself to forgive. Such men, if they could, would prevail with the sun, to shine only upon them and their friends, and to leave all the rest of the world in the dark. This is a very unusual monopoly, and may come within the equity of the law, which makes it treason to imprison the King, when such unfitting bounds are put to his favour, and he confined to the narrow circle of a particular set of men that would enclose him. These honest and only loyal gentlemen, if they may be allowed to bear witness for themselves, make a king their engine and degrade him into a property, at the very time that their flattery would make him believe that they paid divine worship to him.

Besides these, there is a flying squadron on both sides, that are afraid the world should agree; small dabblers in conjuring, that raise angry apparitions to keep men from being reconciled. Like wasps they fly up and down, buzz, and sting, to keep men unquiet, but these insects are commonly short-lived creatures, and no doubt in a little time, mankind will be rid of them. They were giants at least who fought once against Heaven; but for such pygmies as these to contend against it is such a provoking folly that the insolent bunglers ought to be laughed and hissed out of the world for it. They should consider there is a soul in that great body of the people, which may for a time be drowsy and inactive, but when the Leviathan* is roused, it moves like an angry creature, and will neither be convinced nor resisted. The people can never agree to show their united power, till they are extremely tempted and provoked to it, so that to apply cupping glasses to a great beast naturally disposed to sleep, and to force the tame thing, whether it will or no, to be valiant, must be learnt out of some other book than Machiavelli,* who would never have prescribed such a preposterous method.

It is to be remembered, that if princes have law and authority on their side, the people on theirs may have Nature, which is a formidable adversary. Duty, justice, religion, nay even human prudence too, bids the people suffer everything rather than resist; but uncorrected Nature, wherever it feels a smart, will run to the nearest remedy. Men's passions are in this case to be considered, as much as their duty, let it be never so strongly enforced; for if their passions are provoked, they being as much a part of us as any of our limbs, they lead men into a short way of arguing that admits no distinctions, and from the foundation of self-defence, they will draw inferences that will have miserable effects upon the quiet of a government.

Our Trimmer therefore dreads a general discontent, because he thinks it differs from a rebellion only as a spotted fever does from the plague, the same species under a lower degree of malignity. It works several ways, sometimes like a slow poison that has its effects a great distance from the time that it is given, sometimes like dry flax prepared to catch at the first fire, or like seed in the ground, ready to sprout upon the first shower. In every shape it is fatal, and our Trimmer thinks no pains or precaution can be too great to prevent it.

In short he thinks himself in the right, grounding his opinions upon that truth, which equally hates to be under the oppression of wrangling sophistry on the one hand, or the short dictates of mistaken authority on the other.

Our Trimmer adores the goddess Truth, though in all ages she has been scurvily used, as well as those that worshipped her. It is of late become such a ruining virtue, that mankind seems to be agreed to commend and avoid it. Yet the want of practice, which repeals all other laws, has no influence upon the law of Truth, because it has a root in Heaven, and an intrinsic value in itself that can never be impaired. She shows her greatness in this, that her enemies even when they are successful are ashamed to own it. Nothing but powerful Truth has the prerogative of triumphing, not only after victory, but in spite of it, and to put conquest itself out of countenance. She may be kept under and suppressed, but her dignity still remains with her even when she is in chains. Falsehood with all its impudence has not enough to speak ill of her before her face; such majesty she carries about her, that her most prosperous enemies are fain to whisper their treason. All the power upon earth can never extinguish her; she has lived in all ages; and let the mistaken zeal of prevailing authority christen any opposition to it with what name they please, she makes it not only an ugly and unmannerly, but a dangerous thing too, to profess it. She has lived still; very retiredly indeed, nay sometimes so buried that only some few of the more discerning part of mankind could have a glimpse of her: with all that she has eternity in her, she knows not how to die, and from the darkest clouds that can shade or cover her, she breaks out from time to time, with triumph for her friends, and terror to her enemies.

Our Trimmer therefore, inspired by this divine virtue, thinks fit to conclude with these assertions: that our climate is a Trimmer between that part of the world where men are roasted, and the other where they are frozen; that our Church is a Trimmer between the frenzy of fanatic visions, and the lethargic ignorance of Popish dreams; that our laws are Trimmers between the excesses of unbounded power, and the extravagance of liberty not enough restrained; that true virtue has ever been thought a Trimmer, and to have its dwelling in the middle, between the two extremes; that even God Almighty himself is divided between his two great attributes, his mercy and his justice.

In such company our Trimmer is not ashamed of his name, and willingly leaves to the bold champions of either extreme, the honour of contending with no less adversaries than Nature, religion, liberty, prudence, humanity, and common sense.

A CHARACTER OF KING CHARLES II

I. OF HIS RELIGION

A CHARACTER differs from a picture only in this, every part of it must be like, but it is not necessary that every feature should be comprehended in it as in a picture, only some of the most remarkable.

This Prince at his first entrance into the world had adversity for his introducer, which is generally thought to be no ill one, but in his case it proved so, and laid the foundation of most of those misfortunes or errors that were the causes of the great objections made to him.

The first effect it had was in relation to his religion.

The ill-bred familiarity of the Scotch divines had given him a distaste of that part of the Protestant religion. He was left then to the little remnant of the Church of England in the Faubourg St Germain; which made such a kind of figure, as might easily be turned in such a manner as to make him lose his veneration for it.* In a refined country where religion appeared in pomp and splendour, the outward appearance of such unfashionable men was made an argument against their religion; and a young prince not averse to raillery, was the more susceptible of a contempt for it.

The company he kept, the men in his pleasures, and the arguments of state that he should not appear too much a Protestant whilst he expected assistance from a Popish prince; all these, together with a habit encouraged by an application to his pleasures, did so loosen and untie him from his first impressions, that I take it for granted, after the first year or two, he was no more a Protestant. If you ask me what he was, my answer must be, that he was of the religion of a young prince in his warm blood, whose enquiries were more applied to find arguments against believing, than to lay any settled foundations for acknowledging providence, mysteries, &c. A general creed, and no very long one, may be presumed to be the utmost religion of one, whose age and inclination could not well spare any thoughts that did not tend to his pleasures.

In this kind of indifference or unthinkingness, which is too natural in the beginnings of life to be heavily censured, I will suppose he might pass some considerable part of his youth. I must presume too that no occasions were lost, during that time, to insinuate everything to bend him towards Popery. Great art without intermission, against youth and easiness, which are seldom upon their guard, must have its effect. A man is to be admired if he resists, and therefore cannot reasonably be blamed if he yields to them. When the critical minute was, I'll not undertake to determine; but certainly the inward conviction does generally precede the outward declarations: at what distances depends upon men's several complexions and circumstances; no stated period can be fixed.

It will be said that he had not religion enough to have conviction; that is a vulgar error. Conviction indeed is not a proper word but where a man is convinced by reason; but in the common acceptation, it is applied to those who cannot tell why they are so. If men can be at least as positive in a mistake as when they are in the right, they may be as clearly convinced when they do not know why, as when they do.

I must presume that no man of the King's age, and his methods of life, could possibly give a good reason for changing the religion in which he was born, let it be what it will. But our passions are much oftener convinced than our reason. He had but little reading, and that tending to his pleasures more than to his instruction. In the library of a young prince, the solemn folios are not much rumpled; books of a lighter digestion have the dog's ears.

Some pretend to be very precise in the time of his reconciling: the Cardinal de Retz,* &c. I will not enter into it minutely, but whenever it was, it is observable that the government of France did not think it advisable to discover it openly; upon which such obvious reflections may be made that I will not mention them.

Such a secret can never be put into a place which is so closely stopped that there shall be no chinks. Whispers went about, particular men had intimations: Cromwell had his advertisements in other things, and this was as well worth his paying for. There was enough said of it to startle a great many, though not universally diffused; so much, that if the government here had not crumbled of itself, his right alone, with that and other clogs upon it, would hardly have thrown it down. I conclude that when he came into England he was as certainly a Roman Catholic,* as that he was a man of pleasure; both very consistent by visible experience.

It is impertinent to give reasons for men's changing their religion. None can give them but themselves, as every man has quite a different way of arguing: a thing which may very well be accounted for. They are differing kinds of wit, to be quick to find a fault, and to be capable to find out a truth. There must be industry in the last; the first requires only a lively heat, that catches hold of the weak side of anything, but to choose the strong one is another talent. The reason why men of wit are often the laziest in their enquiries is that their heat carries their thoughts so fast that they are apt to be tired, and they faint in the drudgery of a continued application. Have not men of great wit in all times permitted their understandings to give way to their first impressions? It takes off from the diminution when a man does not mind a thing; and the King had then other business. The inferior part of the man was then in possession, and the faculties of the brain, as to serious and painful enquiries, were laid asleep at least, though not extinguished. Careless men are most subject to superstition. Those who do not study reason enough to make it their guide have more unevenness. As they have neglects, so they have starts and frights; dreams will serve the turn; omens and sicknesses have violent and sudden effects upon them. Nor is the strength of an argument so effectual from its intrinsic force, as by its being well suited to the temper of the party.

The genteel part of the Catholic Religion might tempt a prince that had more of the fine gentleman than his governing capacity required: and the exercise of indulgence to sinners being more frequent in it, than of inflicting penance, might be some recommendation. Mistresses of that faith are stronger specifics in this case, than any that are in physic.

The Roman Catholics complained of his breach of promise to them very early.* There were broad peepings out, glimpses so often repeated, that to discerning eyes it was flaring. In the very first year there were such suspicions as produced melancholy shakings of the head, which were very significant. His unwillingness to marry a Protestant was remarkable, though both the Catholic and the Christian Crown would have adopted her. Very early in his youth, when any German princess was proposed, he put off the discourse with raillery. A thousand little circumstances were a kind of accumulative evidence, which in these cases may be admitted.

Men that were earnest Protestants were under the sharpness of his displeasure, expressed by raillery, as well as by other ways. Men near him have made discoveries from sudden breakings out in discourse,

&c., which shewed there was a root. It was not the least skilful part of his concealing himself, to make the world think he leaned towards an indifference in religion.

He had sicknesses before his death, in which he did not trouble any Protestant divines; those who saw him upon his deathbed, saw a great deal.

As to his writing those papers, he might do it.* Though neither his temper nor education made him very fit to be an author, yet in this case (a known topic, so very often repeated), he might write it all himself, and yet not one word of it his own. That Church's argument does so agree with men unwilling to take pains, the temptation of putting an end to all the trouble of enquiring is so great, that it must be very strong reason that can resist. The King had only his mere natural faculties, without any acquisitions to improve them; so that it is no wonder, if an argument which gave such ease and relief to his mind, made such an impression, that with thinking often of it (as men are apt to do of everything they like), he might, by the effect chiefly of his memory, put together a few lines with his own hand, without any help at the time; in which there was nothing extraordinary, but that one so little inclined to write at all, should prevail with himself to do it with the solemnity of a casuist.

II. HIS DISSIMULATION

ONE great objection made to him was the concealing himself, and disguising his thoughts. In this there ought a latitude to be given; it is a defect not to have it at all, and a fault to have it too much. Human nature will not allow the mean: like all other things, as soon as ever men get to do them well, they cannot easily hold from doing them too much. It is the case even in the least things, as singing, &c.

In France, he was to dissemble injuries and neglects, from one reason; in England he was to dissemble too, though for other causes. A king upon the throne has as great temptations (though of another kind) to dissemble, as a king in exile. The King of France might have his times of dissembling as much with him, as he could have to do it with the King of France: so he was in a school.*

No king can be so little inclined to dissemble but he must needs learn it from his subjects, who every day give him such lessons of it.

Dissimulation is like most other qualities, it has two sides; it is necessary, and yet it is dangerous too. To have none at all lays a man open to contempt, to have too much exposes him to suspicion, which is only the less dishonourable inconvenience. If a man does not take very great precautions, he is never so much showed as when he endeavours to hide himself. One man cannot take more pains to hide himself than another will do to see into him, especially in the case of kings.

It is none of the exalted faculties of the mind, since there are chambermaids will do it better than any prince in Christendom. Men given to dissembling are like rooks at play,* they will cheat for shillings they are so used to it. The vulgar definition of dissembling is downright lying; that kind of it which is less ill-bred comes pretty near it. Only princes and persons of honour must have gentler words given to their faults than the nature of them may in themselves deserve.

Princes dissemble with too many not to have it discovered; no wonder then that he carried it so far that it was discovered. Men compared notes, and got evidence; so that those whose morality would give them leave, took it for an excuse for serving him ill. Those who knew his face fixed their eyes there, and thought it of more importance to see, than to hear what he said. His face was as little a blab as most men's, yet though it could not be called a prattling face, it would sometimes tell tales to a good observer. When he thought fit to be angry, he had a very peevish memory; there was hardly a blot that escaped him. At the same time that this showed the strength of his dissimulation, it gave warning too; it fitted his present purpose, but it made a discovery that put men more upon their guard against him. Only self-flattery furnishes perpetual arguments to trust again: the comfortable opinion men have of themselves keeps up human society, which would be more than half destroyed without it.

III. HIS AMOURS, MISTRESSES, &C.

It may be said that his inclinations to love were the effects of health, and a good constitution, with as little mixture of the seraphic part as ever man had. And though from that foundation men often raise their passions, I am apt to think his stayed as much as any man's ever did in the lower region. This made him like easy mistresses: they were generally resigned to him while he was abroad, with an implied bargain. Heroic refined lovers place a good deal of their pleasure in the difficulty, both for the vanity of conquest, and as a better earnest of their kindness.

After he was restored, mistresses were recommended to him; which is no small matter in a court, and not unworthy the thoughts even of a party. A mistress either dexterous in herself, or well-instructed by those that are so, may be very useful to her friends, not only in the immediate hours of her ministry, but by her influences and insinuations at other times. It was resolved generally by others whom he should have in his arms, as well as whom he should have in his councils. Of a man who was so capable of choosing, he chose as seldom as any man that ever lived.

He had more properly, at least in the beginning of his time, a good stomach to his mistresses, than any great passion for them. His taking them from others was never learnt in a romance; and indeed fitter for a philosopher than a knight-errant. His patience for their frailties showed him no exact lover. It is a heresy according to a true lover's creed ever to forgive an infidelity, or the appearance of it. Love of ease will not do it, where the heart is much engaged; but where mere nature is the motive, it is possible for a man to think righter than the common opinion, and to argue that a rival takes away nothing but the heart, and leaves all the rest.

In his latter times he had no love, but insensible engagements that made it harder than most might apprehend to untie them. The politics might have their part; a secret, a commission, a confidence in critical things, though it does not give a lease for a precise term of years, yet there may be difficulties in dismissing them; there may be no love all the while; perhaps the contrary.

He was said to be as little constant as they were thought to be. Though he had no love, he must have some appetite, or else he could not keep them for mere ease, or for the love of sauntering. Mistresses are frequently apt to be uneasy; they are in all respects craving creatures; so that though the taste of those joys might be flattened, yet a man who loved pleasure so as to be very unwilling to part with it, might (with the assistance of his fancy, which does not grow old so fast) reserve some supplemental entertainments, that might make their personal service be still of use to him. The definition of pleasure, is what pleases, and if that which grave men may call a corrupted fancy shall administer any remedies for putting off mourning for the loss of youth, who shall blame it?

The young men seldom apply their censure to these matters; and the elder have an interest to be gentle towards a mistake that seems to make some kind of amends for their decays.

He had wit enough to suspect, and he had wit enough too not to care. The ladies got a great deal more than would have been allowed to be an equal bargain in Chancery, for what they did for it; but neither the manner, nor the measure of pleasure is to be judged by others.

Little inducements at first grew into strong reasons by degrees. Men who do not consider circumstances, but judge at a distance, by a general way of arguing, conclude if a mistress in some cases is not immediately turned off, it must needs be that the gallant is incurably subjected. This will by no means hold in private men, much less in princes, who are under more entanglements, from which they cannot so easily loosen themselves.

His mistresses were as different in their humours, as they were in their looks. They gave matter of very different reflections. The last especially was quite out of the definition of an ordinary mistress;* the causes and the manner of her being first introduced were very different. A very peculiar distinction was spoken of, some extraordinary solemnities that might dignify, though not sanctify her function. Her chamber was the true cabinet council. The King did always by his councils, as he did sometimes by his meals; he sat down out of form with the Queen, but he supped below stairs. To have the secrets of a king, who happens to have too many, is to have a king in chains. He must not only not part with her, but he must in his own defence dissemble his dislike: the less kindness he has, the more he must show. There is great difference between being muffled, and being tied: he was the first, not the last. If he had quarrelled at some times, besides other advantages, this mistress had a powerful second* (one may suppose a kind of a guarantee); this to a man that loved his ease, though his age had not helped, was sufficient.

The thing called sauntering is a stronger temptation to princes than it is to others. The being galled with importunities, pursued from one room to another with asking faces; the dismal sound of unreasonable complaints, and ill-grounded pretences; the deformity of fraud ill-disguised; all these would make any man run away from them; and I used to think it was the motive for making him walk so fast. So it was more properly taking sanctuary. To get into a room, where all business was to stay at the door, excepting such as he was disposed to admit, might be very acceptable to a younger man than he was, and less given to his ease. He slumbered after dinner, had the noise of the company to divert him, without their solicitations to importune him. In these hours where he was more unguarded, no doubt the cunning men of the court took their times to make their observations, and there is as little doubt but he made his upon them too. Where men had chinks he would see through them as soon as any man about him. There was much more real business done there in his politic, than there was in his personal capacity, *stans pede in uno*;* and there was the French part of the government, which was not the least.

In short, without endeavouring to find more arguments, he was used to it. Men do not care to put off a habit, nor do often succeed when they go about it. His was not an unthinkingness; he did not perhaps think so much of his subjects as they might wish; but he was far from being wanting to think of himself.

IV. HIS CONDUCT TO HIS MINISTERS

HE lived with his ministers as he did with his mistresses; he used them, but he was not in love with them. He showed his judgement in this, that he cannot properly be said ever to have had a favourite, though some might look so at a distance. The present use he might have of them, made him throw favours upon them, which might lead the lookers on into that mistake; but he tied himself no more to them than they did to him, which implied a sufficient liberty on either side.

Perhaps he made dear purchases. If he seldom gave profusely, but where he expected some unreasonable thing, great rewards were material evidences against those who received them.

He was free of access to them, which was a very gaining quality. He had at least as good a memory for the faults of his ministers as for their services; and whenever they fell, the whole inventory came out; there was not a slip omitted.

That some of his ministers seemed to have a superiority, did not spring from his resignation to them, but to his ease. He chose rather to be eclipsed than to be troubled.

His brother* was a minister, and he had his jealousies of him. At the same time that he raised him, he was not displeased to have him lessened. The cunning observers found this out, and at the same time that he reigned in the cabinet, he was very familiarly used at the private supper.

A minister turned off is like a lady's waiting-woman, that knows all her washes, and has a shrewd guess at her strayings; so there is danger in turning them off, as well as in keeping them.

He had back stairs to convey informations to him, as well as for other uses; and though such informations are sometimes dangerous (especially to a prince that will not take pains necessary to digest them), yet in the main, that humour of hearing everybody against anybody, kept those about him in more awe than they would have been without it. I do not believe that ever he trusted any man, or any set of men so entirely, as not to have some secrets, in which they had no share; as this might make him less well served, so in some degree it might make him the less imposed upon.

You may reckon under this article his female ministry; for though he had ministers of the council, ministers of the cabinet, and ministers of the *ruelle*,* the *ruelle* was often the last appeal. Those who were not well there, were used because they were necessary at the time, not because they were liked; so that their tenure was a little uncertain. His ministers were to administer business to him as doctors do physic, wrap it up in something to make it less unpleasant; some skilful digressions were so far from being impertinent, that they could not many times fix him to a fair audience without them. His aversion to formality made him dislike a serious discourse, if very long, except it was mixed with something to entertain him. Some even of the graver sort too, used to carry this very far, and rather than fail, use the coarsest kind of youthful talk.

In general, he was upon pretty even terms with his ministers, and could as easily bear their being hanged as some of them could his being abused.

V. OF HIS WIT AND CONVERSATION

HIS wit consisted chiefly in the quickness of his apprehension. His apprehension made him find faults, and that led him to short sayings upon them, not always equal, but often very good.

By his being abroad, he contracted a habit of conversing familiarly which, added to his natural genius, made him very apt to talk; perhaps more than a very nice judgment would approve.

He was apter to make broad allusions upon anything that gave the least occasion, than was altogether suitable with the very good breeding he showed in most other things. The company he kept whilst abroad had so used him to that sort of dialect, that he was so far from thinking it a fault or an indecency, that he made it a matter of raillery upon those who could not prevail upon themselves to join in it. As a man who has a good stomach loves generally to talk of meat, so in the vigour of his age, he began that style, which by degrees grew so natural to him, that after he ceased to do it out of pleasure, he continued to do it out of custom. The hypocrisy of the former times inclined men to think they could not show too great an aversion to it, and that helped to encourage this unbounded liberty of talking, without the restraints of decency which were before observed. In his more familiar conversations with the ladies, even they must be passive, if they would not enter into it. How far sounds as well as objects may have their effects to raise inclination, might be an argument to him to use that style; or whether using liberty at its full stretch, was not the general inducement without any particular motives to it.

The manner of that time of telling stories had drawn him into it; being commended at first for the faculty of telling a tale well, he might insensibly be betrayed to exercise it too often. Stories are dangerous in this, that the best expose a man most, by being oftenest repeated. It might pass for an evidence for the moderns against the ancients, that it is now wholly left off by all that have any pretence to be distinguished by their good sense.

He had the improvements of wine, &c., which made him pleasant and easy in company, where he bore his part, and was acceptable even to those who had no other design than to be merry with him.

The thing called wit, a prince may taste, but it is dangerous for him to take too much of it; it has allurements which by refining his thoughts, take off from their dignity, in applying them less to the governing part. There is a charm in wit, which a prince must resist: and that to him was no easy matter; it was contesting with Nature upon terms of disadvantage.

His wit was not so ill-natured as to put men out of countenance. In the case of a king especially, it is more allowable to speak sharply of them, than to them.

His wit was not acquired by reading; that which he had above his original stock by nature, was from company, in which he was very capable to observe. He could not so properly be said to have a wit very much raised, as a plain, gaining, well-bred, recommending kind of wit.

But of all men that ever liked those who had wit, he could the best endure those who had none. This leans more towards a satire than a compliment, in this respect, that he could not only suffer impertinence, but at some times seemed to be pleased with it.

He encouraged some to talk a good deal more with him than one would have expected from a man of so good a taste. He should rather have ordered his attorney-general to prosecute them for a misdemeanour, in using common sense so scurvily in his presence. However, if this was a fault, it is arrogant for any of his subjects to object to it, since it would look like defying such a piece of indulgence. He must in some degree loosen the strength of his wit, by his condescension to talk with men so very unequal to him. Wit must be used to some equality, which may give it exercise, or else it is apt either to languish, or to grow a little vulgar, by reigning amongst men of a lower size, where there is no awe to keep a man upon his guard.

It fell out rather by accident than choice, that his mistresses were such as did not care that wit of the best kind should have the precedence in their apartments. Sharp and strong wit will not always be so held in by good manners, as not to be a little troublesome in a *ruelle*. But wherever impertinence has wit enough left to be thankful for being well used, it will not only be admitted, but kindly received; such charms everything has that sets us off by comparison.

His affability was a part, and perhaps not the least, of his wit.

It is a quality that must not always spring from the heart; men's pride, as well as their weakness, makes them ready to be deceived by it. They are more ready to believe it a homage paid to their merit, than a bait thrown out to deceive them. Princes have a particular advantage.

There was at first as much of art as nature in his affability, but by habit it became natural. It is an error of the better hand, but the universality takes away a good deal of the force of it. A man that has had a kind look seconded with engaging words, whilst he is chewing the pleasure, if another in his sight should be received just as kindly, that equality would presently alter the relish. The pride of mankind will have distinction, till at last it comes to smile for smile, meaning nothing of either side, without any kind of effect; mere drawing-room compliments; the bow alone would be better without them. He was under some disadvantages of this kind, that grew still in proportion as it came by time to be more known that there was less signification in those things than at first was thought.

The familiarity of his wit must needs have the effect of lessening the distance fit to be kept to him. The freedom used to him whilst abroad, was retained by those who used it longer than either they ought to have kept it, or he have suffered it, and others by their example learned to use the same. A King of Spain that will say nothing but *tiendro cuydado*,* will, to the generality, preserve more respect; an engine that will speak but sometimes, at the same time that it will draw the raillery of the few who judge well, it will create respect in the ill-judging generality. Formality is sufficiently revenged upon the world for being so unreasonably laughed at; it is destroyed it is true, but it has the spiteful satisfaction of seeing everything destroyed with it.

His fine gentlemanship did him no good, encouraged in it by being too much applauded.

His wit was better suited to his condition before he was restored than afterwards. The wit of a gentleman, and that of a crowned head, ought to be different things. As there is a crown law, there is a crown wit too. To use it with reserve is very good, and very rare. There is a dignity in doing things seldom, even without any other circumstance. Where wit will run continually, the spring is apt to fail; so that it grows vulgar, and the more it is practised, the more it is debased.

He was so good at finding out other men's weak sides that it made him less intent to cure his own: that generally happens. It may be called a treacherous talent, for it betrays a man to forget to judge himself, by being so eager to censure others. This does so misguide men the first part of their lives, that the habit of it is not easily recovered, when the greater ripeness of their judgment inclines them to look more into themselves than into other men.

Men love to see themselves in the false looking glass of other men's failings. It makes a man think well of himself at the time, and by sending his thoughts abroad to get food for laughing, they are less at leisure to see faults at home. Men choose rather to make the war in another country, than to keep all well at home.

VI. HIS TALENTS, TEMPER, HABITS, &C.

HE had a mechanical head, which appeared in his inclination to shipping and fortification, &c. This would make one conclude that his thoughts would naturally have been more fixed to business, if his pleasures had not drawn them away from it.

He had a very good memory, though he would not always make equal good use of it. So that if he had accustomed himself to direct his faculties to his business, I see no reason why he might not have been a good deal master of it. His chain of memory was longer than his chain of thought; the first could bear any burden, the other was tired by being carried on too long; it was fit to ride a heat, but it had not wind enough for a long course.

A very great memory often forgets how much time is lost by repeating things of no use. It was one reason of his talking so much; since a great memory will always have something to say, and will be discharging itself, whether in or out of season, if a good judgment does not go along with it, to make it stop and turn. One might say of his memory, that it was a *beauté journaliere*:* sometimes he would make shrewd applications, &c., at others he would bring things out of it, that never deserved to be laid in it.

He grew by age into a pretty exact distribution of his hours, both for his business, pleasures, and the exercise for his health, of which he took as much care as could possibly consist with some liberties he was resolved to indulge in himself. He walked by his watch, and when he pulled it out to look upon it, skilful men would make haste with what they had to say to him.

He was often retained in his personal against his politic capacity. He would speak upon those occasions most dexterously against himself; Charles Stuart would be bribed against the King; and in the distinction, he leaned more to his natural self than his character would allow. He would not suffer himself to be so much fettered by his character as was convenient; he was still starting out of it; the power of nature was too strong for the dignity of his calling, which generally yielded as often as there was a contest.

It was not the best use he made of his back-stairs to admit men to
bribe him against himself, to procure a defalcation, help a lame account-
ant to get off, or side with the farmers against the improvement of the
revenue.* The King was made the instrument to defraud the Crown,
which is somewhat extraordinary.

That which might tempt him to it probably was, his finding that
those about him so often took money upon those occasions; so that he
thought he might do well at least to be a partner. He did not take the
money to hoard it; there were those at court who watched those times,
as the Spaniards do for the coming in of the Plate Fleet.* The beggars
of both sexes helped to empty his cabinet, and to leave room in them
for a new lading upon the next occasion. These negotiators played
double with him too, when it was for their purpose so to do. He knew
it, and went on still; so he gained his present end, at the time, he was
less solicitous to enquire into the consequences.

He could not properly be said to be either covetous or liberal; his
desire to get was not with an intention to be rich; and his spending
was rather an easiness in letting money go, than any premeditated
thought for the distribution of it. He would do as much to throw off
the burden of a present importunity, as he would to relieve a want.

When once the aversion to bear uneasiness takes place in a man's
mind, it does so check all the passions, that they are damped into
a kind of indifference; they grow faint and languishing, and come to
be subordinate to that fundamental maxim, of not purchasing anything at the price of a difficulty. This made that he had as little eagerness to oblige, as he had to hurt men; the motive of his giving bounties
was rather to make men less uneasy to him, than more easy to themselves; and yet no ill nature all this while. He would slide from an
asking face, and could guess very well. It was throwing a man off from
his shoulders, that leaned upon them with his whole weight; so that
the party was not gladder to receive, than he was to give. It was a kind
of implied bargain; though men seldom kept it, being so apt to forget
the advantage they had received, that they would presume the King
would as little remember the good he had done them, so as to make it
an argument against their next request.

This principle of making the love of ease exercise an entire sovereignty in his thoughts, would have been less censured in a private
man, than might be in a prince. The consequence of it to the public
changes the nature of that quality, or else a philosopher in his private

capacity might say a great deal to justify it. The truth is, a king is to be such a distinct creature from a man, that their thoughts are to be put in quite a differing shape, and it is such a disquieting task to reconcile them, that princes might rather expect to be lamented than to be envied, for being in a station that exposes them, if they do not do more to answer men's expectations than human nature will allow.

That men have the less ease for their loving it so much, is so far from a wonder, that it is a natural consequence, especially in the case of a prince. Ease is seldom got without some pains, but it is yet seldomer kept without them. He thought giving would make men more easy to him, whereas he might have known it would certainly make them more troublesome.

When men receive benefits from princes, they attribute less to his generosity than to their own deserts; so that in their own opinion, their merit cannot be bounded; by that mistaken rule, it can as little be satisfied. They would take it for a diminution to have it circumscribed. Merit has a thirst upon it that can never be quenched by golden showers. It is not only still ready, but greedy to receive more. This King Charles found in as many instances as any prince that ever reigned, because the easiness of access introducing the good success of their first request, they were the more encouraged to repeat those importunities, which had been more effectually stopped in the beginning by a short and resolute denial. But his nature did not dispose him to that method, it directed him rather to put off the troublesome minute for the time, and that being his inclination, he did not care to struggle with it.

I am of an opinion, in which I am every day more confirmed by observation, that gratitude is one of those things that cannot be bought. It must be born with men, or else all the obligations in the world will not create it. An outward show may be made to satisfy decency, and to prevent reproach; but a real sense of a kind thing is a gift of Nature, and never was, nor can be acquired.

The love of ease is an opiate, it is pleasing for the time, quiets the spirits, but it has its effects that seldom fail to be most fatal. The immoderate love of ease makes a man's mind pay a passive obedience to anything that happens: it reduces the thoughts from having desire to be content.

It must be allowed he had a little overbalance on the well-natured side, not vigour enough to be earnest to do a kind thing, much less to do a harsh one; but if a hard thing was done to another man, he did not eat his supper the worse for it. It was rather a deadness than severity of nature, whether it proceeded from a dissipation of spirits, or by the habit of living in which he was engaged.

If a king should be born with more tenderness than might suit with his office, he would in time be hardened. The faults of his subjects make severity so necessary, that by the frequent occasions given to use it, it comes to be habitual, and by degrees the resistance that Nature made at first grows fainter, till at last it is in a manner quite extinguished.

In short, this Prince might more properly be said to have gifts than virtues, as affability, easiness of living, inclinations to give, and to forgive; qualities that flowed from his nature rather than from his virtue.

He had not more application to anything than the preservation of his health; it had an entire preference to anything else in his thoughts, and he might be said without aggravation to study that, with as little intermission as any man in the world. He understood it very well, only in this he failed, that he thought it was more reconcilable with his pleasures than it really was. It is natural to have such a mind to reconcile these, that it is the easier for any man that goes about it to be guilty of that mistake.

This made him overdo in point of nourishment, the better to furnish to those entertainments; and then he thought by great exercise to make amends, and to prevent the ill effects of his blood being too much raised. The success he had in this method, whilst he had youth and vigour to support him in it, encouraged him to continue it longer than Nature allowed. Age steals so insensibly upon us, that we do not think of suiting our way of reasoning to the several stages of life; so insensibly that not being able to pitch upon any precise time, when we cease to be young, we either flatter ourselves that we always continue to be so, or at least forget how much we are mistaken in it.

VII. CONCLUSION

AFTER all this, when some rough strokes of the pencil have made several parts of the picture look a little hard, it is a justice that would be due to every man, much more to a prince, to make some amends, and to reconcile men as much as may be to it by the last finishing.

He had as good a claim to a kind interpretation as most men. First as a prince: living and dead, generous and well-bred men will be gentle to them; next as an unfortunate prince in the beginning of his time, and a gentle one in the rest.

A Prince neither sharpened by his misfortunes whilst abroad, nor by his power when restored, is such a shining character, that it is a reproach not to be so dazzled with it, as not to be able to see a fault in its full light. It would be a scandal in this case to have an exact memory. And if all who are akin to his vices should mourn for him, never prince would be better attended to his grave. He is under the protection of common frailty, that must engage men for their own sakes not to be too severe, where they themselves have so much to answer.

What therefore an angry philosopher would call lewdness, let frailer men call a warmth and sweetness of the blood, that would not be confined in the communicating itself; an overflowing of good nature, of which he had such a stream, that it would not be restrained within the banks of a crabbed and unsociable virtue.

If he had sometimes less firmness than might have been wished, let the kindest reason be given, and if that should be wanting, the best excuse. I would assign the cause of it to be his loving at any rate to be easy, and his deserving the more to be indulged in it, by his desiring that everybody else should be so.

If he sometimes let a servant fall, let it be examined whether he did not weigh so much upon his master, as to give him a fair excuse. That yieldingness, whatever foundations it might lay to the disadvantage of posterity, was a specific to preserve us in peace for his own time. If he loved too much to lie upon his own down-bed of ease, his subjects had the pleasure, during his reign, of lolling and stretching upon theirs. As a sword is sooner broken upon a feather-bed than upon a table, so his pliantness broke the blow of a present mischief much better than a more immediate resistance would perhaps have done.

Ruin saw this, and therefore removed him first to make way for further overturnings.*

If he dissembled, let us remember, first, that he was a king, and that dissimulation is a jewel of the Crown; next, that it is very hard for a man not to do sometimes too much of that which he concludes necessary for him to practice. Men should consider that as there would be no false dice, if there were no true ones, so if dissembling is grown universal, it ceases to be foul play, having an implied allowance by the general practice. He that was so often forced to dissemble in his own defence, might the better have the privilege sometimes to be the aggressor, and to deal with men at their own weapon.

Subjects are apt to be as arbitrary in their censure, as the most assuming kings can be in their power. If there might be matter for objections, there is not less reason for excuses; the defects laid to his charge, are such as may claim indulgence from mankind.

Should nobody throw a stone at his faults but those who are free from them, there would be but a slender shower.*

What private man will throw stones at him because he loved? Or what prince, because he dissembled?

If he either trusted, or forgave his enemies, or in some cases neglected his friends, more than could in strictness be allowed, let not those errors be so arraigned as take away the privilege that seems to be due to princely frailties. If princes are under the misfortune of being accused to govern ill, their subjects have the less right to fall hard upon them, since they generally so little deserve to be governed well.

The truth is, the calling of a king, with all its glittering, has such an unreasonable weight upon it, that they may rather expect to be lamented, than to be envied, for being set upon a pinnacle, where they are exposed to censure, if they do not do more to answer men's expectations, than corrupted nature will allow.

It is but justice therefore to this Prince, to give all due softenings to the less shining parts of his life; to offer flowers and leaves to hide, instead of using aggravations to expose them.

Let his royal ashes then lie soft upon him, and cover him from harsh and unkind censures; which though they should not be unjust, can never clear themselves from being indecent.

THE LADY'S NEW YEAR'S GIFT:
OR, ADVICE TO A DAUGHTER

Dear Daughter,

I find, that even our most pleasing thoughts will be unquiet; they will be in motion; and the mind can have no rest whilst it is possessed by a darling passion. You are at present the chief object of my care, as well as of my kindness, which sometimes throws me into visions of your being happy in the world, that are better suited to my partial wishes, than to my reasonable hopes for you. At other times, when my fears prevail, I shrink as if I was struck, at the prospect of danger, to which a young woman must be exposed. By how much the more lively, so much the more liable you are to be hurt; as the finest plants are the soonest nipped by the frost. Whilst you are playing full of innocence, the spiteful world will bite, except you are guarded by your caution. Want of care therefore, my dear child, is never to be excused; since, as to this world, it has the same effect as want of virtue. Such an early sprouting wit requires so much the more to be sheltered by some rules, like something strewed upon tender flowers to preserve them from being blasted. You must take it well to be pruned by so kind a hand as that of a father. There may be some bitterness in mere obedience: the natural love of liberty may help to make the commands of a parent harder to go down; some inward resistance there will be, where power and not choice makes us move. But when a father lays aside his authority, and persuades only by his kindness, you will never answer it to good nature, if it has not weight with you.

A great part of what is said in the following discourse may be above the present growth of your understanding,* but that becoming every day taller, will in a little time reach up to it, so as to make it easy to you. I am willing to begin with you before your mind is quite formed, that being the time in which it is most capable of receiving a colour that will last when it is mixed with it. Few things are well learnt, but by early precepts: those well infused, make them natural; and we are never sure of retaining what is valuable, till by a continued habit we have made it a piece of us.

Whether my skill can draw the picture of a fine woman, may be a question; but it can be none, that I have drawn that of a kind father. If you will take an exact copy, I will so far presume upon my workmanship as to undertake you shall not make an ill figure. Give me so much credit as to try, and I am sure that neither your wishes nor mine shall be disappointed by it.

RELIGION

THE first thing to be considered is religion. It must be the chief object of your thoughts, since it would be a vain thing to direct your behaviour in the world, and forget that which you are to have towards him that made it. In a strict sense, it is the only thing necessary: you must take it into your mind, and from thence throw it into your heart, where you are to embrace it so close, as never to lose the possession of it. But then it is necessary to distinguish between the reality and the pretence.

Religion does not consist in believing the legend of the nursery, where children with their milk are fed with the tales of witches, hobgoblins, prophecies, and miracles. We suck in so greedily these early mistakes, that our riper understanding has much ado to cleanse our minds from this kind of trash: the stories are so entertaining, that we do not only believe them, but relate them; which makes the discovery of the truth somewhat grievous, when it makes us lose such a field of impertinence, where we might have diverted ourselves, besides the throwing some shame upon us, for having ever received them. This is making the world a jest, and imputing to God Almighty that the province he assigns to the Devil is to play at blind man's buff, and show* tricks with mankind; and is so far from being religion that it is not sense, and has right only to be called that kind of devotion of which ignorance is the undoubted mother, without competition or dispute. These mistakes are therefore to be left off with your hanging sleeves;* and you ought to be as much out of countenance to be found with them about you, as to be seen playing with babies* at an age when other things are expected from you.

The next thing to be observed to you, is that religion does as little consist in loud answers and devout convulsions at church, or praying in an extraordinary manner. Some ladies are so extreme stirring at church, that one would swear the worm in their conscience made them so unquiet. Others will have such a divided face, between a devout goggle and an inviting glance, that the unnatural mixture makes even the best looks to be at that time ridiculous. These affected appearances are ever suspected, like very strong perfumes, which are generally thought no very good symptoms in those that make use of them. Let your earnestness therefore be reserved for your closet, where you may have God Almighty to yourself: in public be still and calm, neither indecently careless, nor affected in the other extreme.

It is not true devotion to put on an angry zeal against those who may be of a differing persuasion. Partiality to ourselves makes us often mistake it for a duty to fall hard upon others in that case; and being pushed on by self-conceit, we strike without mercy, believing that the wounds we give are meritorious, and that we are fighting God Almighty's quarrel; when the truth is, we are only setting out ourselves. Our devotion too often breaks out into that shape, which most agrees with our particular temper. The choleric grow into a hardened severity against all who dissent from them; snatch at all the texts of scripture that suit with their complexion; and because God's wrath was sometimes kindled, they conclude that anger is a divine virtue; and are so far from imagining their ill-natured zeal requires an apology, that they value themselves upon it, and triumph in it. Others, whose nature is more credulous than ordinary, admit no bounds or measure to it; they grow as proud of extending their faith, as princes are of enlarging their dominions; not considering, that our faith, like our stomach, is capable of being overcharged; and that as the last is destroyed by taking in more than it can digest, so our reason may be extinguished by oppressing it with the weight of too many strange things; especially if we are forbidden to chew what we are commanded to swallow. The melancholy and sullen are apt to place a great part of their religion in dejected or ill-humoured looks, putting on an unsociable face, and declaiming against the innocent entertainments of life, with as much sharpness as they could bestow upon the greatest crimes. This generally is only a vizard,* there is seldom anything real in it. No other thing is the better for being sour; and it would be hard that religion should be so, which is the best of things. In the meantime it may be said with truth, that this surly kind of devotion has perhaps done little less hurt in the world by frighting, than the most scandalous examples have done by infecting it.

Having told you, in these few instances, to which many more might be added, what is not true religion, it is time to describe to you, what is so. The ordinary definitions of it are no more like it, than the common signposts* are like the princes they would represent. The unskilful daubers in all ages have generally laid on such ill colours, and drawn such harsh lines, that the beauty of it is not easily to be discerned: they have put in all the forbidding features that can be thought of; and in the first place, have made it an irreconcilable enemy to Nature; when, in reality, they are not only friends, but twins, born together at the same time; and it is doing violence to them both, to go about to have them separated. Nothing is so kind and so inviting as true and unsophisticated religion: instead of imposing unnecessary burdens upon our nature, it eases us of the greater weight of our passions and mistakes: instead of subduing us with rigour, it redeems us from the slavery we are in, to ourselves, who are the most severe masters, whilst we are under the usurpation of our appetites let loose, and not restrained.

Religion is a cheerful thing, so far from being always at cuffs with good humour that it is inseparably united to it. Nothing unpleasant belongs to it, though the spiritual cooks have done their unskilful part to give an ill relish to it. A wise epicure would be religious for the sake of pleasure: good sense is the foundation of both; and he is a bungler who aims at true luxury, but where they are joined.

Religion is exalted reason, refined and sifted from the grosser parts of it: it dwells in the upper region of the mind, where there are fewest clouds or mists to darken or offend it. It is both the foundation and the crown of all virtues: it is morality improved and raised to its height, by being carried nearer heaven, the only place where perfection resides. It cleanses the understanding, and brushes off the earth that hangs about our souls. It does not want the hopes and the terrors which are made use of to support it; neither ought it to descend to the borrowing any argument out of itself, since there we may find everything that should invite us. If we were to be hired to religion, it is able to outbid the corrupted world, with all it can offer to us, being so much the richer of the two, in everything where reason is admitted to be judge of the value.

Since this is so, it is worth your pains to make religion your choice, and not make use of it only as a refuge. There are ladies, who finding by the too visible decay of their good looks that they can shine no more by that light, put on the varnish of an affected devotion, to keep up some kind of figure in the world. They take sanctuary in the church, when they are pursued by growing contempt, which will not be stopped, but follows them to the altar. Such late penitence is only a disguise for the tormenting grief of being no more handsome. That is the killing thought which draws the sighs and tears, that appear outwardly to be applied to a better end.

There are many who have an aguish devotion, hot and cold fits, long intermissions, and violent raptures. This unevenness is by all means to be avoided. Let your method be a steady course of good life, that may run like a smooth stream, and be a perpetual spring to furnish to the continued exercise of virtue. Your devotion may be earnest, but it must be unconstrained; and like other duties, you must make it your pleasure too, or else it will have very little efficacy. By this rule you may best judge of your own heart. Whilst those duties are joys, it is an evidence of their being sincere; but when they are a penance, it is a sign that your nature makes some resistance; and whilst that lasts, you can never be entirely secure of yourself.

If you are often unquiet and too nearly touched by the cross accidents of life, your devotion is not of the right standard; there is too much alloy in it. That which is right and unmixed, takes away the sting of everything that would trouble you: it is like a healing balm, that extinguishes the sharpness of the blood; so this softens and dissolves the anguish of the mind. A devout mind has the privilege of being free from passions, as some climates are from all venomous kind of creatures. It will raise you above the little vexations to which others for want of it will be exposed, and bring you to a temper, not of stupid indifference, but of such a wise resignation, that you may live in the world, so as it may hang about you like a loose garment,* and not tied too close to you.

Take heed of running into that common error, of applying God's judgements upon particular occasions. Our weights and measures are not competent to make the distribution either of his mercy or his justice: he has thrown a veil over these things, which makes it not only an impertinence, but a kind of sacrilege, for us to give sentence in them without his commission.

As to your particular faith, keep to the religion that is grown up with you, both as it is the best in itself, and that the reason of staying in it upon that ground is somewhat stronger for your sex, than it will perhaps be allowed to be for ours; in respect that the voluminous enquiries into the truth, by reading, are less expected from you. The best of books will be direction enough to you, not to change; and whilst you are fixed and sufficiently confirmed in your own mind, you will do best to keep vain doubts and scruples at such a distance, that they may give you no disquiet. Let me recommend to you a method of being rightly informed, which can never fail. It is in short this: get understanding, and practise virtue. And if you are so blessed as to have those for your share, it is not surer that there is a God, than it is, that by him all necessary truths will be revealed to you.

HUSBAND

THAT which challenges the next place in your thoughts is, how to live with a husband. And though that is so large a word that few rules can be fixed to it which are unchangeable, the methods being as various as the several tempers of men to which they must be suited, yet I cannot omit some general observations, which, with the help of your own, may the better direct you in the part of your life upon which your happiness most depends.

It is one of the disadvantages belonging to your sex, that young women are seldom permitted to make their own choice; their friends' care and experience are thought safer guides to them, than their own fancy; and their modesty often forbids them to refuse when their parents recommend, though their inward consent may not entirely go along with it. In this case there remains nothing for them to do, but to endeavour to make that easy which falls to their lot, and by a wise use of everything they may dislike in a husband, turn that by degrees to be very supportable, which if neglected, might in time beget an aversion.

You must first lay it down for a foundation in general, that there is inequality in the sexes, and that for the better economy of the world, the men, who were to be the lawgivers, had the larger share of reason bestowed upon them; by which means your sex is the better prepared for the compliance that is necessary for the better performance of those duties which seem to be most properly assigned to it. This looks a little uncourtly at the first appearance; but upon examination it will be found, that Nature is so far from being unjust to you, that she is partial on your side. She has made you such large amends by other advantages, for the seeming injustice of the first distribution, that the right of complaining is come over to our sex. You have it in your power not only to free yourselves, but to subdue your masters, and without violence throw both their natural and legal authority at your feet. We are made of differing tempers, that our defects may the better be mutually supplied: your sex wants our reason for your conduct, and our strength for your protection; ours wants your gentleness to soften, and to entertain us. The first part of our life is a good deal subjected to you in the nursery, where you reign without competition, and by that means have the advantage of giving the first impressions. Afterwards you have stronger influences, which, well managed, have more force in your behalf, than all our privileges and jurisdictions can pretend to have against you. You have more strength in your looks, than we have in our laws; and more power by your tears, than we have by our arguments. It is true that the laws of marriage run in a harsher style towards your sex. 'Obey' is an ungentle word, and less easy to be digested, by making such an unkind distinction in the terms of the contract, and so very unsuitable to the excess of good manners, which generally goes before it. Besides, the universality of the rule seems to be a grievance, and it appears reasonable that there might be an exemption for extraordinary women from ordinary rules, to take away the just exception that lies against the false measure of general equality.

It may be alleged by the counsel retained by your sex, that as there is in all other laws, an appeal from the letter to the equity, in cases that require it, it is as reasonable, that some court of a larger jurisdiction might be erected, where some wives might resort and plead specially. And in such instances, where Nature is so kind as to raise them above the level of their own sex, they might have relief, and obtain a mitigation in their own particular, of a sentence which was given generally against womankind. The causes of separation are now so very coarse, that few are confident enough to buy their liberty at the price of having their modesty so exposed. And for disparity of minds, which above all other things requires a remedy, the laws have made no provision; so little refined are numbers of men, by whom they are compiled. This and a great deal more might be said to give a colour to the complaint.

But the answer to it, in short, is, that the institution of marriage is too sacred to admit a liberty of objecting to it; that the supposition of yours being the weaker sex, having without all doubt a good foundation, makes it reasonable to subject it to the masculine dominion; that no rule can be so perfect, as not to admit some exceptions; but the law presumes there would be so few found in this case, who would have a sufficient right to such a privilege, that it is safer some injustice should be connived at in a very few instances, than to break into an establishment, upon which the order of human society does so much depend.

You are therefore to make your best of what is settled by law and custom, and not vainly imagine, that it will be changed for your sake. But that you may not be discouraged, as if you lay under the weight of an incurable grievance, you are to know, that by a wise and dexterous conduct, it will be in your power to relieve yourself from anything that looks like a disadvantage in it. For your better direction, I will give a hint of the most ordinary causes of dissatisfaction between man and wife, that you may be able by such a warning to live so upon your guard, that when you shall be married, you may know how to cure your husband's mistakes, and to prevent your own.

First then, you are to consider, you live in a time which has rendered some kind of frailties so habitual, that they lay claim to large grains of allowance. The world in this is somewhat unequal, and our sex seems to play the tyrant, in distinguishing partially for ourselves, by making that in the utmost degree criminal in the woman, which in a man passes under a much gentler censure. The root and the excuse of this injustice is the preservation of families from any mixture which may bring a blemish to them: and whilst the point of honour continues to be so placed, it seems unavoidable to give your sex the greater share of the penalty. But if in this it lies under any disadvantage, you are more than recompensed by having the honour of families in your keeping. The consideration so great a trust must give you, makes full amends; and this power the world has lodged in you can hardly fail to restrain the severity of an ill husband, and to improve the kindness and esteem of a good one. This being so, remember, that next to the danger of committing the fault yourself, the greatest is that of seeing it in your husband. Do not seem to look or hear that way; if he is a man of sense, he will reclaim himself; the folly of it, is of itself sufficient to cure him; if he is not so, he will be provoked, but not reformed. To expostulate in these cases looks like declaring war, and preparing reprisals; which to a thinking husband would be a dangerous reflection. Besides, it is so coarse a reason which will be assigned for a lady's too great warmth upon such an occasion, that modesty no less than prudence ought to restrain her; since such an indecent complaint makes a wife much more ridiculous, than the injury that provokes her to it. But it is yet worse, and more unskilful, to blaze it in the world, expecting it should rise up in arms to take her part: whereas she will find, it can have no other effect, than that she will be served up in all companies, as the reigning jest at that time; and will continue to be the common entertainment, till she is rescued by some newer folly that comes upon the stage, and drives her away from it. The impertinence of such methods is so plain, that it does not deserve the pains of being laid open. Be assured, that in these cases your discretion and silence will be the most prevailing reproof. An affected ignorance, which is seldom a virtue, is a great one here: and when your husband sees how unwilling you are to be uneasy, there is no stronger argument to persuade him not to be unjust to you. Besides, it will naturally make him more yielding in other things: and whether it be to cover or to redeem his offence, you may have the good effects of it whilst it lasts, and all that while have the most reasonable ground that can be, of presuming such a behaviour will at last entirely convert him. There is nothing so glorious to a wife, as a victory so gained: a man so reclaimed, is for ever after subjected to her virtue; and her bearing for a time, is more than rewarded by a triumph that will continue as long as her life.

The next thing I will suppose is, that your husband may love wine more than is convenient.* It will be granted, that though there are vices of a deeper dye, there are none that have greater deformity than this, when it is not restrained. But with all this, the same custom which is the more to be lamented for its being so general, should make it less uneasy to everyone in particular who is to suffer by the effects of it. So that in the first place, it will be no new thing, if you should have a drunkard for your husband; and there is by too frequent examples evidence enough, that such a thing may happen, and yet a wife may live too without being miserable. Self-love dictates aggravating words to everything we feel; ruin and misery are the terms we apply to whatever we do not like, forgetting the mixture allotted to us by the condition of human life, by which it is not intended we should be quite exempt from trouble. It is fair, if we can escape such a degree of it as would oppress us, and enjoy so much of the pleasant part as may lessen the ill taste of such things as are unwelcome to us. Everything has two sides, and for our own ease we ought to direct our thoughts to that which may be least liable to exception. To fall upon the worst side of a drunkard, gives so unpleasant a prospect, that it is not possible to dwell upon it. Let us pass then to the more favourable part, as far as a wife is concerned in it.

I am tempted to say (if the irregularity of the expression could in strictness be justified) that a wife is to thank God her husband has faults. Mark the seeming paradox, my dear, for your own instruction, it being intended no further. A husband without faults is a dangerous observer; he has an eye so piercing, and sees everything so plain, that it is exposed to his full censure. And though I will not doubt but that your virtue will disappoint the sharpest enquiries; yet few women can bear the having all they say or do represented in the clear glass of an understanding without faults. Nothing softens the arrogance of our nature like a mixture of some frailties. It is by them we are best told, that we must not strike too hard upon others, because we ourselves do so often deserve blows: they pull our rage by the sleeve, and whisper gentleness to us in our censures, even when they are rightly applied. The faults and passions of husbands bring them down to you, and make them content to live upon less unequal terms, than faultless men would be willing to stoop to; so haughty is mankind till humbled by common weaknesses and defects, which in our corrupted state contribute more towards the reconciling us to one another, than all the precepts of the philosophers and divines. So that where the errors of our nature make amends for the disadvantages of yours, it is more your part to make use of the benefit than to quarrel at the fault.

Thus in case a drunken husband should fall to your share, if you will be wise and patient, his wine shall be of your side; it will throw a veil over your mistakes, and will set out and improve everything you do that he is pleased with. Others will like him less, and by that means he may perhaps like you the more. When after having dined too well, he is received at home without a storm, or so much as a reproaching look, the wine will naturally work out all in kindness, which a wife must encourage, let it be wrapped up in never so much impertinence. On the other side, it would boil up into rage, if the mistaken wife should treat him roughly, like a certain thing called a kind shrew, than which the world, with all its plenty, cannot show a more senseless, ill-bred, forbidding creature. Consider, that where the man will give such frequent intermissions of the use of his reason, the wife insensibly gets a right of governing in the vacancy, and that raises her character and credit in the family, to a higher pitch than perhaps could be done under a sober husband, who never puts himself into an incapacity of holding the reins. If these are not entire consolations, at least they are remedies to some degree. They cannot make drunkenness a virtue, nor a husband given to it a felicity; but you will do yourself no ill office in the endeavouring, by these means, to make the best of such a lot, in case it should happen to be yours, and by the help of a wise observation, to make that very supportable, which would otherwise be a load that would oppress you.

The next case I will put is, that your husband may be choleric or ill-humoured. To this it may be said, that passionate men generally make amends at the foot of the account. Such a man, if he is angry one day without any sense, will the next day be as kind without any reason. So that by marking how the wheels of such a man's head are used to move, you may easily bring over all his passion to your party. Instead of being struck down by his thunder, you shall direct it where and upon whom you shall think it best applied. Thus are the strongest poisons turned to the best remedies; but then there must be art in it, and a skilful hand, else the least bungling makes it mortal. There is a great deal of nice care requisite to deal with a man of this complexion. Choler proceeds from pride, and makes a man so partial to himself, that he swells against contradiction, and thinks he is lessened if he is opposed. You must in this case take heed of increasing the storm by an unwary word, or kindling the fire whilst the wind is in a corner which may blow it in your face: you are dexterously to yield everything till he begins to cool, and then by slow degrees you may rise and gain upon him: your gentleness well timed, will like a charm dispel his anger ill placed; a kind smile will reclaim, when a shrill, pettish answer would provoke him. Rather than fail upon such occasions, when other remedies are too weak, a little flattery may be admitted, which by being necessary, will cease to be criminal.

If ill humour and sullenness, and not open and sudden heat, is his disease, there is a way of treating that too, so as to make it a grievance to be endured. In order to it, you are first to know, that naturally good sense has a mixture of surly in it; and there being so much folly in the world, and for the most part so triumphant, it gives frequent temptations to raise the spleen of men who think right. Therefore that which may generally be called ill humour, is not always a fault; it becomes one when either it is wrong applied, or that it is continued too long, when it is not so: for this reason you must not too hastily fix an ill name upon that which may perhaps not deserve it; and though the case should be, that your husband might too sourly resent anything he dislikes, it may so happen, that more blame shall belong to your mistake, than to his ill humour. If a husband behaves himself sometimes with an indifference that a wife may think offensive, she is in the wrong to put the worst sense upon it, if by any means it will admit a better. Some wives will call it ill humour, if their husbands change their style from that which they used whilst they made their first addresses to them. Others will allow no intermission or abatement in the expressions of kindness to them, not enough distinguishing times, and forgetting that it is impossible for men to keep themselves up all their lives to the height of some extravagant moments. A man may at sometimes be less careful in little things, without any cold or disobliging reason for it; as a wife may be too expecting in smaller matters, without drawing upon herself the inference of being unkind. And if your husband should be really sullen, and have such frequent fits, as might take away the excuse of it, it concerns you to have an eye prepared to discern the first appearances of cloudy weather, and to watch when the fit goes off, which seldom lasts long if it is let alone. But whilst the mind is sore, everything galls it, and that makes it necessary to let the black humour begin to spend itself, before you come in and venture to undertake it.

If in the lottery of the world you should draw a covetous husband, I confess it will not make you proud of your good luck; yet even such a one may be endured too, though there are few passions more intractable then that of avarice. You must first take care that your definition of avarice may not be a mistake. You are to examine every circumstance of your husband's fortune, and weigh the reason of everything you expect from him before you have right to pronounce that sentence. The complaint is now so general against all husbands, that it gives great suspicion of its being often ill-grounded. It is impossible they should all deserve that censure, and therefore it is certain, that it is many times misapplied. He that spares in everything is an inexcusable niggard; he that spares in nothing is as inexcusable a madman. The mean is, to spare in what is least necessary, to lay out more liberally in what is most required in our several circumstances. Yet this will not always satisfy. There are wives who are impatient of the rules of economy, and are apt to call their husbands' kindness in question, if any other measure is put to their expense than that of their own fancy. Be sure to avoid this dangerous error, such a partiality to yourself, which is so offensive to an understanding man, that he will very ill bear a wife's giving herself such an injurious preference to all the family, and whatever belongs to it.

But to admit the worst, and that your husband is really a close-handed wretch, you must in this as in other cases, endeavour to make it less afflicting to you; and first you must observe seasonable hours of speaking. When you offer anything in opposition to this reigning humour, a third hand and a wise friend may often prevail more than you will be allowed to do in your own cause. Sometimes you are dexterously to go along with him in things, where you see that the niggardly part of his mind is most predominant, by which you will have the better opportunity of persuading him in things where he may be more indifferent. Our passions are very unequal, and are apt to be raised or lessened, according as they work upon different objects; they are not to be stopped or restrained in those things where our mind is more particularly engaged. In other matters they are more tractable, and will sometimes give reason a hearing, and admit a fair dispute. More than that, there are few men, even in this instance of avarice, so entirely abandoned to it, that at some hours and upon some occasions, will not forget their nature, and for that time turn prodigal. The same man who will grudge himself what is necessary, let his pride be raised and he shall be profuse: at another time his anger shall have the same effect; a fit of vanity, ambition, and sometimes of kindness, shall open and enlarge his narrow mind; a dose of wine will work upon his tough humour, and for the time dissolve it. Your business must be, if this case happens, to watch these critical moments, and not let one of them slip without making your advantage of it; and a wife may be said to want skill, if by these means, she is not able to secure herself in a good measure against the inconveniences this scurvy quality in a husband might bring upon her, except he should be such an incurable monster, as I hope will never fall to your share.

The last supposition I will make is, that your husband should be weak and incompetent to make use of the privileges that belong to him. It will be yielded, that such a one leaves room for a great many objections. But God Almighty seldom sends a grievance without a remedy, or at least such a mitigation as takes away a great part of the sting, and the smart of it. To make such a misfortune less heavy, you are first to bring to your observation, that a wife very often makes the better figure, for her husband's making no great one: and there seems to be little reason, why the same lady that chooses a waiting woman with worse looks, may not be content with a husband that has less wit; the argument being equal from the advantage of the comparison. If you will be more ashamed in some cases of such a husband, you will be less afraid than you would perhaps be of a wise one. His unseasonable weakness may no doubt sometimes grieve you, but then set against this, that it gives you the dominion, if you will make the right use of it. It is next to his being dead, in which case the wife has right to administer; therefore be sure, if you have such an idiot, that none, except yourself, may have the benefit of the forfeiture: such a fool is a dangerous beast, if others have the keeping of him; and you must be very undexterous, if when your husband shall resolve to be an ass, you do not take care he may be *your* ass. But you must go skilfully about it, and above all things, take heed of distinguishing in public what kind of husband he is: your inward thoughts must not hinder the outward payment of the consideration that is due to him. Your slighting him in company, besides that it would, to a discerning bystander, give too great encouragement for the making nearer applications to you, is in itself such an indecent way of assuming, that it may provoke the tame creature to break loose, and to show his dominion for his credit, which he was content to forget for his ease. In short, the surest and the most approved method will be to do like a wise minister to an easy prince: first give him the orders you afterwards receive from him.

With all this, that which you are to pray for is a wise husband, one that by knowing how to be a master, for that very reason will not let you feel the weight of it; one whose authority is so softened by his kindness, that it gives you ease without abridging your liberty; one that will return so much tenderness for your just esteem of him, that you will never want power, though you will seldom care to use it. Such a husband is as much above all the other kinds of them, as a rational subjection to a prince, great in himself, is to be preferred before the disquiet and uneasiness of unlimited liberty.

Before I leave this head, I must add a little concerning your behaviour to your husband's friends, which requires the most refined part of your understanding to acquit yourself well of it. You are to study how to live with them with more care than you are to apply to any other part of your life; especially at first, that you may not stumble at the first setting out. The family into which you are grafted will generally be apt to expect, that like a stranger in a foreign country, you should conform to their methods, and not bring in a new model by your own authority. The friends in such a case are tempted to rise up in arms as against an unlawful invasion, so that you are with the utmost caution to avoid the least appearances of anything of this kind. And that you may with less difficulty afterwards give your directions, be sure at first to receive them from your husband's friends. Gain them to you by early applying to them, and they will be so satisfied, that as nothing is more thankful than pride, when it is complied with, they will strive which of them shall most recommend you; and when they have helped you to take root in your husband's good opinion, you will have less dependence upon theirs, though you must not neglect any reasonable means of preserving it. You are to consider, that a man governed by his friends, is very easily enflamed by them; and that one who is not so, will yet for his own sake expect to have them considered. It is easily improved to a point of honour in a husband, not to have his relations neglected; and nothing is more dangerous, than to raise an objection, which is grounded upon pride: it is the most stubborn and lasting passion we are subject to, and where it is the first cause of the war, it is very hard to make a secure peace. Your caution in this is of the last importance to you.

And that you may the better succeed in it, carry a strict eye upon the impertinence of your servants; take heed that their ill humour may not engage you to take exceptions, or their too much assuming in small matters, raise consequences which may bring you under great disadvantage. Remember that in the case of a royal bride, those about her are generally so far suspected to bring in a foreign interest, that in most countries they are insensibly reduced to a very small number, and those of so low a figure, that it does not admit the being jealous of them. In little, and in the proportion, this may be the case of every new married woman, and therefore it may be more advisable for you, to gain the servants you find in a family than to tie yourself too fast to those you carry into it. You are not to overlook these small reflections, because they may appear low and inconsiderable; for it may be said, that as the greatest streams are made up of the small drops at the head of the springs from whence they are derived, so the greater circum-stances of your life will be in some degree directed by these seeming trifles, which having the advantage of being the first acts of it, have a greater effect than singly in their own nature they could pretend to.

I will conclude this article with my advice, that you would, as much as Nature will give you leave, endeavour to forget the great indulgence you have found at home. After such a gentle discipline as you have been under, everything you dislike will seem the harsher to you. The tenderness we have had for you, my dear, is of another nature, peculiar to kind parents, and differing from that which you will meet with at first in any family into which you shall be transplanted; and yet they may be very kind too, and afford no justifiable reason to you to complain. You must not be frightened with the first appearances of a differing scene; for when you are used to it, you may like the house you go to, better than that you left; and your husband's kindness will have so much advantage of ours, that we shall yield up all competition, and as well as we love you, be very well contented to surrender to such a rival.

HOUSE, FAMILY, AND CHILDREN

You must lay before you, my dear, there are degrees of care to recommend yourself to the world in the several parts of your life. In many things, though the doing them well may raise your credit and esteem, yet the omission of them would draw no immediate reproach upon you. In others, where your duty is more particularly applied, the neglect of them is amongst those faults which are not forgiven, and will bring you under a censure, which will be much a heavier thing than the trouble you would avoid. Of this kind is the government of your house, family and children, which since it is the province allotted to your sex, and that the discharging it well will for that reason be expected from you, if you either desert it out of laziness, or manage it ill for want of skill, instead of a help you will be an encumbrance to the family where you are placed.

I must tell you, that no respect is lasting, but that which is produced by our being in some degree useful to those that pay it. Where that fails, the homage and the reverence go along with it and fly to others where something may be expected in exchange for them. And upon this principle the respects even of the children and the servants will not stay with one that does not think them worth their care, and the old housekeeper shall make a better figure in the family than the lady with all her fine clothes, if she wilfully relinquishes her title to the government. Therefore take heed of carrying your good breeding to such a height as to be good for nothing, and to be proud of it. Some think it has a great air to be above troubling their thoughts with such ordinary things as their house and family; others dare not admit cares for fear they should hasten wrinkles; mistaken pride makes some think they must keep themselves up, and not descend to these duties, which do not seem enough refined for great ladies to be employed in; forgetting all this while, that it is more than the greatest princes can do, at once to preserve respect, and to neglect their business. No age ever erected altars to insignificant gods; they had all some quality applied to them to draw worship from mankind; this makes it the more unreasonable for a lady to expect to be considered, and at the same time resolve not to deserve it. Good looks alone will not do; they are not such a lasting tenure as to be relied upon; and if they should stay longer than they usually do, it would by no means be safe to depend upon them: for when time has abated the violence of the first liking, and that the nap is a little worn off, though still a good degree of kindness may remain, men recover their sight which before might be dazzled, and allow themselves to object as well as to admire.

In such a case, when a husband sees an empty airy thing sail up and down the house to no kind of purpose, and look as if she came thither only to make a visit; when he finds, that after her emptiness has been extremely busy about some very senseless thing, she eats her breakfast half an hour before dinner, to be at greater liberty to afflict the company with her discourse; then calls for her coach, that she may trouble her acquaintance, who are already cloyed with her; and having some proper dialogues ready to display her foolish eloquence at the top of the stairs, she sets out like a ship out of the harbour, laden with trifles, and comes back with them; at her return she repeats to her faithful waiting woman, the triumphs of that day's impertinence; then wrapped up in flattery and clean linen, goes to bed so satisfied that it throws her into pleasant dreams of her own felicity: such a one is seldom serious but with her tailor; her children and family may now and then have a random thought, but she never takes aim but at something very impertinent. I say when a husband, whose province is without doors, and to whom the economy of the house would be in some degree indecent, finds no order nor quiet in his family, meets with complaints of all kinds springing from this root, the mistaken lady who thinks to make amends for all this, by having a well-chosen petticoat, will at last be convinced of her error, and with grief be forced to undergo the penalties that belong to those who are wilfully insignificant. When this scurvy hour comes upon her, she first grows angry; then when the time of it is past, would perhaps grow wiser, not remembering that we can no more have wisdom than grace, whenever we think fit to call for it. There are times and periods fixed for both; and when they are too long neglected, the punishment is, that they are irrecoverable, and nothing remains but a useless grief for the folly of having thrown them out of our power. You are to think what a mean figure a woman makes, when she is so degraded by her own fault; whereas there is nothing in those duties which are expected from you, that can be a lessening to you, except your want of conduct makes it so.

You may love your children without living in the nursery, and you may have a competent and discreet care of them, without letting it break out upon the company, or exposing yourself by turning your discourse that way, which is a kind of laying children to the parish, and it can hardly be done anywhere, that those who hear it will be so forgiving, as not to think they are overcharged with them. A woman's tenderness to her children is one of the least deceitful evidences of her virtue; but yet the way of expressing it must be subject to the rules of good breeding: and though a woman of quality ought not to be less kind to them than mothers of the meanest rank are to theirs, yet she may distinguish herself in the manner, and avoid the coarse methods, which in women of a lower size might be more excusable.

You must begin early to make them love you, that they may obey you. This mixture is nowhere more necessary than in children. And I must tell you, that you are not to expect returns of kindness from yours, if ever you have any, without grains of allowance; and yet it is not so much a defect in their good nature, as a shortness of thought in them. Their first insufficiency makes them lean so entirely upon their parents for what is necessary, that the habit of it makes them continue the same expectations for what is unreasonable; and as often as they are denied, so often they think they are injured; and whilst their desires are strong, and their reason yet in the cradle, their anger looks no further than the thing they long for and cannot have: and to be displeased for their own good, is a maxim they are very slow to understand: so that you may conclude, the first thoughts of your children will have no small mixture of mutiny; which being so natural, you must not be angry, except you would increase it. You must deny them as seldom as you can, and when there is no avoiding it, you must do it gently; you must flatter away their ill humour, and take the next opportunity of pleasing them in some other thing before they either ask or look for it: this will strengthen your authority, by making it soft to them; and confirm their obedience, by making it their interest.

You are to have as strict a guard upon yourself amongst your children, as if you were amongst your enemies. They are apt to make wrong inferences, to take encouragement from half words, and misapply what you may say or do, so as either to lessen their duty, or to extend their liberty further than is convenient. Let them be more in awe of your kindness than of your power. And above all, take heed of supporting a favourite child in its impertinence, which will give a right to the rest of claiming the same privilege. If you have a divided number, leave the boys to the father's more peculiar care, that you may with the greater justice pretend to a more immediate jurisdiction over those of your own sex. You are to live so with them, that they may never choose to avoid you, except when they have offended; and then let them tremble, that they may distinguish: but their penance must not continue so long as to grow too sour upon their stomachs, that it may not harden instead of correcting them: the kind and severe parts must have their several turns, seasonably applied; but your indulgence is to have the broader mixture, that love, rather than fear, may be the root of their obedience.

Your servants are in the next place to be considered; and you must remember not to fall into the mistake of thinking, that because they receive wages, and are so much inferior to you, therefore they are below your care to know how to manage them. It would be as good reason for a master workman to despise the wheels of his engine because they are made of wood. These are the wheels of your family; and let your directions be never so faultless, yet if these engines stop or move wrong, the whole order of your house is either at a stand, or discomposed. Besides, the inequality which is between you, must not make you forget, that Nature makes no such distinction, but that servants may be looked upon as humble friends, and that returns of kindness and good usage are as much due to such of them as deserve it, as their service is due to us when we require it. A foolish haughtiness in the style of speaking, or in the manner of commanding them, is in itself very indecent; besides that it begets an aversion in them, of which the least ill effect to be expected is that they will be slow and careless in all that is enjoined them: and you will find it true by your experience, that you will be so much the more obeyed as you are less imperious. Be not too hasty in giving your orders, nor too angry when they are not altogether observed; much less are you to be loud, and too much disturbed: an evenness in distinguishing when they do well or ill, is that which will make your family move by a rule, and without noise, and will the better set out your skill in conducting it with ease and silence, that it may be like a well-disciplined army, which knows how to anticipate the orders that are fit to be given them. You are never to neglect the duty of the present hour, to do another thing, which though it may be better in itself, is not to be unseasonably preferred. Allot well-chosen hours for the inspection of your family, which may be so distinguished from the rest of your time, that the necessary cares may come in their proper place, without any influence upon your good humour, or interruption to other things. By these methods you will put yourself in possession of being valued by your servants, and then their obedience will naturally follow.

I must not forget one of the greatest articles belonging to a family, which is the expense. It must not be such as by failing either in the time or measure of it, may rather draw censure than gain applause. If it was well examined, there is more money given to be laughed at, than for any other thing in the world, though the purchasers do not think so. A well-stated rule is like the Line,* when that is once past we are under another Pole; so the first straying from a rule, is a step towards making that which was before a virtue, to change its nature, and to grow either into a vice, or at least an impertinence. The art of laying out money wisely, is not attained to without a great deal of thought; and it is yet more difficult in the case of a wife, who is accountable to her husband for her mistakes in it. It is not only his money, his credit too is at stake, if what lies under the wife's care is managed, either with indecent thrift, or too loose profusion. You are therefore to keep the mean between these two extremes, and it being hardly possible to hold the balance exactly even, let it rather incline towards the liberal side, as more suitable to your quality, and less subject to reproach. Of the two, a little money misspent is sooner recovered, than the credit which is lost, by having it unhandsomely saved; and a wise husband will less forgive a shameful piece of parsimony, than a little extravagance, if it be not too often repeated. His mind in this must be your chief direction; and his temper, when once known, will in great measure justify your part in the management, if he is pleased with it.

In your clothes avoid too much gaudy; do not value yourself upon an embroidered gown; and remember, that a reasonable word, or an obliging look, will gain you more respect, than all your fine trappings. This is not said to restrain you from a decent compliance with the world, provided you take the wiser, and not the foolisher part of your sex for your pattern. Some distinctions are to be allowed, whilst they are well suited to your quality and fortune, and in the distribution of the expense it seems to me that a full attendance and well-chosen ornaments for your house, will make you a better figure, than too much glittering in what you wear, which may with more ease be imitated by those that are below you. Yet this must not tempt you to starve everything but your own apartment; or in order to more abundance there, give just cause to the least servant you have, to complain of the want of what is necessary. Above all, fix it in your thoughts, as an unchangeable maxim, that nothing is truly fine but what is fit, and that just so much as is proper for your circumstances of their several kinds, is much finer than all you can add to it.

When you once break through those bounds, you launch into a wide sea of extravagance. Everything will become necessary, because you have a mind to it; and you have a mind to it, not because it is fit for you, but because somebody else has it. This lady's logic sets reason upon its head, by carrying the rule from things to persons, and appeals from what is right to every fool that is in the wrong. The word necessary is miserably applied; it disorders families, and overturns governments, by being so abused. Remember, that children and fools want everything because they want wit to distinguish: and therefore there is no stronger evidence of a crazy understanding, than the making too large a catalogue of things necessary, when in truth there are so very few things that have a right to be placed in it. Try everything first in your judgement, before you allow it a place in your desire; else your husband may think it as necessary for him to deny, as it is for you to have whatever is unreasonable; and if you shall too often give him that advantage, the habit of refusing may perhaps reach to things that are not unfit for you.

There are unthinking ladies, who do not enough consider, how little their own figure agrees with the fine things they are so proud of. Others when they have them will hardly allow them to be visible; they cannot be seen without light, and that is many times so saucy and so prying, that like a too forward gallant it is to be forbid the chamber.

Some, when you are ushered into their dark *ruelle*,* it is with such solemnity, that a man would swear there was something in it, till the unskilful lady breaks silence, and begins a chat, which discovers it is a puppet play with magnificent scenes. Many esteem things rather as they are hard to be got, than that they are worth getting: this looks as if they had an interest to pursue that maxim, because a great part of their own value depends upon it. Truth in these cases would be often unmannerly, and might derogate from the prerogative great ladies would assume to themselves, of being distinct creatures from those of their sex who are inferior, and of less difficult access.

In other things too, your condition must give the rule to you, and therefore it is not a wife's part to aim at more than a bounded liberality; the further extent of that quality, otherwise to be commended, belongs to the husband, who has better means for it. Generosity wrong placed becomes a vice. It is no more a virtue when it grows into an inconvenience. Virtues must be enlarged or restrained according to differing circumstances. A princely mind will undo a private family. Therefore things must be suited, or else they will not deserve to be commended, let them in themselves be never so valuable; and the expectations of the world are best answered when we acquit ourselves in that manner which seems to be prescribed to our several conditions, without usurping upon those duties which do not so particularly belong to us.

I will close the consideration of this article of expense, with this short word. Do not fetter yourself with such restraint in it as may make you remarkable; but remember that virtue is the greatest ornament, and good sense the best equipage.

BEHAVIOUR AND CONVERSATION

IT is time now to lead you out of your house into the world. A dangerous step; where your virtue alone will not secure you, except it is attended with a great deal of prudence. You must have both for your guard, and not stir without them. The enemy is abroad and you are sure to be taken, if you are found straggling. Your behaviour is therefore to incline strongly towards the reserved part; your character is to be immovably fixed upon that bottom, not excluding any mixture of greater freedom, as far as it may be innocent and well timed. The extravagances of the age have made caution more necessary; and by the same reason that the too great licence of ill men has by consequence in many things restrained the lawful liberty of those who did not abuse it, the unjustifiable freedoms of some of your sex have involved the rest in the penalty of being reduced. And though this cannot so alter the nature of things as to make that criminal which in itself is indifferent, yet if it makes it dangerous, that alone is sufficient to justify the restraint. A close behaviour is the fittest to receive virtue for its constant guest, because there, and there only, it can be secure. Proper reserves are the outworks, and must never be deserted by those who intend to keep the place; they keep off the possibility not only of being taken, but of being attempted; and if a woman sees danger though at never so remote a distance, she is for that time to shorten her line of liberty. She who will allow herself to go to the utmost extent of everything that is lawful, is so very near going further, that those who lie at watch will begin to count upon her.

Mankind, from the double temptation of vanity and desire, is apt to turn everything a woman does to the hopeful side; and there are few who dare make an impudent application, till they discern something which they are willing to take for an encouragement. It is safer therefore to prevent such forwardness, than to go about to cure it. It gathers strength by the first allowances, and claims a right from having been at any time suffered with impunity. Therefore nothing is with more care to be avoided, than such a kind of civility as may be mistaken for invitation; and it will not be enough for you to keep yourself free from any criminal engagements; for if you do that which either raises hopes or creates discourse, there is a spot thrown upon your good name; and those kind of stains are the harder to be taken out, being dropped upon you by the man's vanity, as well as by the woman's malice.

Most men are in one sense platonic lovers, though they are not willing to own that character. They are so far philosophers, as to allow, that the greatest part of pleasure lies in the mind; and in pursuance of that maxim, there are few who do not place the felicity more in the opinion of the world, of their being prosperous lovers, than in the blessing itself, how much soever they appear to value it. This being so, you must be very cautious not to gratify those chameleons at the price of bringing a cloud upon your reputation, which may be deeply wounded, though your conscience is unconcerned.

Your own sex too will not fail to help the least appearance that gives a handle to be ill turned. The best of them will not be displeased to improve their own value, by laying others under a disadvantage, when there is a fair occasion given for it. It distinguishes them still the more: their own credit is more exalted, and, like a picture set off with shades, shines more when a lady, either less innocent, or less discreet, is set near, to make them appear so much the brighter. If these lend their breath to blast such as are so unwary as to give them this advantage, you may be sure there will be a stronger gale from those, who, besides malice or emulation, have an interest too, to strike hard upon a virtuous woman. It seems to them, that their load of infamy is lessened, by throwing part of it upon others: so that they will not only improve when it lies in their way, but take pains to find out the least mistake an innocent woman commits, in revenge of the injury she does in leading a life which is a reproach to them. With these you must be extremely wary, and neither provoke them to be angry, nor invite them to be intimate.

To the men you are to have a behaviour which may secure you, without offending them. No ill-bred affected shyness, nor a roughness unsuitable to your sex, and unnecessary to your virtue; but a way of living that may prevent all coarse railleries or unmannerly freedoms; looks that forbid without rudeness, and oblige without invitation, or leaving room for the saucy inferences men's vanity suggests to them upon the least encouragements. This is so very nice, that it must engage you to have a perpetual watch upon your eyes, and to remember that one careless glance gives more advantage than a hundred words not enough considered; the language of the eyes being very much the most significant, and the most observed.

Your civility, which is always to be preserved, must not be carried to a compliance, which may betray you into irrecoverable mistakes. This French ambiguous word *complaisance** has led your sex into more blame, than all other things put together. It carries them by degrees into a certain thing called 'a good kind of woman', an easy idle creature, that does neither good nor ill but by chance, has no choice, but leaves that to the company she keeps. Time, which by degrees adds to the signification of words, has made her, according to the modern style, little better than one who thinks it a rudeness to deny, when civilly required, either her service in person, or her friendly assistance, to those who would have a meeting, or want a confidant. She is a certain thing always at hand, an easy companion, who has ever a great compassion for distressed lovers: she censures nothing but rigour, and is never without a plaster for a wounded reputation, in which chiefly lies her skill in chirurgery:* she seldom has the propriety of any particular gallant, but lives upon brokerage,* and waits for the scraps her friends are content to leave her.

There is another character not quite so criminal, yet not less ridiculous; which is that of 'a good-humoured woman', one who thinks she must always be in a laugh, or a broad smile, because good humour is an obliging quality, thinks it less ill manners to talk impertinently, than to be silent in company. When such a prating engine rides admiral,* and carries the lantern in a circle of fools, a cheerful coxcomb coming in for a recruit, the chattering of monkeys is a better noise than such a concert of senseless merriment. If she is applauded in it, she is so encouraged, that, like a ballad singer, who if commended, breaks his lungs, she lets herself loose, and overflows upon the company. She conceives that mirth is to have no intermission, and therefore she will carry it about with her, though it be to a funeral; and if a man should put a familiar question, she does not know very well how to be angry, for then she would be no more that pretty thing called a good-humoured woman.

This necessity of appearing at all times to be so infinitely pleased is a grievous mistake, since in a handsome woman that invitation is unnecessary; and in one who is not so, ridiculous. It is not intended by this, that you should forswear laughing; but remember, that fools being always painted in that posture, it may fright those who are wise from doing it too frequently, and going too near a copy which is so little inviting, and much more from doing it loud, which is an unnatural sound, and looks so much like another sex, that few things are more offensive. That boisterous kind of jollity is as contrary to wit and good manners, as it is to modesty and virtue. Besides, it is a coarse kind of quality, that throws a woman into a lower form, and degrades her from the rank of those who are more refined. Some ladies speak loud and make a noise to be the more minded, which looks as if they beat their drums for volunteers,* and if by misfortune none come in to them, they may, not without reason, be a good deal out of countenance.

There is one thing yet more to be avoided, which is the example of those who intend nothing further than the vanity of conquest, and think themselves secure of not having their honour tainted by it.

Some are apt to believe their virtue is too obscure, and not enough known, except it is exposed to a broader light, and set out to its best advantage, by some public trials. These are dangerous experiments, and generally fail, being built upon so weak a foundation as that of a too great confidence in ourselves. It is as safe to play with fire, as to dally with gallantry. Love is a passion that has friends in the garrison, and for that reason must by a woman be kept at such a distance that she may not be within the danger of doing the most usual thing in the world, which is conspiring against herself: else the humble gallant, who is only admitted as a trophy, very often becomes the conqueror; he puts on the style of victory, and from an admirer, grows into a master, for so he may be called from the moment he is in possession. The first resolutions of stopping at good opinion and esteem, grow weaker by degrees against the charms of courtship skilfully applied. A lady is apt to think a man speaks so much reason whilst he is commending her, that she has much ado to believe him in the wrong when he is making love to her: and when besides the natural inducements your sex has to be merciful, she is bribed by well-chosen flattery, the poor creature is in danger of being caught like a bird listening to the whistle of one that has a snare for it.

Conquest is so tempting a thing, that it often makes women mistake men's submissions, which with all their fair appearance, have generally less respect than art in them. You are to remember, that men who say extreme fine things, many times say them most for their own sakes; and that the vain gallant is often as well pleased with his own compliments, as he could be with the kindest answer. Where there is not that ostentation, you are to suspect there is a design. And as strong perfumes are seldom used but where they are necessary to smother an unwelcome scent, so excessive good words leave room to believe they are strewed to cover something, which is to gain admittance under a disguise. You must therefore be upon your guard, and consider, that of the two, respect is more dangerous than anger. It puts even the best understandings out of their place for the time, till their second thoughts restore them; it steals upon us insensibly, throws down our defences, and makes it too late to resist, after we have given it that advantage. Whereas railing goes away in sound; it has so much noise in it, that by giving warning it bespeaks caution. Respect is a slow and sure poison, and like poison swells us within ourselves. Where it prevails too much, it grows to be a kind of apoplexy in the mind, turns it quite round, and after it has once seized the understanding, becomes mortal to it. For these reasons, the safest way is to treat it like a sly enemy, and to be perpetually upon the watch against it.

I will add one advice to conclude this head, which is, that you will let every seven years make some alteration in you towards the graver side, and not be like the girls of 50, who resolve to be always young, whatever time with his iron teeth has determined to the contrary. Unnatural things carry a deformity in them never to be disguised; the liveliness of youth in a riper age looks like a new patch upon an old gown; so that a gay matron, a cheerful old fool, may be reasonably put into the list of the tamer kind of monsters. There is a certain creature called a grave hobby-horse, a kind of a she-numps,* that pretends to be pulled to a play, and must needs go to Bartholomew Fair,* to look after the young folks, whom she only seems to make her care; in reality she takes them for her excuse. Such an old butterfly is of all creatures the most ridiculous, and the soonest found out. It is good to be early in your caution, to avoid anything that comes within distance of such despicable patterns, and not like some ladies, who defer their conversion till they have been so long in possession of being laughed at, that the world does not know how to change their style, even when they are reclaimed from that which gave the first occasion for it. The advantages of being reserved are too many to be set down; I will only say, that it is a guard to a good woman, and a disguise to an ill one. It is of so much use to both, that those ought to use it as an artifice, who refuse to practise it as a virtue.

FRIENDSHIPS

I MUST in a particular manner recommend to you a strict care in the choice of your friendships. Perhaps the best are not without their objections, but however, be sure that yours may not stray from the rules which the wiser part of the world has set to them. The leagues offensive and defensive, seldom hold in politics, and much less in friendships. The violent intimacies, when once broken, of which they scarce ever fail, make such a noise: the bag of secrets untied, they fly about like birds let loose from a cage, and become the entertainment of the town. Besides, these great dearnesses by degrees grow injurious to the rest of your acquaintance, and throw them off from you. There is such an offensive distinction when the dear friend comes into the room, that it is flinging stones at the company, who are not apt to forgive it. Do not lay out your friendship too lavishly at first, since it will, like other things, be so much the sooner spent; neither let it be of too sudden a growth; for as the plants which shoot up too fast are not of that continuance, as those which take more time for it; so too swift a progress in pouring out your kindness, is a certain sign that by the course of nature it will not be long lived.

You will be responsible to the world, if you pitch upon such friends as at the time are under the weight of any criminal objection. In that case you will bring yourself under the disadvantages of their character, and must bear your part of it. Choosing implies approving; and if you fix upon a lady for your friend against whom the world shall have given judgement, it is not so well natured as to believe you are altogether averse to her way of living, since it does not discourage you from admitting her into your kindness. And resemblance of inclinations being thought none of the least inducements to friendship, you will be looked upon at least as a well-wisher if not a partner with her in her faults. If you can forgive them in another, it may be presumed you will not be less gentle to yourself; and therefore you must not take it ill, if you are reckoned a *croupière*,* and condemned to pay an equal share with such a friend of the reputation she has lost.

If it happens that your friend should fall from the state of innocence after your kindness was engaged to her, you may be slow in your belief in the beginning of the discovery: but as soon as you are convinced by a rational evidence, you must, without breaking too roughly, make a fair and a quick retreat from such a mistaken acquaintance; else by moving too slowly from one that is so tainted, the contagion may reach you so far as to give you part of the scandal, though not of the guilt. This matter is so nice, that as you must not be too hasty to join in the censure upon your friend when she is accused, so you are not on the other side to defend her with too much warmth; for if she should happen to deserve the report of common fame, besides the vexation that belongs to such a mistake, you will draw an ill appearance upon yourself, and it will be thought you pleaded for her not without some consideration of yourself. The anger which must be put on to vindicate the reputation of an injured friend, may incline the company to suspect you would not be so zealous, if there was not a possibility that the case might be your own. For this reason you are not to carry your dearness so far, as absolutely to lose your sight, where your friend is concerned. Because malice is too quick-sighted, it does not follow that friendship is to be blind: there must be a mean between these two extremes, else your excess of good nature may betray you into a very ridiculous figure, and by degrees you may be preferred into such offices as you will not be proud of. Your ignorance may lessen the guilt, but will improve the jest upon you, who shall be kindly solicitous to procure a meeting, and innocently contribute to the ills you would avoid: whilst the contriving lovers, when they are alone, shall make you the subject of their mirth, and perhaps (with respect to the goddess of love be it spoken) it is not the worst part of their entertainment, at least it is the most lasting, to laugh at the believing friend, who was so easily deluded.

Let the good sense of your friends be a chief ingredient in your choice of them; else let your reputation be never so clear, it may be clouded by their impertinence. It is like our houses being in the power of a drunken or a careless neighbour; only so much the worse, as that there will be no insurance here to make you amends, as there is in the case of fire.

To conclude this paragraph: if formality is to be allowed in any instance, it is to be put on to resist the invasion of such forward women as shall press themselves into your friendship, where, if admitted, they will either be a snare or an encumbrance.

CENSURE

I WILL come next to the consideration, how you are to manage your censure; in which both care and skill will be a good deal required. To distinguish is not only natural but necessary; and the effect of it is, that we cannot avoid giving judgement in our minds, either to absolve or to condemn as the case requires. The difficulty is, to know when and where it is fit to proclaim the sentence. An aversion to what is criminal, and a contempt of what is ridiculous, are the inseparable companions of understanding and virtue; but the letting them go further than our own thoughts, has so much danger in it, that though it is neither possible nor fit to suppress them entirely, yet it is necessary they should be kept under very great restraint. An unlimited liberty of this kind is little less than sending a herald and proclaiming war to the world, which is an angry beast when so provoked. The contest will be unequal, though you are never so much in the right; and if you begin against such an adversary, it will tear you in pieces, with this justification, that it is done in its own defence.

You must therefore take heed of laughing, except in company that is very sure. It is throwing snowballs against bullets; and it is the disadvantage of a woman, that the malice of the world will help the brutality of those who will throw a slovenly untruth upon her. You are for this reason to suppress your impatience for fools, who, besides that they are too strong a party to be unnecessarily provoked, are of all others the most dangerous in this case. A blockhead in his rage will return a dull jest that will lie heavy, though there is not a grain of wit in it. Others will do it with more art, and you must not think yourself secure because your reputation may perhaps be out of the reach of ill will; for if it finds that part guarded, it will seek one which is more exposed. It flies like a corrupt humour in the body, to the weakest part. If you have a tender side, the world will be sure to find it, and to put the worst colour upon all you say or do, give an aggravation to everything that may lessen you, and a spiteful turn to everything that might recommend you.

Anger lays open those defects which friendship would not see and civility might be willing to forget. Malice needs no such invitation to encourage it, neither are any pains more superfluous than those we take to be ill spoken of. If envy, which never dies, and seldom sleeps, is content sometimes to be in a slumber, it is very unskilful to make a noise to awaken it. Besides, your wit will be misapplied if it is wholly directed to discern the faults of others, when it is so necessary to be often used to mend and prevent your own. The sending our thoughts too much abroad has the same effect as when a family never stays at home; neglect and disorder naturally follows, as it must do within ourselves, if we do not frequently turn our eyes inward, to see what is amiss with us; where it is a sign we have an unwelcome prospect, when we do not care to look upon it, but rather seek our consolations in the faults of those we converse with.

Avoid being the first in fixing a hard censure, let it be confirmed by the general voice before you give into it; neither are you then to give sentence like a magistrate, or as if you had a special authority to bestow a good or ill name at your discretion. Do not dwell too long upon a weak side, touch and go away; take pleasure to stay longer where you commend, like bees that fix only upon those herbs out of which they may extract the juices of which their honey is composed. A virtue stuck with bristles is too rough for this age; it must be adorned with some flowers, or else it will be unwillingly entertained; so that even where it may be fit to strike, do it like a lady, gently; and assure yourself, that where you care to do it, you will wound others more, and hurt yourself less, by soft strokes, than by being harsh or violent.

The triumph of wit is to make your good nature subdue your censure; to be quick in seeing faults, and slow in exposing them. You are to consider, that the invisible thing called a good name, is made up of the breath of numbers that speak well of you; so that if by a disobliging word you silence the meanest, the gale will be less strong which is to bear up your esteem. And though nothing is so vain as the eager pursuit of empty applause, yet to be well thought of, and to be kindly used by the world, is like a glory about a woman's head; it is a perfume she carries about with her, and leaves wherever she goes; it is a charm against ill will. Malice may empty her quiver, but cannot wound; the dirt will not stick, the jests will not take; without the consent of the world a scandal does not go deep: it is only a slight stroke upon the injured party, and returns with the greater force upon those that gave it.

VANITY AND AFFECTATION

I MUST with more than ordinary earnestness give you caution against vanity, it being the fault to which your sex seems to be the most inclined; and since affectation for the most part attends it, I do not know how to divide them. I will not call them twins, because more properly vanity is the mother, and affectation is the darling daughter; vanity is the sin, and affectation is the punishment; the first may be called the root of self-love, the other the fruit; vanity is never at its full growth, till it spreads into affectation, and then it is complete.

Not to dwell any longer upon the definition of them, I will pass to the means and motives to avoid them. In order to it, you are to consider, that the world challenges the right of distributing esteem and applause; so that where any assume by their single authority to be their own carvers, it grows angry, and never fails to seek revenge. And if we may measure a fault by the greatness of the penalty, there are few of a higher size than vanity, as there is scarce a punishment which can be heavier than that of being laughed at.

Vanity makes a woman tainted with it, so top-full of herself, that she spills it upon the company. And because her own thoughts are entirely employed in self-contemplation, she endeavours, by a cruel mistake, to confine her acquaintance to the same narrow circle of that which only concerns her ladyship, forgetting that she is not of half the importance to the world that she is to herself, so mistaken she is in her value, by being her own appraiser. She will fetch such a compass in discourse to bring in her beloved self, and rather than fail, her fine petticoat, that there can hardly be a better scene than such a trial of ridiculous ingenuity. It is a pleasure to see her angle for commendations, and rise so dissatisfied with the ill-bred company, if they will not bite. To observe her throwing her eyes about to fetch in prisoners, and go about cruising like a privateer,* and so out of countenance if she returns without booty, is no ill piece of comedy. She is so eager to draw respect, that she always misses it, yet thinks it so much her due, that when she fails, she grows waspish, not considering that it is impossible to commit a rape upon the will; that it must be fairly gained, and will not be taken by storm; and that in this case, the tax ever rises highest by a benevolence.

If the world instead of admiring her imaginary excellences, takes the liberty to laugh at them, she appeals from it to herself, for whom she gives sentence, and proclaims it in all companies. On the other side, if encouraged by a civil word, she is so obliged, that she will give thanks for being laughed at, in good language. She takes a compliment for a demonstration, and sets it up as an evidence, even against her looking glass. But the good lady being all this while in a most profound ignorance of herself, forgets that men would not let her talk upon them, and throw so many senseless words at their heads, if they did not intend to put her person to fine and ransom for her impertinence. Good words of any other lady, are so many stones thrown at her, she can by no means bear them; they make her so uneasy, that she cannot keep her seat, but up she rises, and goes home half burst with anger and strait-lacing. If by great chance she says anything that has sense in it, she expects such an excessive rate in commendations, that to her thinking the company ever rises in her debt.

She looks upon rules as things made for the common people, and not for persons of her rank; and this opinion sometimes tempts her to extend her prerogative to the dispensing with the commandments. If by great fortune she happens, in spite of her vanity, to be honest, she is so troublesome with it, that as far as in her lies, she makes a scurvy thing of it. Her bragging of her virtue looks as if it cost her so much pains to get the better of herself, that the inferences are very ridiculous. Her good humour is generally applied to the laughing at good sense. It would do one good to see how heartily she despises anything that is fit for her to do. The greatest part of her fancy is laid out in choosing her gown, as her discretion is chiefly employed in not paying for it. She is faithful to the fashion, to which not only her opinion but her senses are wholly resigned. So obsequious she is to it, that she would be ready to be reconciled even to virtue, with all its faults, if she had her dancing master's word that it was practised at court.

To a woman so composed, when affectation comes in to improve her character, it is then raised to the highest perfection. She first sets up for a fine thing, and for that reason, will distinguish herself, right or wrong, in everything she does. She would have it thought that she is made of so much the finer clay, and so much more sifted than ordinary, that she has no common earth about her. To this end she must neither move nor speak like other women, because it would be vulgar; and therefore must have a language of her own, since ordinary English is too coarse for her. The looking glass in the morning dictates to her all the motions of the day, which by how much the more studied, are so much the more mistaken. She comes into a room as if her limbs were set on with ill-made screws, which makes the company fear the pretty thing should leave some of its artificial person upon the floor. She does not like herself as God Almighty made her, but will have some of her own workmanship; which is so far from making her a better thing than a woman, that it turns her into a worse creature than a monkey. She falls out with Nature, against which she makes war without admitting a truce, those moments excepted in which her gallant may reconcile her to it.

When she has a mind to be soft and languishing, there is something so unnatural in that affected easiness, that her frowns could not be by many degrees so forbidding. When she would appear unreasonably humble, one may see she is so excessively proud, that there is no enduring it. There is such an impertinent smile, such a satisfied simper, when she faintly disowns some fulsome commendation a man happens to bestow upon her against his conscience, that her thanks for it are more visible under such a thin disguise, than they would be if she should print them. If a handsomer woman takes any liberty of dressing out of the ordinary rules, the mistaken lady follows, without distinguishing the unequal pattern, and makes herself uglier by an example misplaced; either forgetting the privilege of good looks in another, or presuming, without sufficient reason, upon her own.

Her discourse is a senseless chime of empty words, a heap of compliments so equally applied to differing persons, that they are neither valued nor believed. Her eyes keep pace with her tongue, and are therefore always in motion. One may discern that they generally incline to the compassionate side, and that, notwithstanding her pretence to virtue, she is gentle to distressed lovers, and ladies that are merciful. She will repeat the tender part of a play so feelingly, that the company may guess, without injustice, she was not altogether a disinterested spectator. She thinks that paint and sin are concealed by railing at them. Upon the latter she is less hard, and being divided between the two opposite prides of her beauty and her virtue, she is often tempted to give broad hints that somebody is dying for her; and of the two, she is less unwilling to let the world think she may be sometimes profaned, than that she is never worshipped.

Very great beauty may perhaps so dazzle for a time, that men may not so clearly see the deformity of these affectations: but when the brightness goes off, and that the lover's eyes are by that means set at liberty to see things as they are, he will naturally return to his lost senses, and recover the mistake into which the lady's good looks had at first engaged him; and being once undeceived, ceases to worship that as a goddess which he sees is only an artificial shrine, moved by wheels and springs, to delude him. Such women please only like the first opening of a scene, that has nothing to recommend it but the being new. They may be compared to flies, that have pretty shining wings for two or three hot months, but the first cold weather makes an end of them. So the latter season of these fluttering creatures is dismal: from their nearest friends they receive a very faint respect; from the rest of the world, the utmost degree of contempt.

Let this picture supply the place of any other rules which might be given to prevent your resemblance to it. The deformity of it, well considered, is instruction enough; from the same reason, that the sight of a drunkard is a better sermon against that vice, than the best that was ever preached upon that subject.

PRIDE

AFTER having said this against vanity, I do not intend to apply the same censure to pride, well placed, and rightly defined. It is an ambiguous word; one kind of it is as much a virtue, as the other is a vice: but we are naturally so apt to choose the worst, that it is become dangerous to commend the best side of it.

A woman is not to be proud of her fine gown; nor when she has less wit than her neighbours, to comfort herself that she has more lace. Some ladies put so much weight upon ornaments, that if one could see into their hearts, it would be found, that even the thought of death is made less heavy to them by the contemplation of their being laid out in state, and honourably attended to the grave. One may come a good deal short of such an extreme, and yet still be sufficiently impertinent, by setting a wrong value upon things which ought to be used with more indifference. A lady must not appear solicitous to engross respect to herself, but be content with a reasonable distribution, and allow it to others, that she may have it returned to her. She is not to be troublesomely nice, nor distinguish herself by being too delicate, as if ordinary things were too coarse for her; this is an unmannerly and an offensive pride, and where it is practised, deserves to be mortified, of which it seldom fails. She is not to lean too much upon her quality, much less to despise those who are below it.

Some make quality an idol, and then their reason must fall down and worship it. They would have the world think, that no amends can ever be made for want of a great title, or an ancient coat of arms: they imagine, that with these advantages they stand upon the higher ground, which makes them look down upon merit and virtue, as things inferior to them. This mistake is not only senseless, but criminal too, in putting a greater price upon that which is a piece of good luck, than upon things which are valuable in themselves. Laughing is not enough for such a folly; it must be severely whipped, as it justly deserves. It will be confessed, there are frequent temptations given by pert upstarts to be angry, and by that to have our judgements corrupted in these cases: but they are to be resisted; and the utmost that is to be allowed, is, when those of a new edition will forget themselves, so as either to brag of their weak side, or to endeavour to hide their meanness by their insolence, to cure them by a little seasonable raillery, a little sharpness well placed, without dwelling too long upon it.

These and many other kinds of pride are to be avoided. That which is to be recommended to you, is an emulation to raise yourself to a character, by which you may be distinguished; an eagerness for precedence in virtue, and all such other things as may gain you a greater share of the good opinion of the world. Esteem to virtue is like a cherishing air to plants and flowers, which makes them blow and prosper; and for that reason it may be allowed to be in some degree the cause as well as the reward of it. That pride which leads to a good end, cannot be a vice, since it is the beginning of a virtue; and to be pleased with just applause is so far from a fault, that it would be an ill symptom in a woman who should not place the greatest part of her satisfaction in it. Humility is no doubt a great virtue; but it ceases to be so, when it is afraid to scorn an ill thing. Against vice and folly it is becoming your sex to be haughty; but you must not carry the contempt of things to arrogance towards persons; and it must be done with fitting distinctions, else it may be inconvenient by being unseasonable. A pride that raises a little anger to be outdone in anything that is good, will have so good an effect, that it is very hard to allow it to be a fault. It is no easy matter to carry even between these differing kinds so described; but remember, that it is safer for a woman to be thought too proud, than too familiar.

DIVERSIONS

THE last thing I shall recommend to you, is a wise and a safe method of using diversions. To be too eager in the pursuit of pleasure whilst you are young, is dangerous; to catch at it in riper years, is grasping a shadow; it will not be held. Besides that, by being less natural it grows to be indecent. Diversions are most properly applied to ease and relieve those who are oppressed, by being too much employed. Those that are idle have no need of them, and yet they, above all others, give themselves up to them. To unbend our thoughts, when they are too much stretched by our cares, is not more natural than it is necessary, but to turn our whole life into a holiday is not only ridiculous, but destroys pleasure instead of promoting it. The mind, like the body, is tired by being always in one posture; too serious breaks, and too diverting loosens it: it is variety that gives the relish; so that diversions too frequently repeated grow first to be indifferent, and at last tedious. Whilst they are well chosen and well timed, they are never to be blamed; but when they are used to an excess, though very innocent at first, they often grow to be criminal, and never fail to be impertinent.

Some ladies are bespoken for merry meetings, as Bessus was for duels.* They are engaged in a circle of idleness, where they turn round for the whole year, without the interruption of a serious hour. They know all the players' names, and are intimately acquainted with all the booths in Bartholomew Fair. No soldier is more obedient to the sound of his captain's trumpet, than they are to that which summons them to a puppet play or a monster. The spring which brings out flies, and fools, makes them inhabitants of Hyde Park; in winter they are an encumbrance to the playhouse, and the ballast of the drawing room. The streets all this while are so weary of these daily faces, that men's eyes are overlaid with them. The sight is glutted with fine things as the stomach with sweet ones; and when a fair lady will give too much of herself to the world, she grows luscious, and oppresses instead of pleasing. These jolly ladies do so continually seek diversion, that in a little time they grow into a jest, yet are unwilling to remember, that if they were seldom seen they would not be so often laughed at. Besides, they make themselves cheap, than which there cannot be an unkinder word bestowed upon your sex.

To play sometimes, to entertain company, or to divert yourself, is not to be disallowed; but to do it so often as to be called a gamester is to be avoided, next to the things that are most criminal. It has consequences of several kinds not to be endured; it will engage you into a habit of idleness and ill hours, draw you into ill-mixed company, make you neglect your civilities abroad and your business at home, and impose into your acquaintance such as will do you no credit. To deep play there will be yet greater objections. It will give occasion to the world to ask spiteful questions; how you dare venture to lose, and what means you have to pay such great sums. If you pay exactly, it will be required from whence the money comes. If you owe, and especially to a man, you must be so very civil to him for his forbearance, that it lays a ground of having it further improved, if the gentleman is so disposed; who will be thought no unfair creditor, if where the estate fails he seizes upon the person. Besides, if a lady could see her own face upon an ill game, at a deep stake, she would certainly forswear anything that could put her looks under such a disadvantage.

To dance sometimes will not be imputed to you as a fault; but remember that the end of your learning it was, that you might the better know how to move gracefully. It is only an advantage so far. When it goes beyond it, one may call it excelling in a mistake, which is no very great commendation. It is better for a woman never to dance, because she has no skill in it, than to do it too often, because she does it well. The easiest as well as the safest method of doing it, is in private companies, amongst particular friends, and then carelessly, like a diversion, rather than with solemnity, as if it was a business, or had anything in it to deserve a month's preparation by serious conference with a dancing master.

Much more might be said to all these heads, and many more might be added to them. But I must restrain my thoughts, which are full of my dear child, and would overflow into a volume, which would not be fit for a New Year's gift. I will conclude with my warmest wishes for all that is good to you. That you may live so as to be an ornament to your family, and a pattern to your sex; that you may be blessed with a husband that may value, and with children that may inherit your virtue; that you may shine in the world by a true light, and silence envy by deserving to be esteemed; that wit and virtue may both conspire to make you a great figure. When they are separated, the first is so empty, and the other so faint, that they scarce have right to be commended. May they therefore meet and never part; let them be your guardian angels, and be sure never to stray out of the distance of their joint protection. May you so raise your character, that you may help to make the next age a better thing, and leave posterity in your debt for the advantage it shall receive by your example.

Let me conjure you, my dearest, to comply with this kind ambition of a father, whose thoughts are so engaged in your behalf, that he reckons your happiness to be the greatest part of his own.

A LETTER TO A DISSENTER, UPON OCCASION OF HIS MAJESTY'S LATE GRACIOUS DECLARATION OF INDULGENCE

SIR,

Since addresses are in fashion, give me leave to make one to you. This is neither the effect of fear, interest, or resentment; therefore you may be sure it is sincere: and for that reason it may expect to be kindly received. Whether it will have power enough to convince, depends upon the reasons, of which you are to judge; and upon your preparation of mind, to be persuaded by truth, whenever it appears to you. It ought not to be the less welcome for coming from a friendly hand, one whose kindness to you is not lessened by difference of opinion, and who will not let his thoughts for the public be so tied or confined to this or that subdivision of Protestants, as to stifle the charity which, besides all other arguments, is at this time become necessary to preserve us.

I am neither surprised nor provoked, to see that in the condition you were put into by the laws, and the ill circumstances you lay under, by having the exclusion and rebellion* laid to your charge, you were desirous to make yourselves less uneasy and obnoxious to authority. Men who are sore, run to the nearest remedy with too much haste to consider all the consequences. Grains of allowance are to be given, where Nature gives such strong influences. When to men under sufferings it offers ease, the present pain will hardly allow time to examine the remedies; and the strongest reason can hardly gain a fair audience from our mind, whilst so possessed, till the smart is a little allayed.

I do not know whether the warmth that naturally belongs to new friendships, may not make it a harder task for me to persuade you. It is like telling lovers, in the beginning of their joys, that they will in a little time have an end. Such an unwelcome style does not easily find credit: but I will suppose you are not so far gone in your new passion, but that you will hear still; and therefore I am under the less discouragement, when I offer to your consideration two things. The first is, the cause you have to suspect your new friends.* The second, the duty incumbent upon you, in Christianity and prudence, not to hazard the public safety, neither by desire of ease, nor of revenge.

To the first: consider that notwithstanding the smooth language which is now put on to engage you, these new friends did not make you their choice, but their refuge. They have ever made their first courtships to the Church of England, and when they were rejected there, they made their application to you in the second place. The instances of this might be given in all times. I do not repeat them, because whatsoever is unnecessary must be tedious, the truth of this assertion being so plain, as not to admit a dispute. You cannot therefore reasonably flatter yourselves, that there is any inclination to you. They never pretended to allow you any quarter, but to usher in liberty for themselves under that shelter. I refer you to *Mr Coleman's Letters*,* and to the *Journals of Parliament*, where you may be convinced, if you can be so mistaken as to doubt; nay, at this very hour, they can hardly forbear, in the height of their courtship, to let fall hard words of you. So little is Nature to be restrained; it will start out sometimes, disdaining to submit to the usurpation of art and interest.

This alliance, between liberty and infallibility, is bringing together the two most contrary things that are in the world. The Church of Rome does not only dislike the allowing liberty, but by its principles it cannot do it. Wine is not more expressly forbidden to the Mahometans, than giving heretics liberty is to the Papists: they are no more able to make good their vows to you, than men married before, and their wife alive, can confirm their contract with another. The continuance of their kindness, would be a habit of sin, of which they are to repent, and their absolution is to be had upon no other terms than their promise to destroy you. You are therefore to be hugged now, only that you may be the better squeezed at another time. There must be something extraordinary, when the Church of Rome sets up bills, and offers plasters, for tender consciences. By all that has hitherto appeared, her skill in chirurgery lies chiefly in a quick hand, to cut off limbs; but she is the worst at healing, of any that ever pretended to it.

To come so quick from another extreme, is such an unnatural motion, that you ought to be upon your guard; the other day you were sons of Belial, now you are angels of light. This is a violent change, and it will be fit for you to pause upon it, before you believe it. If your features are not altered, neither is their opinion of you, whatever may be pretended. Do you believe less than you did, that there is idolatry in the Church of Rome? Sure you do not. See then, how they treat both in words and writing, those who entertain that opinion. Conclude from hence, how inconsistent their favour is with this single article, except they give you a dispensation for this too, and by a *non obstante*,* secure you that they will not think the worse of you.

Think a little how dangerous it is to build upon a foundation of paradoxes. Popery now is the only friend to liberty, and the known enemy to persecution. The men of Taunton and Tiverton* are above all other eminent for loyalty. The Quakers, from being declared by the Papists not to be Christians, are now made favourites, and taken into their particular protection; they are on a sudden grown the most accomplished men of the kingdom, in good breeding, and give thanks with the best grace, in double refined language. So that I should not wonder, though a man of that persuasion, in spite of his hat, should be master of the ceremonies.* Not to say harsher words, these are such very new things, that it is impossible not to suspend our belief, till by a little more experience we may be informed whether they are realities or apparitions. We have been under shameful mistakes, if these opinions are true; but for the present, we are apt to be incredulous; except we could be convinced, that the priests' words in this case too are able to make such a sudden and effectual change; and that their power is not limited to the sacrament, but that it extends to alter the nature of all other things, as often as they are so disposed.

Let me now speak of the instruments of your friendship, and then leave you to judge, whether they do not afford matter of suspicion. No sharpness is to be mingled where healing only is intended; so nothing will be said to expose particular men, how strong so ever the temptation may be, or how clear the proofs to make it out. A word or two in general, for your better caution, shall suffice: suppose then, for argument's sake, that the mediators of this new alliance, should be such as have been formerly employed in treaties of the same kind, and there detected to have acted by order, and to have been empowered to give encouragements and rewards. Would not this be an argument to suspect them?

If they should plainly be under engagements to one side, their arguments to the other ought to be received accordingly; their fair pretences are to be looked upon as part of their commission, which may not improbably give them a dispensation in the case of truth, when it may bring a prejudice upon the service of those by whom they are employed.

If there should be men who, having formerly had means and authority to persuade by secular arguments, have in pursuance of that power, sprinkled money amongst the Dissenting ministers;* and if those very men should now have the same authority, practice the same methods, and disburse, where they cannot otherwise persuade, it seems to me to be rather an evidence than a presumption of the deceit.

If there should be ministers amongst you who, by having fallen under temptations of this kind, are in some sort engaged to continue their frailty by the awe they are in lest it should be exposed, the persuasions of these unfortunate men must sure have the less force, and their arguments, though never so specious, are to be suspected, when they come from men who have mortgaged themselves to severe creditors that expect a rigorous observation of the contract, let it be never so unwarrantable.

If these, or any others, should at this time preach up anger and vengeance against the Church of England, may it not without injustice be suspected, that a thing so plainly out of season springs rather from corruption than mistake; and that those who act this choleric part, do not believe themselves, but only pursue higher directions, and endeavour to make good that part of their contract which obliges them, upon a forfeiture, to make use of their inflaming eloquence? They might apprehend their wages would be retrenched if they should be moderate. And therefore whilst violence is their interest, those who have not the same arguments have no reason to follow such a partial example.

If there should be men who, by the load of their crimes against the government, have been bowed down to comply with it against their conscience; who by incurring the want of a pardon, have drawn upon themselves the necessity of an entire resignation; such men are to be lamented, but not to be believed.* Nay, they themselves, when they have discharged their unwelcome task, will be inwardly glad that their forced endeavours do not succeed, and are pleased when men resist their insinuations, which are far from being voluntary or sincere, but are squeezed out of them by the weight of their being so obnoxious.

If in the height of this great dearness, by comparing things, it should happen that at this instant there is much a surer friendship with those who are so far from allowing liberty that they allow no living to a Protestant under them, let the scene lie in what part of the world it will, the argument will come home, and sure it will afford sufficient ground to suspect. Apparent contradictions must strike us; neither Nature nor reason can digest them. Self-flattery, and the desire to deceive ourselves to gratify a present appetite, with all their power, which is great, cannot get the better of such broad conviction, as some things carry along with them. Will you call these vain and empty suspicions? Have you been at all times so void of fears and jealousies as to justify your being so unreasonably valiant in having none upon this occasion? Such an extraordinary courage at this unseasonable time, to say no more, is too dangerous a virtue to be commended.

If then, for these and a thousand other reasons, there is cause to suspect, sure your new friends are not to dictate to you, or advise you; for instance, the addresses that fly abroad every week, and murder us with *Another to the same*;* the first draughts are made by those who are not very proper to be secretaries to the Protestant religion; and it is your part only to write them out fairer again. Strange! that you who have been formerly so much against set forms, should now be content the priests should indict for you. The nature of thanks is an unavoidable consequence of being pleased or obliged; they grow in the heart, and from thence show themselves either in looks, speech, writing, or action. No man was ever thankful because he was bid to be so, but because he had, or thought he had, some reason for it. If then there is cause in this case to pay such extravagant acknowledgements, they will flow naturally, without taking such pains to procure them; and it is unkindly done to tire all the post-horses with carrying circular letters to solicit that which would be done without any trouble or constraint. If it is really in itself such a favour, what needs so much pressing men to be thankful, and with such eager circumstances, that where persuasions cannot delude, threatenings are employed to fright them into a compliance? Thanks must be voluntary, not only unconstrained, but unsolicited, else they are either trifles or snares; they either signify nothing, or a great deal more than is intended by those that give them. If an inference should be made, that whosoever thanks the King for his Declaration, is by that engaged to justify it in point of law, it is a greater stride than, I presume, all those care to make who are persuaded to address. If it shall be supposed, that all the thankers will be repealers of the Test, whenever a Parliament shall meet, such an expectation is better prevented before, than disappointed afterwards; and the surest way to avoid the lying under such a scandal, is not to do anything that may give a colour to the mistake. These bespoken thanks are little less improper than love letters that were solicited by the lady to whom they are to be directed: so, that besides the little ground there is to give them, the manner of getting them does extremely lessen their value. It might be wished that you would have suppressed your impatience, and have been content for the sake of religion, to enjoy it within yourselves, without the liberty of a public exercise, till a Parliament had allowed it; but since that could not be, and that the artifices of some amongst you have made use of the well-meant zeal of the generality to draw them into this mistake, I am so far from blaming you with that sharpness which, perhaps, the matter in strictness would bear, that I am ready to err on the side of the more gentle construction.

There is a great difference between enjoying quietly the advantages of an act irregularly done by others, and the going about to support it against the laws in being: the law is so sacred, that no trespass against it is to be defended; yet frailties may in some measure be excused, when they cannot be justified. The desire of enjoying a liberty from which men have been so long restrained, may be a temptation that their reason is not at all times able to resist. If in such a case, some objections are leapt over, indifferent men will be more inclined to lament the occasion than to fall too hard upon the fault, whilst it is covered with the apology of a good intention; but where, to rescue yourselves from the severity of one law, you give a blow to all the laws by which your religion and liberty are to be protected; and instead of silently receiving the benefit of this indulgence, you set up for advocates to support it, you become voluntary aggressors, and look like counsel retained by the prerogative against your old friend Magna Carta, who has done nothing to deserve her falling thus under your displeasure.

If the case then should be, that the price expected from you for this liberty, is giving up your right in the laws, sure you will think twice, before you go any further in such a losing bargain. After giving thanks for the breach of one law, you lose the right of complaining of the breach of all the rest; you will not very well know how to defend yourselves, when you are pressed; and having given up the question, when it was for your advantage, you cannot recall it when it shall be to your prejudice. If you will set up at one time a power to help you, which at another time by parity of reason shall be made use of to destroy you, you will neither be pitied, nor relieved against a mischief you draw upon yourselves, by being so unreasonably thankful. It is like calling in auxiliaries to help, who are strong enough to subdue you: in such a case your complaints will come too late to be heard, and your sufferings will raise mirth instead of compassion.

If you think, for your excuse, to expound your thanks so as to restrain them to this particular case, others, for their ends, will extend them further; and in these differing interpretations, that which is backed by authority will be the most likely to prevail; especially when by the advantage you have given them, they have in truth the better of the argument, and that the inferences from your own concessions are very strong, and express against you. This is so far from being a groundless supposition, that there was a late instance of it, the last session of Parliament, in the House of Lords, where the first thanks, though things of course, were interpreted to be the approbation of the King's whole speech, and a restraint from the further examination of any part of it, though never so much disliked; and it was with difficulty obtained, not to be excluded from the liberty of objecting to this mighty prerogative of dispensing, merely by this innocent and usual piece of good manners, by which no such thing could possibly be intended.*

This shows, that some bounds are to be put to your good breeding, and that the constitution of England is too valuable a thing to be ventured upon a compliment. Now that you have for some time enjoyed the benefit of the end, it is time for you to look into the danger of the means. The same reason that made you desirous to get liberty, must make you solicitous to preserve it; so that the next thought will naturally be, not to engage yourself beyond retreat, and to agree so far with the principles of all religions, as not to rely upon a death-bed repentance.

There are certain periods of time, which being once past, make all cautions ineffectual, and all remedies desperate. Our understandings are apt to be hurried on by the first heats, which, if not restrained in time, do not give us leave to look back, till it is too late. Consider this in the case of your anger against the Church of England, and take warning by their mistake in the same kind, when after the late King's Restoration, they preserved so long the bitter taste of your rough usage to them in other times, that it made them forget their interest, and sacrifice it to their revenge.

Either you will blame this proceeding in them, and for that reason not follow it, or if you allow it, you have no reason to be offended with them; so that you must either dismiss your anger, or lose your excuse; except you should argue more partially than will be supposed of men of your morality and understanding.

If you had now to do with those rigid prelates, who made it a matter of conscience to give you the least indulgence, but kept you at an uncharitable distance, and even to your more reasonable scruples continued stiff and inexorable, the argument might be fairer on your side; but since the common danger has so laid open that mistake, that all the former haughtiness towards you is for ever extinguished, and that it has turned the spirit of persecution into a spirit of peace, charity, and condescension; shall this happy change only affect the Church of England? And are you so in love with separation, as not to be moved by this example? It ought to be followed, were there no other reason than that it is a virtue; but when besides that, it is become necessary to your preservation, it is impossible to fail the having its effect upon you.

If it should be said, that the Church of England is never humble, but when she is out of power, and therefore loses the right of being believed when she pretends to it; the answer is, first, it would be an uncharitable objection, and very much mistimed; an unseasonable triumph, not only ungenerous, but unsafe; so that in these respects it cannot be urged, without scandal, even though it could be said with truth. Secondly, this is not so in fact, and the argument must fall, being built upon a false foundation; for whatever may be told you, at this very hour, and in the heat and glare of your present sunshine, the Church of England can in a moment bring clouds again; and turn the royal thunder upon your heads, blow you off the stage with a breath, if she would give but a smile or a kind word; the least glimpse of her compliance would throw you back into the state of suffering, and draw upon you all the arrears of severity, which have accrued during the time of this kindness to you, and yet the Church of England, with all her faults, will not allow herself to be rescued by such unjustifiable means, but chooses to bear the weight of power, rather than lie under the burden of being criminal.

It cannot be said, that she is unprovoked: books and letters come out every day, to call for answers, yet she will not be stirred. From the supposed authors, and the style, one would swear they were undertakers, and had made a contract to fall out with the Church of England. There are lashes in every address, challenges to draw the pen in every pamphlet; in short, the fairest occasions in the world given to quarrel; but she wisely distinguishes between the body of Dissenters, whom she will suppose to act, as they do, with no ill intent; and these small skirmishers picked and sent out to picqueer,* and to begin a fray* amongst the Protestants, for the entertainment, as well as the advantage, of the Church of Rome.

This conduct is so good, that it will be scandalous not to applaud it. It is not equal dealing, to blame our adversaries for doing ill, and not commend them when they do well.

To hate them because they persecuted, and not to be reconciled to them when they are ready to suffer, rather than receive all the advantages that can be gained by a criminal compliance, is a principle no sort of Christians can own, since it would give an objection to them never to be answered.

Think a little, who they were that promoted your former persecutions, and then consider how it will look to be angry with the instruments, and at the same time to make a league with the authors of your sufferings.

Have you enough considered what would be expected from you? Are you ready to stand in every borough by virtue of a *congé d'elire,** and instead of election, be satisfied if you are returned?

Will you in Parliament, justify the dispensing power, with all its consequences, and repeal the Test, by which you will make way for the repeal of all the laws that were made to preserve your religion, and to enact others that shall destroy it?

Are you disposed to change the liberty of debate into the merit of obedience, and to be made instruments to repeal or enact laws, when the Roman consistory* are Lords of the Articles?*

Are you so linked with your new friends, as to reject any indulgence a Parliament shall offer you, if it shall not be so comprehensive as to include the Papists in it?

Consider that the implied conditions of your new treaty are no less, than that you are to do everything you are desired, without examining, and that for this pretended liberty of conscience, your real freedom is to be sacrificed. Your former faults hang like chains still about you, you are let loose only upon bail; the first act of non-compliance, sends you to jail again.

You may see that the Papists themselves do not rely upon the legality of this power, which you are to justify, since the being so very earnest to get it established by a law, and the doing such very hard things in order, as they think to obtain it, is a clear evidence, that they do not think that the single power of the Crown is in this case a good foundation; especially when this is done under a Prince, so very tender of all the rights of sovereignty, that he would think it a diminution to his prerogative, where he conceives it strong enough to go alone, to call in the legislative help to strengthen and support it.

You have formerly blamed the Church of England, and not without reason, for going so far as they did in their compliance;* and yet as soon as they stopped, you see they are not only deserted, but prosecuted. Conclude then from this example, that you must either break off your friendship, or resolve to have no bounds in it. If they do not succeed in their design, they will leave you first; if they do, you must either leave them, when it will be too late for your safety, or else after the queasiness of starting at a surplice, you must be forced to swallow transubstantiation.

Remember that the other day those of the Church of England were Trimmers for enduring you, and now by a sudden turn, you are become the favourites; do not deceive yourselves, it is not the nature of lasting plants thus to shoot up in a night; you may look gay and green for a little time, but you want a root to give you a continuance. It is not so long since, as to be forgotten, that the maxim was, 'It is impossible for a Dissenter not to be a rebel'.* Consider at this time in France, even the new converts are so far from being employed that they are disarmed; their sudden change makes them still to be distrusted, notwithstanding that they are reconciled. What are you to expect then from your dear friends, to whom, whenever they shall think fit to throw you off again, you have in other times given such arguments for their excuse?

Besides all this, you act very unskilfully against your visible interest, if you throw away the advantages, of which you can hardly fail in the next probable revolution. Things tend naturally to what you would have, if you would let them alone, and not by an unseasonable activity lose the influences of your good star, which promises you everything that is prosperous.

The Church of England convinced of its error in being severe to you; the Parliament, whenever it meets, sure to be gentle to you; the next heir bred in the country which you have so often quoted for a pattern of indulgence;* a general agreement of all thinking men, that we must no more cut ourselves off from the Protestants abroad, but rather enlarge the foundations upon which we are to build our defences against the common enemy; so that in truth, all things seem to conspire to give you ease and satisfaction, if by too much haste to anticipate your good fortune, you do not destroy it.

The Protestants have but one article of human strength to oppose the power which is now against them, and that is, not to lose the advantage of their numbers, by being so unwary as to let themselves be divided.

We all agree in our duty to our Prince; our objections to his belief, do not hinder us from seeing his virtues; and our not complying with his religion, has no effect upon our allegiance; we are not to be laughed out of our passive obedience, and the doctrine of non-resistance, though even those who perhaps owe the best part of their security to that principle, are apt to make a jest of it.

So that if we give no advantage by the fatal mistake of misapplying our anger, by the natural course of things this danger will pass away like a shower of hail; fair weather will succeed, as lowering as the sky now looks, and all by this plain and easy receipt.* Let us be still, quiet, and undivided, firm at the same time to our religion, our loyalty, and our laws, and so long as we continue this method, it is next to impossible, that the odds of two hundred to one should lose the bet; except the Church of Rome, which has been so long barren of miracles, should now in her declining age be brought to bed of one that would outdo the best she can brag of in her *Legend*.*

To conclude, the short question will be, whether you will join with those who must in the end run the same fate with you. If Protestants of all sorts, in their behaviour to one another, have been to blame, they are upon the more equal terms, and for that very reason it is fitter for them now to be reconciled. Our disunion is not only a reproach, but a danger to us; those who believe in modern miracles have more right, or at least more excuse, to neglect all secular cautions; but for us, it is as justifiable to have no religion, as wilfully to throw away the human means of preserving it. I am,

Dear Sir,
Your most Affectionate
Humble Servant,
T.W.

THE ANATOMY OF AN EQUIVALENT

I. THE world has of late years never been without some extraordinary word to furnish the coffee-houses* and fill the pamphlets. Sometimes it is a new one invented, and sometimes an old one revived. They are usually fitted to some present purpose, with intentions as differing as the various designs several parties may have, either to delude the people, or to expose their adversaries. They are not of long continuance, but after they have passed a little while, and that they are grown nauseous by being so often repeated, they give place to something that is newer. Thus, after 'Whig', 'Tory', and 'Trimmer' have had their time, now they are dead and forgotten, being supplanted by the word 'Equivalent', which reigns in their stead.

The birth of it is in short this: after many repeated essays to dispose men to the repeal of Oaths and Tests,* made for the security of the Protestant religion, the general aversion to comply in it was found to be so great, that it was thought advisable to try another manner of attempting it, and to see whether by putting the same thing into another mould, and softening a harsh proposition by a plausible term, they might not have better success.

To this end, instead of an absolute quitting of these laws, without any condition, which was the first proposal, now it is put into gentler language, and runs thus: If you will take away the Oaths and Tests,* you shall have as good a thing for them. This put into the fashionable word, is now called an 'Equivalent'.

II. So much to the word itself. I will now endeavour in short to examine and explain, in order to the having it fully understood,

First, what is the nature of a true Equivalent; and

In the next place, what things are not to be admitted under that denomination.

I shall treat these as general propositions, and though I cannot undertake how far they may be convincing, I may safely do it that they are impartial; of which there can be no greater evidence than that I make neither inference nor application, but leave that part entirely to the reader, according as his own thoughts shall direct and dispose him.

III. I will first take notice, that this word, by the application which has been made of it in some modern instances, lies under some disadvantage, not to say some scandal. It is transmitted hither from France; and if, as in most other things that we take from them, we carry them beyond the pattern, it should prove so in this, we should get into a more partial style than the principles of English justice will I hope ever allow us to be guilty of.

The French King's Equivalents in Flanders are very extraordinary bargains; his manner of proposing and obtaining them is very differing from the usual methods of equal dealing. In a later instance, Denmark, by the encouragement as well as by the example of France, has proposed things to the Duke of Holstein which are called Equivalents; but that they are so, the world is not yet sufficiently convinced, and probably the parties concerned do not think them to be so, and consequently do not appear to be at all disposed to accept them. Princes enjoin and prescribe such things when they have strength and power to supply the want of arguments; and according to practice in these cases, the weaker are never thought to have an ill bargain, if they have anything left them. So that the first qualification of an Equivalent must be, that the appraisers be indifferent, else it is only a sound, there can be nothing real in it. For, where the same party that proposes a bargain, claims a right to set the value; or which is worse, has power too to make it good; the other may be forced to submit to the conditions, but he can by no means ever be persuaded to treat upon them.

IV. The next thing to be considered is, that to make an Equivalent in reality an equal thing in the proposer, it must be a better thing than that which is required by him; just as good is subject to the hazard of not being quite so good. It is not easy to have such an even hand as to make the value exactly equal; besides, according to the maxim in law, *melior conditio possidentis*,* the offer is not fair, except the thing offered is better in value than the thing demanded. There must be allowance for removing what is fixed, and there must be something that may be a justification for changing. The value of things very often depends more upon other circumstances, than upon what is merely intrinsic to them; therefore the calculation must be made upon that foot, perhaps in most cases; and particularly the want which one of the parties may have of the thing he requires, makes it more valuable to him than it is in itself. If the party proposing does not want the thing he would have in exchange, his requiring it is impertinent; if he does, his want of it must go into the appraisement, and by consequence every proposer of an Equivalent must offer a better thing, or else he must not take it unkindly to be refused, except the other party has an equal want of the same thing, which is very improbable, since naturally he that wants most will speak first.

V. Another thing necessary to the making a fair bargain is, that let the parties who treat, be they never so unequal in themselves, yet as to the particular thing proposed, there must be an exact equality, as far as it relates to the full liberty of taking or refusing, concurring or objecting, without any consequence of revenge, or so much as dissatisfaction. For it is impossible to treat where it is an affront to differ; in that case there is no mean between the two extremes, either an open quarrel or an entire submission. The way of bargaining must be equal, else the bargain itself cannot be so. For example, the proposer is not only to use equal terms as to the matter, but fair ones in the manner too. There must be no intimations of anger in case of refusal, much less any open threatening. Such a style is so ill-suited to the usual way of treating, that it looks more like a breach of the peace, than the making a bargain. It would be yet more improper and less agreeing with the nature of an Equivalent if, whilst two men are chaffering* about the price, one of them should actually take the thing in question at his own rate, and afterwards desire to have his possession confirmed by a formal agreement. Such a proceeding would not only destroy that particular contract, but make it impossible to have any other with the party that could be guilty of such a practice.

VI. Violence preceding destroys all contract, and even though the party that offers it should have a right to the thing he so takes, yet it is to be obtained by legal means, else it may be forfeited by his irregularity in the pursuit of it. The law is such an enemy to violence, and so little to be reconciled to it, that in the case of a rape, the punishment is not taken off though the party injured afterwards consents. The justice of the law has its eye upon the first act, and the maxim of *volenti non fit injuria** does not in this case help the offender, it being a plea subsequent to the crime, which makes it to be rejected as a thing wrong dated and out of time.

In taking away goods or money it is the same thing. The party robbed, by giving them afterwards to the taker, does not exempt him from the punishment of the violence. Quite contrary, the man from whom they were taken is punishable, if h● does not prosecute. If the case should be, that a man thus taking away a thing without price, claims a right to take it, then whether it is well or ill founded is not the question; but sure, the party from whom it is so taken, whilst he is treating to sell or exchange it, can never make a bargain with so arbitrary a chapman,* there being no room left after that to talk of the value.

VII. To make an equal bargain there must be a liberty of differing, not only in everything that is really essential, but in everything that is thought so by either party, and most especially by him who is in possession of the thing demanded. His opinion must be a rule to him, and even his mistake in the value, though it may not convince the man he has to deal with, yet he will be justified for not accepting what is offered, till that mistake is fairly rectified and overruled.

When a security is desired to be changed, that side which desires it must not pretend to impose upon the other, so as to dictate to them, and tell them without debate that they are safe in what is proposed, since of that the counsel on the other side must certainly be the most competent judges. The hand it comes from is a great circumstance, either to invite or discourage in all matters of contract; the qualifications of the party offering must suit with the proposition itself, else let it be never so fair, there is ground for suspicion.

VIII. When men are of a temper that they think they have wrong done them, if they have not always the better side of a bargain; if they happen to be such as by experience have been found to have an ill memory for their word; if the character they bear, does not recommend their justice, wherever their interest is concerned: In these cases, thinking men will avoid dealing, not only to prevent surprise, but to cut off the occasions of difficulty or dispute.

It is yet more discouraging when there are, either a precedent practice, or standing maxims of gross partiality, in assuming a privilege of exemption from the usual methods of equal dealing.

To illustrate this by an instance, suppose that in any case, the Church of Rome should have an interest to promote a bargain; let her way of dealing be a little examined, which will direct those with whom she treats, how far they are to rely upon what she proposes to them. We may begin with the quality in the world, the least consisting with equal dealing, *viz.* an incurable partiality to herself; which, that it may arrive to its full perfection, is crowned with infallibility. At the first setting out, she makes herself incapable of dealing upon terms of equality, by the power she claims of binding and loosing, which has been so often applied to treaties, as well as to sins.

If the definition of justice is to deal equally, she cannot be guilty of it without betraying her prerogative, and according to her principles, she gives up the superiority derived to her by apostolical succession, if she degrades herself so as to be judged by the rules of common right, especially if the bargain should be with heretics, who in her opinion have forfeited the claim they might otherwise have had to it.

IX. Besides, her taste has been so spoiled by unreasonable bargains, that she can never bring down her palate to anything that is fair or equal. She has not only judged it an Equivalent, but a great bargain for the other side, to give them absolutions and indulgences for the real payment of great sums, for which she has drawn bills to have them repaid with interest in Purgatory.

This spiritual bank has carried on such a trade upon these advantageous terms, that it can never submit to the small profits an ordinary bargain would produce.

The several popes have in exchange for the Peter Pence,* and all their other rents and fines out of England, sent sanctified roses, relics, and other such wonder-working trifles. And by virtue of their character of Holy Fathers, have used princes like children, by sending them such rattles to play with, which they made them buy at extravagant rates. Besides which, they were to be thankful too, into the bargain.

A chip of the Cross, a piece of St Laurence's gridiron, a hair of St Peter, have been thought Equivalents for much more substantial things. The popes, being masters of the jewel-house, have set the rates upon them, and they have passed; though the whole shop would not take up the value of a bodkin in Lombard Street* upon the credit of them.

They are unconscionable purchasers, for they get all the money from the living by praying for them when they are dead. And it is observable, that the northern part of Christendom, which best understands trade, were the first that refused to make any more bargains with them; so that it looks as if the chief quarrel to the heretics was not as they were ill Christians, but as they were unkind merchants, in so discourteously rejecting the commodities of the growth of Rome.

To conclude this head, there is no bartering with infallibility, it being so much above equality that it cannot bear the indignity of a true Equivalent.

X. In all bargains there is a necessity of looking back, and reflecting how far a present proposal is reconcilable with a former practice: for example, if at any time a thing is offered quite differing from the arguments used by the proposer, and inconsistent with the maxims held out by him at other times. Or in a public case, if the same men who promote and press a thing with the utmost violence, do in a little time after with as much violence press the contrary, and profess a detestation of the very thing for which they had before employed all their interest and authority. Or if in the case of a law already made, there should be a privilege claimed to exempt those from the obligation of observing it, who yet should afterwards desire and press to have a new law made in exchange for the old one, by which they would not be bound; and that they should propose a security by a thing of the very same nature as that which they did not allow to be any before. These incoherences must naturally have the effect of raising suspicion, or rather they are a certain proof, that in such circumstances it is irrational for men to expect an effectual Equivalent.

XI. If whatsoever is more than ordinary is suspicious, everything that is unnatural is more so. It is not only unnecessary but unnatural too to persuade with violence what it is folly to refuse; to push men with eagerness into a good bargain for themselves, is a style very much unsuitable to the nature of the thing. But it goes further and is yet more absurd, to grow angry with men for not receiving a proposal that is for their advantage; men ought to be content with the generosity of offering good bargains, and should give their compassion to those who do not understand them. But by carrying their good nature so far as to be choleric in such a case, they would follow the example of the Church of Rome, where the definition of charity is very extraordinary. In her language, the writ *de Haeretico Comburendo** is a love letter, and burning men for differing with them in opinion, howsoever miscalled cruelty, is as they understand it, the perfection of flaming charity.

When anger in these cases lasts long, it is most probable that it is for our own sakes. Good nature for others is one of those diseases that is cured by time, and especially where it is offered and rejected; but for ourselves it never fails, and cannot be extinguished but with our life. It is fair if men can believe that their friends love them next to themselves, to love them better is too much; the expression is so unnatural that it is cloying, and men must have no sense, who in this case have no suspicion.

XII. Another circumstance necessary to a fair bargain is, that there must be openness and freedom allowed, as the effect of that equality which is the foundation of contracting. There must be full liberty of objecting, and making doubts and scruples. If they are such as can be answered, the party convinced is so much the more confirmed and encouraged to deal, instead of being hindered by them; but if instead of an answer to satisfy, there is nothing but anger for a reply, it is impossible not to conclude that there is never a good one to give; so that the objection remaining without being fully confuted, there is an absolute bar put to any further treaty.

There can be no dealing where one side assumes a privilege to impose, so as to make an offer and not bear the examination of it: this is giving judgement, not making a bargain. Where it is called unmannerly to object, or criminal to refuse, the surest way is for men to stay where they are, rather than treat upon such disadvantage.

If it should happen to be in any country where the governing power should allow men of liberty of conscience in the choice of their religion, it would be strange to deny them liberty of speech in making a bargain. Such a contradiction would be so discouraging, that they must be unreasonably sanguine, who in that case can entertain the hopes of a fair Equivalent.

XIII. An equal bargain must not be a mystery nor a secret. The purchaser or proposer is to tell directly and plainly, what it is he intends to give in exchange for that which he requires. It must be viewed and considered by the other party, that he may judge of the value; for without knowing what it is, he cannot determine whether he shall take or leave it. An assertion in general, that it shall be as good or a better thing, is not in this a sufficient excuse for the mistake of dealing upon such uncertain terms. In all things that are dark and not enough explained, suspicion naturally follows. A secret generally implies a defect or a deceit; and if a false light is an objection, no light at all is yet a greater. To pretend to give a better thing, and to refuse to show it, is very near saying, it is not so good a one; at least so it will be taken in common construction. A mystery is yet a more discouraging thing to a Protestant, especially if the proposition should come from a Papist; it being one of his great objections to that Church, that there are so many of them invisible and impossible, which are so violently thrust upon their understandings, that they are overlaid with them. They think that rational creatures are to be convinced only by reason, and that reason must be visible and freely exposed; else they will think themselves used with contempt instead of equality, and will never allow such a suspected secrecy to be a fit preface to a real Equivalent.

XIV. In matters of contract not only the present value, but the contingencies and consequences, as far as they can be fairly supposed, are to be considered. For example, if there should be a possibility, that one of the parties may be ruined by accepting, and the other only disappointed by his refusing, the consequences are so extremely unequal, that it is not imaginable, a man should take that for an Equivalent, which has such a fatal possibility at the heels of it.

If it should happen in a public case, that such a proposal should come from the minor part of an assembly or nation, to the greater, it is very just, that the hazard of such a possibility should more or less likely fall upon the lesser part, rather than upon the greater, for whose sake and advantage things are and must be calculated in all public constitutions. Suppose in any mixed government, the chief magistrate should propose upon a condition, in the senate, diet, or other supreme assembly, either to enact or abrogate one or more laws, by which a possibility might be let in of destroying their religion and property, which in other language signifies no less than soul and body; where could be the Equivalent in the case, not only for the real loss, but even for the fear of losing them? Men can fall no lower than to lose all, and if losing all destroys them, the venturing all must fright them.

In an instance when men are secure, that how far soever they may be overrun by violence, yet they can never be undone by law, except they give their assistance to make it possible; though it should neither be likely nor intended, still the consequence which may happen is too big for any present thing to make amends for it. Whilst the word 'possible' remains, it must forbid the bargain. Wherever it falls out therefore, that in an example of a public nature, the changing, enacting, or repealing a law, may naturally tend to the misplacing the legislative power in the hands of those who have a separate interest from the body of a people, there can be no treating, till it is demonstrably made out that such a consequence shall be absolutely impossible; for if that shall be denied by those who make the proposal, if it is because they cannot do it, the motion at first was very unfair. If they can and will not, it would be yet less reasonable to expect that such partial dealers would ever give an Equivalent fit to be accepted.

XV. It is necessary in all dealing to be assured in the first place, that the party proposing is in a condition to make good his offer; that he is neither under any former obligations or pretended claims, which may render him incapable of performing it; else he is so far in the condition of a minor, that whatever he disposes by sale or exchange may be afterwards resumed, and the contract becomes void, being originally defective, for want of a sufficient legal power in him that made it.

In the case of a strict settlement, where the party is only tenant for life, there is no possibility of treating with one under such fetters; no purchase or exchange of lands or anything else can be good, where there is such an incapacity of making out a title; the interest vested in him being so limited, that he can do little more than pronounce the words of a contract, he can by no means perform the effect of it.

In more public instances, the impossibility is yet more express; as suppose in any kingdom, where the people have so much liberty left them, as that they may make contracts with the Crown, there should be some peculiar rights claimed to be so fixed to the royal function, that no king for the time being could have power to part with them, being so fundamentally tied to the office that they can never be separated. Such rights can upon no occasion be received in exchange for anything the Crown may desire from the people. That can never be taken in payment which cannot lawfully be given, so that if they should part with that which is required upon those terms, it must be a gift, it cannot be a bargain.

There is not in the whole dictionary a more intractable word than 'inherent', and less to be reconciled to the word 'Equivalent'.

The party that will contract in spite of such a claim, is content to take what is impossible to grant, and if he complains of his disappointment, he neither can have remedy, nor deserves it.

If a right so claimed happens to be of so comprehensive a nature, as that by a clear inference it may extend to everything else, as well as to the particular matter in question, as often as the supreme magistrate shall be so disposed, there can in that case be no treating with a prerogative that swallows all the right the people can pretend to; and if they have no right to anything of which they are possessed, it is a jest and not a bargain, to observe any formality in parting with it.

A claim may be so stated, that by the power and advantage of interpreting, it shall have such a murdering eye, that if it looks upon a law, like a basilisk* it shall strike it dead. Where is the possibility of treating, where such a right is assumed? Nay, let it be supposed, that such a claim is not well founded in law, and that upon a free disquisition it could not be made out; yet even in this case, none that are well advised will conclude a bargain, till it is fully stated and cleared, or indeed, so much as engage in a treaty, till by way of preliminary all possibility shall be removed of any trouble or dispute.

XVI. There is a collateral circumstance in making a contract, which yet deserves to be considered, as much as anything that belongs to it; and that is the character and figure of the parties contracting, if they treat only by themselves, and if by others, the qualifications of the instruments they employ.

The proposer especially, must not be so low as to want credit, nor so raised as to carry him above the reach of ordinary dealing. In the first, there is scandal; in the other, danger. There is no rule without some exception, but generally speaking the means should be suited to the end, and since all men who treat, pretend an equal bargain, it is desirable that there may be equality in the persons as well as in the thing.

The manner of doing things has such an influence upon the matter, that men may guess at the end by the instruments that are used to obtain it, who are a very good direction how far to rely upon or suspect the sincerity of that which is proposed. An absurdity in the way of carrying on a treaty, in any one circumstance, if it is very gross, is enough to persuade a thinking man to break off, and take warning from such an ill appearance. Some things are so glaring that it is impossible not to see, and consequently not to suspect them; as suppose in a private case, there should be a treaty of marriage between two honourable families, and the proposing side should think fit to send a woman that had been carted,* to persuade the young lady to an approbation and consent; the unfitness of the messenger must naturally dispose the other party to distrust the message, and to resist the temptation of the best match that could be offered, when conveyed by that hand, and ushered in by such a discouraging preliminary.

In a public instance the suspicion arising from unfit mediators still grows more reasonable in proportion as the consequence is much greater of being deceived. If a Jew should be employed to solicit all sorts of Christians to unite and agree, the contrariety of his profession would not allow men to stay till they heard his arguments; they would conclude from his religion, that either the man himself was mad, or that he thought those to be so, whom he had the impudence to endeavour to persuade.

Or suppose an Adamite* should be very solicitous and active, in all places, and with all sorts of persons, to settle the Church of England in particular, and a fair liberty of conscience for all Dissenters; though nothing in the world has more to be said for it than naked truth, yet if such a man should run up and down without clothes, let his arguments be never so good, or his commission never so authentic, his figure would be such a contradiction to his business, that how serious soever that might be in itself, his interposition would make a jest of it.

Though it should not go so far as this, yet if men have contrarieties in their way of living not to be reconciled; as if they should pretend infinite zeal for liberty, and at that time be in great favour and employed by those who will not endure it; if they are affectedly singular, and conform to the generality of the world in no one thing, but in playing the knave; if demonstration is a familiar word with them, most especially where the thing is impossible; if they quote authority to supply their want of sense, and justify the value of their arguments, not by reason, but by their being paid for them (in which, by the way, those who pay them have probably a very melancholy Equivalent); if they brandish a prince's word like a sword in a crowd, to make way for their own impertinence, and in dispute, as criminals formerly fled to the statue of the prince for sanctuary; if they should now, when baffled, creep under the protection of a king's name, where out of respect they are no further to be pursued—in these cases, though the propositions should be really good, they will be corrupted by passing through such conduits, and it would be a sufficient mistake to enter into a treaty; but it would be little less than madness from such hands to expect an Equivalent.

XVII. Having touched upon these particulars as necessary in order to the stating the nature of an equal bargain, and the circumstances belonging to it, let it now be examined in two or three instances, what things are not to be admitted by way of contract, to pass under the name of an Equivalent.

First, though it will be allowed, that in the general corruption of mankind, which will not admit justice alone to be a sufficient tie to make good a contract, that a punishment added for the breach of it is a fitting or rather a necessary circumstance; yet it does not follow, that in all cases, a great penalty upon the party offending is an absolute and an entire security. It must be considered in every particular case, how far the circumstances may rationally lead a man to rely more or less upon it.

In a private instance, the penalty inflicted upon the breach of contract must be first, such a one as the party injured can enforce, and secondly, such a one as he will enforce, when it is in his power.

If the offending party is in a capacity of hindering the other from bringing the vengeance of the law upon him; if he has strength or privilege sufficient to overrule the letter of the contract; in that case, a penalty is but a word, there is no consequence belonging to it. Secondly, the forfeiture or punishment must be such as the man aggrieved will take. For example, if upon a bargain, one of the parties shall stipulate to subject himself, in case of his failure, to have his ears cut or his nose slit by the other, with security given that he shall not be prosecuted for executing this part of the agreement, the penalty is no doubt heavy enough to discourage a man from breaking his contract; but on the other side it is of such a kind, that the other, how much soever he may be provoked, will not in cold blood care to inflict it. Such an extravagant clause would seem to be made only for show and sound, and no man would think himself safer by a thing which one way or other is sure to prove ineffectual.

In a public case, suppose in a government so constituted that a law may be made in the nature of a bargain, it is in itself no more than a dead letter, the life is given to it by the execution of what it contains; so that let it in itself be never so perfect, it depends upon those who are entrusted with seeing it observed.

If it is in any country, where the chief magistrate chooses the judges, and the judges interpret the laws; a penalty in any one particular law can have no effect but what is precarious. It may have a loud voice to threaten, but it has not a hand to give a blow; for as long as the governing power is in possession of this prerogative, let who will choose the meat, if they choose the cooks, it is they that will give the taste to it. So that it is clear that the rigour of a penalty will not in all cases fix a bargain, neither is it universally a true position, that the increase of punishment for the breach of a new law, is an Equivalent for the consent to part with an old one.

XVIII. In most bargains there is a reference to the time to come, which is therefore to be considered as well as that which comes within the compass of the present valuation.

Where the party contracting has not a full power to dispose what belongs to him or them in reversion, who shall succeed after him in his right, he cannot make any part of what is so limited to be the condition of the contract. Further, he cannot enjoin the heir or successor to forbear the exercise of any right that is inherent to him, as he is a man; neither can he restrain him, without his own consent, from doing any act which in itself is lawful, and liable to no objection. For example, a father cannot stipulate with any other man, that in consideration of such a thing done, or to be done, his son shall never marry; because marriage is an institution established by the laws of God and man, and therefore nobody can be so restrained by any power from doing such an act, when he thinks fit, being warranted by an authority that is not to be controlled.

XIX. Now, as there are rights inherent in men's persons in their single capacities, there are rights as much fixed to the body politic, which is a creature that never dies. For instance, there can be no government without a supreme power; that power is not always in the same hands, it is in different shapes and dresses, but still wherever it is lodged, it must be unlimited. It has a jurisdiction over everything else, but it cannot have it above itself. Supreme power can no more be limited than infinity can be measured; because it ceases to be the thing; its very being is dissolved, when any bounds can be put to it.

Where this supreme power is mixed, or divided, the shape only differs, the argument is still the same.

The present State of Venice cannot restrain those who succeed them in the same power, from having an entire and unlimited sovereignty; they may indeed make present laws which shall retrench their present power, if they are so disposed, and those laws, if not repealed by the same authority that enacted them, are to be observed by the succeeding senate till they think fit to abrogate them, and no longer; for if the supreme power shall still reside in the senate, perhaps composed of other men, or of other minds (which will be sufficient) the necessary consequence is, that one senate must have as much right to alter such a law, as another could have to make it.

XX. Suppose the supreme power in any state should make a law to enjoin all subsequent lawmakers to take an oath never to alter it, it would produce these following absurdities.

First, all supreme power being instituted to promote the safety and benefit, and to prevent the prejudice and danger which may fall upon those who live under the protection of it; the consequence of such an oath would be, that all men who are so trusted, shall take God to witness, that such a law once made, being judged at the time to be advantageous for the public, though afterwards by the vicissitude of times, or the variety of accidents or interests, it should plainly appear to them to be destructive, they will suffer it to have its course, and will never repeal it.

Secondly, if there could in any nation be found a set of men, who having a part in the supreme legislative power, should as much as in them lies, betray their country by such a criminal engagement, so directly opposite to the nature of their power, and to the trust reposed in them; if these men have their power only for life, when they are dead such an oath can operate no further; and though that would be too long a lease for the life of such a monster as an oath so composed, yet it must then certainly give up the ghost. It could bind none but the first makers of it, another generation would never be tied up by it.

Thirdly, in those countries where the supreme assemblies are not constant standing courts, but called together upon occasions, and composed of such as the people choose for that time only, with a trust and character that remains no longer with them than till that assembly is regularly dissolved; such an oath taken by the members of a senate, diet, or other assembly so chosen, can have very little effect, because at the next meeting there may be quite another set of men who will be under no obligation of that kind. The eternity intended to that law by those that made it, will be cut off by new men who shall succeed them in their power, if they have a differing taste, or another interest.

XXI. To put it yet further, suppose a clause in such a law, that it shall be criminal in the last degree for any man chosen in a subsequent assembly to propose the repealing it; and since nothing can be enacted which is not first proposed, by this means it seems as if a law might be created which should never die. But let this be examined.

First, such a clause would be so destructive to the being of such a constitution, as that it would be as reasonable to say, that a king had right to give or sell his kingdom to a foreign prince, as that any number of men who are entrusted with the supreme power, or any part of it, should have a right to impose such shackles upon the liberty of those who are to succeed them in the same trust. The ground of that trust is, that every man who is chosen into such an assembly is to do all that in him lies for the good of those who chose him. The English of such a clause would be, that he is not to do his best for those that chose him, because though he should be convinced that it might be very fatal to continue that law, and therefore very necessary to repeal it, yet he must not repeal it, because it is made a crime, and attended with a penalty.

But secondly, to show the emptiness as well as injustice of such a clause, it is clear, that although such an invasion of right should be imposed, it will never be obeyed. There will only be deformity in the monster, it will neither sting nor bite. Such lawgivers would only have the honour of attempting a contradiction which can never have any success; for as such a law in itself would be a madness, so the penalty would be a jest; which may be thus made out.

XXII. A law that carries in itself reason enough to support it, is so far from wanting the protection of such a clause, or from needing to take such an extraordinary receipt for long life, that the admitting it must certainly be the likeliest and the shortest way to destroy it; such a clause in a law must imply an opinion that the greatest part of mankind is against it, since it is impossible such an exorbitance should be done for its own sake; the end of it must be to force men by a penalty, to that which they could not be persuaded to, whilst their reason is left at liberty. This position being granted, which I think can hardly be denied, put the case that a law should be made with this imaginary clause of immortality, after which another assembly is chosen, and if the majority of the electors shall be against this law, the greater part of the elected must be so too, if the choice is fair and regular; which must be presumed, since the supposition of the contrary is not to come within this argument. When these men shall meet, the majority will be visible beforehand of those who are against such a law, so that there will be no hazard to any single man in proposing the repeal of it, when he cannot be punished but by the majority, and he has such a kind of assurance as comes near a demonstration, that the greater number will be of his mind, and consequently, that for their own sakes they will secure him from any danger.

For these reasons, wherever in order to the making a bargain, a proposition is advanced to make a new law, which is to tie up those who neither can nor will be bound by it, it may be a good jest, but it will never be a good Equivalent.

XXIII. In the last place, let it be examined how far a promise ought to be taken for a security in a bargain.

There is great variety of methods for the security of those that deal, according to their dispositions and interests; some are binding, others inducing circumstances, and are to be so distinguished.

First, ready payment is without exception, so of that there can be no dispute; in default of that, the good opinion men may have of one another is a great ingredient to supply the want of immediate performances. Where the trust is grounded upon inclination only, the generosity is not always returned; but where it springs from a long experience it is a better foundation, and yet that is not always secure. In ordinary dealing, one promise may be an Equivalent to another, but it is not so for a thing actually granted or conveyed; especially if the thing required in exchange for it is of great value, either in itself or in its consequences. A bare promise as a single security in such a case is not an equal proposal; if it is offered by way of addition, it generally gives cause to doubt the title is crazy, where so slender a thing is brought in to be a supplement.

XXIV. The earnest of making good a promise, must be such a behaviour preceding as may encourage the party to whom it is made to depend upon it. Where instead of that, there has been want of kindness, and which is worse, an invasion of right, a promise has no persuading force; and till the objection to such a proceeding is forgotten (which can only be the work of time), and the skin is a little grown over the tender part, the wound must not be touched. There must be some intermission at least to abate the smart of unkind usage, or else a promise in the eye of the party injured is so far from strengthening a security that it raises more doubts, and gives more justifiable cause to suspect it.

A word is not like a bone, that being broken and well set again, is said to be sometimes stronger in that very part: it is far from being so in a word given and not made good. Every single act either weakens or improves our credit with other men; and as a habit of being just to our word will confirm, so a habit of too freely dispensing with it must necessarily destroy it. A promise has its effect to persuade a man to lay some weight upon it, where the promiser has not only the power, but may reasonably be supposed to have the will of performing it; and further, that there be no visible interest of the party promising to excuse himself from it, or to evade it.

All obligations are comparative, and where they seem to be opposite, or between the greater and the lesser, which of them ought to have precedence in all respects every man is apt to be his own judge.

XXV. If it should fall out that the promiser, with full intent at the time to perform, might by the interposition of new arguments, or differing advice, think himself obliged to turn the matter of conscience on the other side, and should look upon it to be much a greater fault to keep his word than to break it; such a belief will untie the strictest promise that can be made, and though the party thus absolving himself should do it without the mixture or temptation of private interest, being moved to it merely by his conscience, as then informed; yet how far soever that might diminish the fault in him, it would in no degree lessen the inconveniences to the party who is disappointed, by the breach of an engagement upon which he relied.

XXVI. A promise is to be understood in the plain and natural sense of the words, and to be sure not in his who made it, if it was given as part of a bargain. That would be like giving a man power to raise the value of his money in the payment of his debt, by which, though he paid but half or less, he might pretend according to the letter to have made good the contract.

The power of interpreting a promise entirely takes away the virtue of it. A merchant who should once assume that privilege, would save himself the trouble of making any more bargains.

It is still worse if this jurisdiction over a man's promise should be lodged in hands that have power to support such an extraordinary claim; and if in other cases forbearing to deal upon those terms is advisable, in this it becomes absolutely necessary.

XXVII. There must in all respects be a full liberty to claim a promise, to make it reasonable to take it in any part of payment; else it would be like agreeing for a rent, and at the same time making it criminal to demand it.

A superiority of dignity or power in the party promising makes it a more tender thing for the other party to treat upon that security. The first makes it a nice thing to claim, the latter makes it a difficult thing to obtain.

In some cases, a promise is in the nature of a covenant, and then between equal parties the breach of it will bear a suit; but where the greatness of the promiser is very much raised above the level of equality, there is no forfeiture to be taken. It is so far from the party grieved his being able to sue or recover damages, that he will not be allowed to explain or expostulate, and instead of his being relieved against the breach of promise, he will run the hazard of being punished for breach of good manners. Such a difficulty is putting all or part of the payment in the fire, where men must burn their fingers before they can come at it.

That cannot properly be called good payment, which the party to whom it is due may not receive with ease and safety. It was a King's brother of England* who refused to lend the Pope money, for this reason, That he would never take the bond of one upon whom he could not distrain.*

The argument is still stronger against the validity of a promise, when the contract is made between a prince and a subject. The very offering a king's word in mortgage is rather a threatening in case of refusal, than an inducing argument to accept it; it is unfair at first, and by that gives greater cause to be cautious, especially if a thing of that value and dignity as a king's word ought to be, should be put into the hands of state brokers to strike up a bargain with it.

XXVIII. When God Almighty makes covenants with mankind, his promise is a sufficient security, notwithstanding his superiority and his power; because first, he can neither err nor do injustice. It is the only exception to his omnipotence, that by the perfection of his being he is incapacitated to do wrong.* Secondly, at the instant of his promise, by the extent of his foresight, which cannot fail, there is no room left for the possibility of anything to intervene which might change his mind. Lastly, he is above the receiving either benefit or inconvenience, and therefore can have no interest or temptation to vary from his word, when once he has granted it.

Now though princes are God's vicegerents, yet their commission not being so large, as that these qualifications are devolved to them, it is quite another case, and since the offering a security implies it to be examined by the party to whom it is proposed, it must not be taken ill that objections are made to it, even though the prince himself should be the immediate proposer.

Let a familiar case be put: suppose a prince, tempted by a passion too strong for him to resist, should descend so as to promise marriage to one of his subjects,* and as men are naturally in great haste upon such occasions, should press to take possession before the necessary forms could be complied with;* would the poor lady's scruples be called criminal for not taking the security of the royal word? Or would her allegiance be tainted by her resisting the sacred person of her sovereign, because he was impatient of delay? Courtesy in this case might persuade her to accept it, if she was so disposed, but sure the just exercise of power can never claim it.

XXIX. There is one case where it is more particularly a duty to use very great caution in accepting the security of a promise, and that is when men are authorized and trusted by others to act for them. This puts them under much greater restraints than those who are at liberty to treat for themselves. It is lawful, though it is not prudent, for any man to make an ill bargain for himself, but it is neither the one nor the other, where the party contracting treats on behalf of another, by whom he is entrusted. Men who will unwarily accept an ill security, if it is for themselves, forfeit their own discretion, and undergo the penalty, but they are not responsible to anybody else. They lie under the mortification and the loss of committing the error, by which though they may expose their judgement to some censure, yet their morality suffers no reproach by it.

But those who are deputed by others to treat for them, upon terms of best advantage, though the confidence placed in them should prevent the putting any limits to their power in their commission, yet the condition implied if not expressed, is that the persons so trusted shall neither make an ill bargain, nor accept a slight security.

The obligation is yet more binding when the trust is of a public nature. The aggravation of disappointing a body of men that rely upon them, carries the fault as high as it can go, and perhaps no crime of any kind can outdo such a deliberate breach of trust, or would more justly make men forfeit the protection of human society.

XXX. I will add one thing more upon this head, which is, that it is not always a true proposition, that it is safe to rely upon a promise, if at the time of making it, it is the interest of the promiser to make it good. This, though many times it is a good inducement, yet it has these exceptions to it. First, if the proposer has at other times gone plainly against his visible interest, the argument will turn the other way, and his former mistakes are so many warnings to others, not to come within the danger of any more: let the inducements to those mistakes be never so great and generous, that does not alter the nature, they are mistakes still.

Interest is an uncertain thing, it goes and comes, and varies according to times and circumstances; as good build upon a quicksand, as upon a presumption that interest shall not alter. Where are the men so distinguished from the rest of mankind, that it is impossible for them to mistake their interest? Who are they that have such an exemption from human frailty, as that it can never happen to them not to see their interest for want of understanding, or not to leap over it by excess of zeal?*

Above all, princes are the most liable to mistake; not out of any defect in their nature, which might put them under such an unfortunate distinction; quite contrary, the blood they derive from wise and great ancestors does rather distinguish them on the better side; besides that their great character and office of governing gives a noble exercise to their reason, which can very hardly fail to raise and improve it. But there is one circumstance annexed to their glorious calling, which in this respect is sufficient to outweigh all those advantages; it is that mankind, divided in most things else, agree in this, to conspire in their endeavours to deceive and mislead them; which makes it above the power of human understanding to be so exactly guarded as never to admit a surprise, and the highest applause that could ever yet be given to the greatest men that ever wore a crown, is that they were no oftener deceived.

Thus I have ventured to lay down my thoughts of the nature of a bargain, and the due circumstances belonging to an Equivalent, and will now conclude with this short word: 'Where distrusting may be the cause of provoking anger, and trusting may be the cause of bringing ruin, the choice is too easy to need the being explained.'

MAXIMS OF THE GREAT ALMANSOR

THE following maxims were found by a Jew amongst the papers of the Great Almansor;* and though they must lose a good deal of their original spirit by the translation, yet they seem to be so applicable to all times that it is thought no disservice to mankind to make them public.

1. That a prince who falls out with his laws breaks with his best friends.

2. That his exalting his own authority above his laws is like his letting in an enemy to surprise his guards; the laws are the only guards he can be sure will never run away from him.

3. A prince that will say he can do no good except he may do everything, teaches the people to say they are slaves if they may not do whatever they have a mind to.

4. That power and liberty are like heat and moisture: where they are well mixed everything prospers; where they are single they are destructive.

5. That arbitrary power is like most other things that are very hard, they are also very apt to break.

6. That the profit of places should be measured as they are more or less conducing to the public service, and if business is more necessary than splendour, the instruments of it ought in proportion to be better paid; that the contrary method is as impertinent as it would be to let the carving of a ship cost more than all the rest of it.

7. That where the least useful part of the people have the most credit with the prince, men will conclude the way to get everything is to be good for nothing.

8. That an extravagant gift to any one man raises the market to everybody else; so that in consequence the unlimited bounty of an unthinking prince makes him a beggar, let him have never so much money.

9. That if ordinary beggars are whipped, the daily beggars in fine clothes, out of a proportionable respect to their quality, ought to be hanged.

10. That pride is as loud a beggar as want, and a great deal more saucy.

11. That a prince who will give more to importunity than to merit had as good set out a proclamation to all his loving subjects forbidding them to serve well upon the penalty of their being undone for it.

12. That a wise prince will not oblige his courtiers who are birds of prey so as to disoblige his people who are beasts of burden.

13. That it is safer for a prince to judge of men by what they do to one another, than by what they do to him.

14. That it is a gross mistake to think that a knave between man and man, can be honest to a king, whom of all others men generally make the least scruple to deceive.

15. That a prince who can ever trust the man that has once deceived him loses the right of being faithfully dealt with by anybody else.*

16. That it is not possible for a prince to find out such an honest knave as will let nobody else cheat him.

17. That if a prince does not show an aversion to knaves there will be an inference that will be natural, let it be never so unmannerly.

18. That a prince who forms his opinion too soon is in danger of repenting it too late.

19. That it is less dangerous for a prince to mind too much what the people say than too little.

20. That a prince is to take care the greater part of the people may not be angry at the same time, for though the first beginnings of their ill humour should be against one another, yet if not stopped it will naturally end in anger against him.

21. That if princes would reflect how much they are in the power of their ministers they would be more circumspect in the choice of them.

22. That a wise prince will support good servants against men's anger, and not support ill ones against their complaints.

23. That parties in a state generally, like freebooters,* hang out false colours; the pretence is the public good, the real business is to catch prizes. Like Tartars whenever they succeed, instead of improving their victory, they presently fall upon the baggage.

24. That a prince may play so long between two parties that they may in time join together to be in earnest with him.

25. That there is more dignity in open violence than in the unskilful cunning of a prince who goes about to impose upon the people.

26. That the people will ever suspect the remedies for the diseases of the state, where they are wholly excluded from seeing how they are prepared.

27. That changing hands without changing measures is as if a drunkard in a dropsy should change his doctors and not his diet.

28. That a prince is to watch that his reason may not be subdued by his nature, as not to be so much a man of peace as to be a jest in an army, nor so much a man of war as to be out of his element in the council.

29. That a man who cannot mind his own business is never to be trusted with the king's.

30. That quality alone should only serve to make a show in the embroidered part of the government; but that ignorance, though never so well born, should never be admitted to spoil the public business.

31. That he who thinks his place below him, will mind it so little that he will certainly be below his place.

32. That when a prince's example ceases to have the force of a law, it is a sure sign that his power is wasting and that there will be but a little distance between men's neglecting to imitate and their refusing to obey.

33. That a people may let a king fall yet still remain a people; but if a king lets his people slip from him he is no more a king.

A ROUGH DRAUGHT OF A NEW
MODEL AT SEA

I WILL make no other introduction to the following discourse, than that the importance of our being strong at sea, as it was ever very great, so in our present circumstances it is grown to be much greater; whereas formerly, our force in shipping contributed to our trade, and was our safety, now it is become indispensably necessary to our very being. It may be said now to England, 'Martha, Martha thou art busy about many things, but one thing is necessary':* To the question, What shall we do to be saved in this world? there is no other answer, but look to your moat.

The first article of an Englishman's political creed must be, that he believes in the sea, &c.; without that there needs no general council to pronounce him incapable of salvation.

We are in an island, restrained to it by God Almighty, not as a penalty, but a grace, and one of the greatest that can be given to mankind. Happy confinement! that has made us free, rich, and quiet; a fair portion in this world, and very well worth the preserving; a figure that has ever been envied and could never be imitated by our neighbours.

Our situation has made greatness abroad by land conquests unnatural things to us. It is true we have made excursions, and glorious ones too, which make our name great in history, but they did not last. Admit the English to be giants in courage, yet they must not hope to succeed in making war against Heaven, which seems to have enjoined them to acquiesce in being happy within their own circle. In short, it is no paradox to say that England has its root in the sea, and a deep root too, from whence it sends its branches into both the Indies. We may say further in our present case, that if allegiance is due to protection, ours to the sea is due from that rule, since by that and that alone we are to be protected; and if we have of late suffered the usurpation of other methods, contrary to the homage we owe to that which must preserve us, it is time now to restore the sea to its right; and as there is no repentance effectual without amendment, there is not a moment to be lost in the going about it.

It is not pretended to launch into such a voluminous treatise as to set down everything to which so comprehensive a subject might lead me. For as the sea has little less variety in it than the land, so the naval force of England extends itself into a great many branches, each of which are important enough to require a discourse apart, and peculiarly applied to it. But there must be a preference to some considerations above others, when the weight of them is so visibly superior that it cannot be contested. It is there first, that the foundations are to be laid of our naval economy. Amongst these, there is one article which in its own nature must be allowed to be the cornerstone of the building, *viz.* the choice of officers, with the discipline and encouragements belonging to them. Upon this head only, I shall then take the liberty to venture my opinion into the world, with a real and unaffected submission to those who may offer anything better for the advantage of the public.

The first question then will be, out of what sort of men the officers of the fleet are to be chosen, and this immediately leads us to the present controversy between the gentlemen and the tarpaulins.*

The usual objections on both sides are too general to be relied upon. Partiality and common prejudices direct most men's opinions, without entering into the particular reasons which ought to be the grounds of it; there is so much ease in acquiescing in generals,* that the ignorance of those who cannot distinguish, and the laziness of those that will not, make men very apt to decline the trouble of stricter enquiries, which they think too great a price for being in the right, let it be never so valuable. This makes them judge in the lump, and either let their opinions swim along with the stream of the world, or give them up to be wholly directed by success; the effect of it is that they change their minds upon every present uneasiness, wanting a steady foundation upon which their judgement should be formed. This is perching upon the twigs of things, and not going to the root; but sure the matter in question deserves to be examined in another manner, since so much depends upon it.

To state the thing impartially, it must be owned that it seems to lie fairest for the tarpaulin. It gives an impression that must have so much weight as to make a man's opinion lean very much on that side. It carries so much authority with it; it seems to be so unquestionable that those are fittest to command at sea who have not only made it their calling but their element, that there must naturally be a prejudice to anything that can be said against it; there must therefore be some reason very extraordinary to support the argument on the other side, or else the gentlemen could never enter the lists against such a violent objection, which seems not to be resisted. I will introduce my argument with an assertion, which as I take to be true almost in all cases, so it is necessary to be explained and enforced in this: the assertion is, that there is hardly a single proposition to be made which is not deceitful, and the tying our reason too close to it may in many cases be destructive. Circumstances must come in, and are to be made a part of the matter of which we are to judge; positive* decisions are always dangerous, and more especially in politics. A man who will be master of an argument must do like a skilful general, who sends scouts on all sides, to see whether there may not be an enemy, so he must look round to see what objections can be made, and not go on in a straight line, which is the ready way to lead him into a mistake. Before then, that we conclude what sort of men are fittest to command at sea, a principle is to be laid down, that there is a differing consideration to be had of such a subject matter as is in itself distinct and independent, and of such a one as being a limb of a body, or a wheel of a frame, there is a necessity of suiting it to the rest, and preserving the harmony of the whole. A man must not in that case restrain himself to the separate consideration of that single part, but must take care it may fall in and agree with the shape of the whole creature of which it is a member.

According to this position, which I take to be indisputable, it will not, I hope, appear an affectation, or an extravagant fit of unseasonable politics, if before I enter into the particular state of the present question I say something of the government of England, and make that the groundwork of determining what sort of men are most proper to be made use of to command at sea.

The forms of government to which England must be subjected, are either absolute monarchy, a commonwealth, or a mixed monarchy, as it now is, with those natural alterations that the exigency of affairs may, from time to time, suggest.

As to absolute monarchy, I will not allow myself to be transported into such invectives as are generally made against it; neither am I ready to enter into the aggravating style of calling everything slavery that restrains men in any part of their freedom. One may discern in this, as in most other things, the good and the bad of it. We see by too near an instance what France does by it; it does not only struggle with the rest of Christendom, but is in a fair way of giving law to it.

This is owing in great measure to the strength of a despotic and an undivided power; the uncontrollable authority of the directing councils makes everything move without disorder or opposition, which must give an advantage that is plain enough of itself, without being further proved by the melancholy experience we have of it at this time. I see and admire this, yet I consider at the same time that all things of this kind are comparative; that as on one side, without government men cannot enjoy what belongs to them in particular, nor can a nation secure or preserve itself in general; so on the other side, the end of government being that mankind should live in some competent state of freedom, it is very unnatural to have the end destroyed by the means that were originally made use of to attain it.

In this respect, something is to be ventured, rather than submit to such a precarious state of life as would make it a burden to a reasonable creature, and therefore, after I have owned the advantages in some kinds of an unlimited government, yet whilst they are attended with so many other discouraging circumstances, I cannot think but that they may be bought too dear. And if it should be so, that it is not possible for a state to be great and glorious except the subjects are wretchedly miserable, I am not ashamed to own my low-spirited frailty in preferring such a model of government as may agree with the reasonable enjoyments of a free people, before such a one by which empire is to be extended at such an unnatural price. Besides, whatever men's opinions may be one way or another in the general question, there is an argument in our case that shuts the door to any answer to it; *viz.* we cannot subsist under a despotic power. Our very being would be destroyed by it; for we are to consider we are a very little spot in the map of the world, and made a great figure only by trade, which is the creature of liberty; one destroyed, the other falls to the ground by a natural consequence that will not admit a dispute.

If we should be measured by our acres, we are a poor, inconsiderable people; we are exalted above our natural size by our good laws, and our excellent constitution. By this we are not only happy at home but considerable abroad. Our situation, our humour, our trade, do all concur to strengthen this argument, so that all other reasons must give place to such a one, as makes it out, that there is no mean between being a free nation, and no nation. We are no more a people, nor England can no longer keep its name, from the moment, that by our liberty being extinguished, the vital strength that should support us is withdrawn. We should then be no more than the carcass of a nation, with no other security than that of contempt, and to subsist upon no other tenure, than that we should be below the giving temptation to our stronger neighbours to devour us. In my judgement, therefore, there is such a short decision to be made upon this subject, that in relation to England an absolute monarchy is as unreasonable a thing to be wished, as I hope it will be impossible ever to be obtained.

It must be considered in the next place, whether England is likely to be turned into a commonwealth. It is hard at any time to determine what will be the shape of the next revolution; much more at this time would it be inexcusably arrogant to undertake it. Who can foresee whether it shall be from without, or from within, or from both? Whether with or without the concurrence of the people, whether regularly produced or violently imposed? I shall not therefore magisterially declare it impossible that a commonwealth should be settled here, but I may give my humble opinion, that according to all appearances, it is very improbable.

I will first lay it down for a principle, that it is not a sound way of arguing, to say, that if it can be made out, that the form of a commonwealth will best suit with the interest of the nation, it must, for that reason, of necessity prevail.

I will not deny but that 'Interest will not lie'* is a right maxim, wherever it is sure to be understood; else one had as good affirm that no man in particular, nor mankind in general, can ever be mistaken. A nation is a great while before they see, and generally they must feel first, before their sight is quite cleared. This makes it so long before they see their interest, that for the most part it is too late for them to pursue it. If men must be supposed always to follow their true interest, it must be meant of a new manufacture of mankind by God Almighty; there is to be some new clay, the old stuff never yet made any such infallible creature.

This being premised, it is to be enquired whether instead of an inclination or a leaning towards a commonwealth, there is not in England a general dislike to it. If this is so, as I take it to be, by a very great disparity in numbers, it will be in vain to dispute by reason whilst humour is against it. Allowing the weight that is due to the arguments which may be alleged for it, yet if the herd is against it, the going about to convince them would have no other effect than to show that nothing can be more impertinent than good reasons, when they are misplaced or ill-timed.

I must observe that there must be previous dispositions in all great changes, to facilitate and to make way for them; and I think it not at all absurd to affirm, that such revolutions are seldom made at all, except by the general preparation of men's minds they are half made, before it is plainly visible that men go about them.

This makes all the republican schemes, whether borrowed from the ancient, or invented by the modern doctors in politics, to be no more than dreams, when they are attempted to be put in practice, where a nation is so generally prepossessed against them.

Though it seems to me that this argument alone makes all others unnecessary, yet I must take notice, that besides what has been said upon this subject, there are certain preliminaries to the first building a commonwealth, some materials absolutely necessary for the carrying on such a fabric, which are at present wanting amongst us; I mean virtue, morality, diligence, religion, or at the least hypocrisy. Now this age is so plain dealing as not to dissemble so far as to an outward pretence to qualities which seem at present to be so unfashionable, and under so much discountenance.

From hence we may draw a plain and a natural inference that a commonwealth is not fit for us, because we are not fit for a commonwealth.

This being granted, the supposition of this form of government in England, with all its consequences to the present question, must be excluded, and absolute monarchy having been so too, by the reasons above alleged, it will, without further examination, fall to a mixed government as we now are. I will not say, that there is never to be any alteration; the constitution of the several parts that concur to make up the frame of the present government may be altered in many things; in some for the better, and in others perhaps for the worse, according as circumstances shall arise to induce a change, and as passion and interest shall have more or less influence upon the public councils; but still if it remains in the whole so far a mixed monarchy that there shall be a restraint upon the prince as to the exercise of a despotic power, it is enough to make it a groundwork for the present question.

It appears then that a bounded monarchy is that kind of government which most probably will prevail and continue in England, from whence it must follow (as has been hinted before) that every considerable part ought to be so composed, as the better to conduce to the preserving the harmony of the whole constitution. The navy is of so great importance, that it would be disparaged by calling it less than the life and soul of the government. Therefore, to apply the argument to the subject we are upon, in case the officers should be all tarpaulins, it would either be in reality, or at least it would be thought too great a tendency to a commonwealth. Such a part of the constitution being democratically disposed may be suspected to endeavour to bring it into that shape; and where the influences must be so strong, the supposition will be the more justifiable. In short, if the maritime force, which is the only thing that can defend us, should be wholly directed by the lower sort of men, with an entire exclusion of the nobility and gentry, it will not be easy to answer the arguments supported by so great a probability, that such a scheme would not only lean towards a democracy, but directly lead us into it.

Let us now examine the contrary proposition; *viz.* that all the officers should be gentlemen.

Here the objection lies so fair, of its introducing an arbitrary government, that it is as little to be answered in that respect, as the former is in the other. Gentlemen in a general definition will be suspected to lie more than other men under the temptations of being made instruments of unlimited power; their relations, their way of living, their taste of the entertainments of the court, inspire an ambition that generally draws their inclinations towards it, besides the gratifying of their interests. Men of quality are often taken with the ornaments of government; the splendour dazzles them so, as that their judgements are surprised by it; and there will be always some that have so little remorse for invading other men's liberties, that it makes them less solicitous to preserve their own.

These things throw them naturally into such a dependence as might give a dangerous bias, if they alone were in command at sea; it would make that great wheel turn by an irregular motion, and instead of being the chief means of preserving the whole frame, might come to be the chief instrument to discompose and dissolve it.

The two former exclusive propositions being necessarily to be excluded in this question, there remains no other expedient, neither can any other conclusion be drawn from the argument as it has been stated, than that there must be a mixture in the navy of gentlemen and tarpaulins, as there is in the constitution of the government of power and liberty. This mixture is not to be so rigorously defined as to set down the exact proportion there is to be of each; the greater or lesser number must be directed by circumstances of which the government is to judge, and which make it improper to set such bounds as that upon no occasion it shall on either side be lessened or enlarged.

It is possible the men of Wapping* may think they are injured, by giving them any partners in the dominion of the sea. They may take it unkindly to be jostled in their own element by men of such a different education that they may be said to be of another species. They will be apt to think it a usurpation upon them, and notwithstanding the instances that are against them, and which give a kind of prescription on the other side, they will not easily acquiesce in what they conceive to be a hardship to them.

But I shall in a good measure reconcile myself to them by what follows, *viz.* the gentlemen shall not be capable of bearing office at sea, except they are tarpaulins too; that is to say, except they are so trained up by a continued habit of living at sea, that they may have a right to be admitted free denizens of Wapping. Upon this depends the whole matter, and indeed here lies the difficulty, because the gentlemen brought up under the connivance of a looser discipline, and of an easier admittance, will take it heavily to be reduced within the fetters of such a new model, and I conclude they will be so extremely averse to that which they will call an unreasonable yoke upon them, that their original consent is never to be expected. But if it appears to be convenient, and which is more, that it is necessary for the preservation of the whole, that it should be so, the government must be called in aid to suppress these first boilings of discontent; the rules must be imposed with such authority, and the execution of them must be so well supported, that by degrees their impatience will be subdued, and they will concur in an establishment to which they will be every day more reconciled.

They will find it will take away the objections which are now thrown upon them, of setting up for masters without having ever been apprentices, or at least, without having served out their time.

Mankind naturally swells against favour and partiality; their belief of their own merit makes men object them to a prosperous competitor, even where there is no pretence for it; but where there is the least handle offered, to be sure, it will be taken. So in this case, when a gentleman is preferred at sea, the tarpaulin is very apt to impute it to friends or favour; but if that gentleman has before his preferment passed through all the steps which ought to lead to it, that he smells as much of pitch and tar as those that were swaddled in a sail cloth, his having an escutcheon will be so far from doing him harm that it will set him upon the advantage ground. It will draw a real respect to his quality when so supported, and give him an influence and an authority infinitely superior to that which the mere seaman can ever pretend to.

When a gentleman has learnt how to obey, he will grow very much fitter to command; his own memory will advise him not to exact unreasonable things, and for smaller faults not to inflict too rigorous punishments. He will better resist the temptations of authority (which are great) when he reflects how much he has at other times wished it might be gently exercised, when he was liable to the rigour of it.

When the undistinguishing discipline of a ship has tamed the young mastership which is apt to arise from a gentleman's birth and education, he then grows proud in the right place, and values himself first upon knowing his duty, and then upon doing it.

In plain English, men of quality in their several degrees must either restore themselves to a better opinion both for morality and diligence, or else quality itself will be in danger of being extinguished. The original gentleman is almost lost. In strictness, when posterity does not still further adorn, by their own virtue, the escutcheon their ancestors first got for them by their merit, they deserve the penalty of being deprived of it.

To expect that quality alone should waft men up into places and employments, is as unreasonable as to think that a ship, because it is carved and gilded, should be fit to go to sea, without sails or tackling; but when a gentleman makes no other use of his quality than to incite him the more to do his duty, it will give him such a true and settled superiority as must destroy all competition from those that are below him.

It is time now to go to the probationary qualifications of an officer at sea. And I have some to offer, which I have digested in my thoughts, I hope so impartially, that they may not be speculative notions, but things easy and practicable, if the directing powers will give due countenance and encouragement to the execution of them. But whilst I am going about to set them down, though this little essay was made to no other end than to introduce them, I am upon better recollection induced to put a restraint upon myself, and rather retract the promise

I made at the beginning, than, by explaining the particular methods by which I conceive the good end that is aimed at may be obtained, to incur the imputation of the thing of the world of which I would least be guilty, which is of anticipating by my private opinion the judgement of the Parliament, or seeming out of my slender stock of reason to dictate to the supreme wisdom of the nation. They will, no doubt, consider the present establishments for the discipline at sea, which are many of them very good, and if well executed might go a great way in the present question; but I will not say they are so perfect, but that more may be added to make them more effectual, and that some more supplemental expedients may be necessary to complete what is yet defective. And whenever the Parliament shall think fit to take this matter into their consideration, I am sure they will not want for their direction the auxiliary reason of any man without doors,* much less of one whose thoughts are so entirely and unaffectedly resigned to whatever they shall determine in this or anything else relating to the public.

SOME CAUTIONS OFFERED TO THE CONSIDERATION OF THOSE WHO ARE TO CHOOSE MEMBERS TO SERVE IN THE NEXT PARLIAMENT

I WILL make no other introduction, than that it is hoped the counties and boroughs will remember, in general, that besides other consequences, they will have the credit or the scandal that belongs to an unfitting choice. The creators will be thought like their creatures, and therefore an ill choice will either be a disparagement of their understanding or their morality. There cannot be a fuller approbation of a thing than the choosing it; so that the faults of the Members chosen, if known beforehand, will be judged to be of the growth of that county or borough, after such a solemn approbation of them. In short, those who send up their picture* to Westminster should take care it may be such a one as will do them right. Now to the particulars:

1. A very extraordinary earnestness to be chosen is no very good symptom.

A desire to serve the nation in Parliament is an Englishman's ambition, always to be encouraged and never to be disapproved. A man may not only be willing to stand, but he may declare that willingness to his friends, that they may assist him, and by all the means becoming a modest and a prudent man, he may endeavour to succeed, and prevent the being disappointed in it. But there is a wide difference between this and raising a kind of a petty war in a county or corporation; entering the lists rather for a combat than an election, throwing fire-balls to put men in a heat, and omitting to spread no scandal, whether true or false, which may give an advantage by laying a blemish upon a competitor.

These methods will ever be suspicious; it never will be thought a natural thing for men to take such extravagant pains for the mere sake of doing good to others. To be content to suffer something for a good end is that which many would do without any great repugnance, but where a man can honestly propose to himself nothing except trouble, charge, and loss, by absence from his own affairs, to be so violent in the pursuit of so ill a bargain is not at all suited to the languishing virtue of mankind so corrupted. Such a self-denying zeal in such a self-seeking age is so little to be imagined that it may without injury be suspected; therefore when these blustering pretenders come upon the stage, their natural temper and other circumstances ought to be very well considered, before men trust them with the disposal of their money or their liberty; and I am apt to believe there could hardly be found one single man whose other qualifications would overbalance the objections that lie against such importunate suitors.

2. Recommending letters ought to have no effect upon elections.

In this I must distinguish; for though, in strictness, perhaps there should be no exception, yet in compliance with long practice, and out of an indulgence that is necessary in a time when mankind is too much loosened from severe rules to be kept close up to them, letters sent only from equal men; doing good men right by giving evidence in their behalf; offering them as fitly qualified, when they really are so; and freeing them from unjust aspersions, may be still allowed. The letters I mean, are from men of power, where it may be beneficial to comply, and inconvenient to oppose.

Choice must not only be free from force, but from influence, which is a degree of force; there must be no difficulty; no apprehension that a refusal will be ill taken or resented. The freeholders must be freemen too; they are to have no shackles upon their votes in an election, and the men who stand should carry their own letters of recommendation about them, which are their good character and behaviour in the world, without borrowing evidence, especially when it comes from suspected hands.

Those who make use of these epistles ought to have no more advantage from them than the Muscovites have from the letters put into their hands when they are buried, to recommend them to St Nicholas;* the first should as little get admittance for men into the Parliament as these latter can introduce the bearers into Heaven. The scandal of such letters lies first in the arrogant imposing of those that write them, and next in the wretched meanness of those that need them. Men must be fallen very low in their credit, who upon such an occasion have recourse to power to support it; their enemies could not give stronger evidence of their not being fit for that which they pretend to, and if the electors judge otherwise, they will be pretty sure in a little time to see their mistake and to repent it.

3. Non-attendance in former Parliaments ought to be a bar against the choice of men who have been guilty of it.

It is one of the worst kinds of non-residence and the least to be excused; it is very hard that men should despise a duty which perhaps is the only ground of the respect that is paid to them. It is such a piece of sauciness for anyone to press for the honour of serving in Parliament and then to be careless in attending it, that in a house where there were so many officers,* the penalty had not been improper to have made them ride the wooden horse for it.*

If men forbear to come out of laziness, let them be gratified by taking their ease at home without interruption; if out of small cunning to avoid difficulties, and to escape from the inconvenience of voting in critical cases, let them enjoy that despicable pitch of wisdom and never pretend to make a figure where the public is to be served. If it would not be thought advisable to trust a man immediately after he has been drawn out of a jail, it may be as reasonable to look upon one who for his non-attendance in the House has been sent for in custody, as a kind of bankrupt, which puts him upon unequal terms with those who have been assiduous in the discharge of their duty. They who thought fit in one session to neglect the public business, may be justly suspected by their standing in the next, to intend their own.

Besides these more deliberate offenders, there are some, who do not attend even when they are in the House; absent in their thoughts, for want of comprehending the business that is doing, and therefore diverted from it by anything that is trivial. Such men are nuisances to a serious assembly, and when they are numerous, it amounts almost to a dissolution, it being scarce possible for good sense to be heard, whilst a noise is made by the buzzing of these horseflies. The Roman censors, who degraded a senator for yawning whilst there was a debate, would have much more abundant matter here upon which they might exercise their jurisdiction.

To conclude upon this head, there are so few that ever mended in these cases, that after the first experiment, it is not at all reasonable to take them upon a new trial.

4. Men who are unquiet and busy in their nature are to give more than ordinary proofs of their integrity, before the electing them into a public trust can be justified. As a hot summer breeds greater swarms of flies, so an active time breeds a greater number of these stirring gentlemen.

It is pretty sure that men who cannot allow themselves to be at rest will let nobody else be at quiet. Such a perpetual activity is apt by degrees to be applied to the pursuit of their private interest; and their thoughts being in a continual motion, they have not time to dwell long enough upon anything to entertain a scruple, so that they are generally at full liberty to do what is most convenient for them, without being fettered by any restraint. Nay further, whenever it happens that there is an impunity for cheating, these nimble gentlemen are apt to think it a disparagement to their understandings not to go into it. I doubt it is not a wrong to the present age, to say that a knave is a less unpopular calling than it has been in former times; and to say truth it would be ingratitude in some men to turn honest, when they owe all they have to their knavery.

The people are in this respect unhappy; they are too many to do their own business. Their numbers, which make their strength, are at the same time the cause of their weakness. They are too unwieldy to move, and for this reason nothing can ever redeem them from this incurable impotency; so that they must have solicitors to pursue and look after their interests, who are too often disposed to dispense with the fidelity they owe to those that trust them, especially if the government will pay their bills without abatement. It is better these gentlemen's dexterity should be employed anywhere than in Parliament, where the ill consequence of their being Members is too much diffused, and not restrained to the county or borough who shall be so unwary as to choose them.

5. Great drinkers are less fit to serve in Parliament than is generally apprehended.

Men's virtue as well as their understanding is apt to be tainted by it. The appearance of it is sociable and well-natured, but it is by no means to be relied upon. Nothing is more frail than a man too far engaged in wet popularity. The habit of it makes men careless of their business, and that naturally leads them into circumstances that make them liable to temptation. It is seldom seen that any principles have such a root, as that they can be proof against the continual droppings of a bottle.

As to the faculties of the mind, there is not less objection. The vapours of wine may sometimes throw out sparks of wit, but they are like scattered pieces of ore; there is no vein to work upon. Such wit, even the best of it, is like paying great fines, in which case there must of necessity be an abatement of the constant rent.* Nothing sure is a greater enemy to the brain, than too much moisture; it can the least of anything bear the being continually steeped, and it may be said that thought may be resembled to some creatures which can live only in a dry country. Yet so arrogant are some men, as to think they are so much masters of business as that they can play with it; they imagine they can drown their reason once a day, and that it shall not be the worse for it, forgetting that by too often diving, the understanding at last grows too weak to rise up again.

I will suppose this fault was less frequent, when Solon* made it one of his laws, that it was lawful to kill a magistrate if he was found drunk;* such a liberty taken in this age, either in the Parliament or out of it, would do terrible execution. I cannot but mention a petition in the year 1647 from the County of Devon, to the House of Commons, against the undue election of burgesses who are strong in wine and weak in wisdom. The cause of such petitions is best prevented by choosing such as shall not give any handle for them.

6. Wanting* men give such cause of suspicion wherever they deal, that surely the choosers will be upon their guard as often as such dangerous pretenders make their application to them.

Let the behaviour of such men be never so plausible and untainted, yet they who are to pitch upon those they are to trust with all they have, may be excused if they do not only consider what they are, but what they may be. As we pray ourselves that we may not be led into temptation, we ought not by any means to thrust others into it, even though our own interest was not concerned; and sure when it is, the argument has not less force.

If a man has a small estate, and a numerous family, where it happens that a man has as many children as he has tenants, it is not a recommending circumstance for his election. When it comes to be the question with such a man, whether he shall be just to the public or cruel to his family, it is very possible the decision may be on the side of corrupted nature. It is a compliment to this age which it does not deserve, to suppose men are so tied to morality as that they cannot be pinched out of it, especially now, when it is called starving not to be embroidered or served in plate. The men chosen to serve their country should not be laden with suits that may tempt them to assume privilege, much less under such necessities as may more immediately prepare them for corruption.

Men who need a parliament for their own particular interest have much more reason to offer their service than others have to accept it. And though I do not doubt but that there may be some whose virtue would triumph over their wants, let them be never so pressing; yet to expose the public to the hazard of being deceived, is that which can never be justified by those that choose; and though it must be allowed possible for a wanting man to be honest, yet it is impossible for a man to be wise that will depend upon it.

7. There is a sort of men that have a tinsel wit, which makes them shine amongst those who cannot judge. Club, and coffee-house gentlemen; petty merchants of small conceits, who have an empty habit of prating without meaning; they always aim at wit, and generally make false fire. Their business is less to learn than to set themselves out, which makes them choose to be with such as can only be witnesses of their small ingenuity, rather than with such as might improve it. There is a subordinate wit, as much inferior to a governing genius as the jingling of a Jew's harp is to the lofty sound of an organ.*

Men of this size are in no degree suited to the business of redressing grievances and making laws. There is a parliament wit to be distinguished from all other kinds. Those who have it do not stuff their heads only with cavils and objections. They have a deliberate and an observing wit, a head turned to public things; men who place their greater pleasure in mending a fault than in finding it. Their understanding directs them to object in the right place, and not like those who go by no other rule than to conclude, that must be the best counsel which was not taken. These wholesale judges show such a gross and peevish ignorance, and it appears so openly in all they say or do, that they give loud warning to all considering men, not to choose them.

8. The dislike of slight, airy men must not go so far as to recommend heaviness in opposition to it, especially where men are convicted of it by experience in former sessions.

As a lively coxcomb will seldom fail to lay in his claim for wit, so a blockhead is as apt to pretend that his heaviness is a proof of his judgement. Some have a universal lethargy spread upon the understanding without exception; others have an insufficiency *quoad hoc*,* as in some cases men have *quoad hanc*;* these last can never so turn their thoughts to public business as to give the attention that is necessary to comprehend it.

There are those who have such a thick shell upon the brain that their ignorance is impenetrable, and makes such a stout resistance against common sense that it will never be subdued by it: true *heart of oak* ignorance that will never yield, let reason beat never so hard upon it; and though their kind neighbours have at several elections sent them up to school again, they have still returned the same incurable dunces.

There is a false gravity that is a very ill symptom, and it may be said that as rivers which run very slowly have always the most mud at the bottom, so a solid stiffness in the constant course of a man's life is a sign of a thick bed of mud at the bottom of his brain. A dull man is so near to a dead man that he is hardly to be ranked in the list of the living; and as he is not to be buried whilst he is half alive, he is as little to be employed whilst he is half dead.

Parliaments are now grown to be quite other things than they were formerly. In ancient times, they were little more than a great assizes; a roll of grievances; Magna Carta confirmed; privileges of Holy Church preserved; so many sacks of wool given, and away. Now there are traps and gins laid for the well-meaning country gentleman; he is to grapple with the cunning of men in town, which is not a little improved by being rewarded and encouraged; so that men whose good intentions are not seconded and supported by some degree of ability are as much more dangerous as they are less criminal than cunning knaves. Their honest mistakes, for want of distinguishing, either give a countenance, or at least lessen the scandal of the injurious things that are done to the public; and with leave asked for so odd an expression, their innocent guilt is as mischievous to the laws and liberties as the most deliberate malice of those that would destroy them.

9. There is an abuse which daily increases of sending such to serve in Parliament as are scarce old enough to be sent to the university.

I would not in this restrain the definition of these boys to the age of 21.* If my opinion might take place, I should wish that none might be chosen into the House of Commons under 30, and to make some equality I should, from the same motive, think it convenient that no lord should have a vote in judicature under that age. But to leave this digression, I cannot see why the choosers should not at least make it a rule to themselves not to send any man to represent them under the age of 25, which is the time of majority in most other places of the world. Surely it is not that we are earlier plants than our neighbours; such a supposition could neither be justified by our climate, nor by the degree of latitude in which we are placed; I must therefore attribute it to the haste our ancestors had (and not without reason) to free themselves so much sooner from the severity of wardships.*

But whether this or anything else was the cause of our earlier stepping into man's estate, so it is now, that according to our laws, 21 is the age of discretion, and the young man is then vested with a *legal* how defective soever he may be in his *natural* understanding. With all this, there ought to be a difference made between coming out of pupillage, and leaping into legislatorship. It is perhaps inconvenient enough that a man should be so soon let loose to destroy his own estate, but it is yet worse that he should then have power of giving away other men's.

The law must make general rules, to which there always will be some objection. If there were triers* appointed to judge when leading strings* should be left off, many would wear them a very great while, and some perhaps even with their grey hairs, there being no small number of old boys in all times, and especially in this. It is necessary therefore to make exceptions to this general rule, where the case so much requires it, as it does in the matter in question. The ground of sending these minors to Parliament ought not to recommend the continuance of it to those who are lovers of liberty, since it was by the authority and influence of great men that their stripling sons were first received by the humble depending boroughs or the complying counties.

They called it, as many do still, the best school for young men.* Now, experience has showed us that it is like a school only in this respect, that these youngsters, when they are admitted, deserve to be whipped in it. If the House of Commons is a school, it must be so for men of a riper age; these are too young to learn there, and being elevated by a mistaken smattering in small politics, they grow too supercilious to learn anywhere else; so that instead of improving young promising plants, they are destroyed by being misplaced.

If then they do themselves hurt by it, it is surer yet, that they do the House no good by coming into it. They were not green geese that are said to have saved the Capitol;* they were certainly of full age, or else their cackling could not have been heard, so as to give warning. Indeed it looks now, since the fashion is introduced of long continued Parliaments,* as if we might plant a boy in the House with a prospect that he might continue there till he had grey hairs, and that the same sapling might have such a root as that he might grow up to be timber, without being removed. If these young men had skill enough to pitch upon somebody in the House, to whom they might resign their opinion, and upon whose judgement they might lean without reserve, there might be less objection. But to speak truth, they as little know how to choose, as they did who elected them, so that there is no other expedient left than the letting them alone.

One may say, speaking generally, that a young man's being too soon qualified for the serious business of Parliament would really be no good symptom. It is a sign of too much phlegm and too little fire. In the beginnings of age, if men have not a little more heat than is convenient, as they grow older, they will run a hazard of not having so much as is necessary. The truth is, the vigour of youth is softened and misapplied when it is not spent either in war or close study; all other courses have an idle mixture that comes to nothing, and makes them like trees which for want of pruning run up to wood, and seldom or never bear any fruit.

To conclude this head, it must be owned that there is no age of our life which does not carry arguments along with it to humble us; and therefore it would be well for the business of the world if young men would stay longer before they went into it, and old men not so long before they went out of it.

10. Next to these may be ranked a sort of superfine gentlemen, carpet-knights,* men whose heads may be said to be only appurtenances to their periwigs, which entirely engross all their care and application.

Their understanding is so strictly appropriated to their dress that no part of it is, upon pain of their utmost displeasure, to be diverted to any other use. It is not by this intended to recommend an affected clown, or to make it a necessary qualification for a Member of

Parliament that he must renounce clean linen or good manners; but surely a too earnest application to make everything sit right about them strikes too deep into their small stock of thought to allow it to furnish anything else.

To do right to these fine-spun gentlemen, business is too coarse a thing for them, which makes it an unreasonable hardship upon them to oppress them with it; so that, in tenderness to them, no less than out of care to the public, it is best to leave them to their tailors, with whom they will live in much better correspondence, when the danger is prevented of their falling out about privilege.*

11. Men of injustice and violence in their private dealings are not to be trusted by the people with a commission to treat for them in Parliament.

In the 4th. of Ed. 3,* the King commands in his writs not to choose any knights who had been guilty of crime, or maintenance.* These warm men seldom fail to run into maintenance, taken in a larger extent. It is an unnatural sound to come from a man that is arbitrary in his neighbourhood, to talk of laws and liberties at Westminster; he is not a proper vehicle for such words, which ought never to be profaned. A habitual breaker of the law, to be made one of the lawmakers, is as if the benches in Westminster Hall should be filled with men sent out of Newgate.*

Those who are of this temper cannot change their nature out of respect to their country. Quite contrary, they will less scruple to do wrong to a nation, where nobody takes it to himself, than to particular men, to whose resentments they are more immediately exposed. In short, they lie under such strong objections, that the over-balance of better men cannot altogether purify an assembly where these unclean beasts are admitted.

12. Excessive spenders and unreasonable savers are to be excluded, being both greedy from differing causes. They are both of them diseases of infection, and for that reason are not to be admitted into public assemblies. A prodigal man must be greedy, because he thinks he can never spend enough; the wretch must be so because he will never think he can hoard enough.

The world first admires men's wisdom for getting money, and then rails at them if they do not throw it away; so that the prodigal man is only the less unpopular extreme; he is every jot as well prepared as the miser to fall out with morality, when a good temptation is offered for it.

On the other side, some rich men are as eager to overtake those that are richer, as a running horse is to get to the race-post before the other that contends with him. Men often desire to heap rather because others have more, than that they know what to do with that which they covet with so much impatience; so that it is plain, the fancy has as great a share in this imaginary pleasure of gathering as it has in love, ambition, or any other passion.

It is pretty sure, that as no man was ever the richer for having a good estate if he did not look after it, neither will he be the honester if he has never so much. Want of care will always create want of money, so that whether a man is a beggar because he never had any money, or because he can never keep any, it is all one to those who are to trust him.

Upon this head of prodigality, it may be no unreasonable caution to be afraid of those who in former sessions have been extravagantly liberal of the public money. Trusting is so hazardous a thing, that it should never be done but where it is necessary; so that when trustees are found upon trial to be very lavish (even without examining into the causes of it, which are generally very suspicious), it is a reasonable part of preventing wit to change hands, or else the choosers will pay the penalty that belongs to good nature so misplaced, and the consequences will be attended with the aggravation of their not being made wiser by such a severe and costly warning.

13. It would be of very great use to take a general resolution throughout the kingdom, that none should be chosen for a county, but such as have, either in possession or reversion, a considerable estate in it; nor for a borough, except he is resident, or that he has some estate in the county, in possession or expectancy.

There have been eminent men of law who were of opinion, that in the case of a burgess of a town not resident, the court is to give judgement according to the statute, notwithstanding custom to the contrary. But not to insist now upon that, the prudential part is argument enough to set up a rule to abrogate an ill custom. There is not perhaps a greater cause of the corruption of Parliaments than the adopting Members who may be said to have no title to it by their birth. The juries are by the law to be *ex vicineto*,* and shall there be less care that the representatives of the people shall be so too? Surely the interest of the county is best placed in the hands of such as have some share in it. The outliers are not so easily kept within the pale of the laws.

They are often chosen without being known, which is more like choosing valentines,* than Members of Parliament. The motive of their standing may be rather supposed that they may redress their own grievances, which they know, than those of the county, to which they are strangers. They are chosen at London to serve in Cornwall, &c., and are often parties, before they come to be representatives. One would think the reproach it is to a county not to have men within their own circle to serve them in Parliament should be argument enough to reject these trespassers, without urging the ill consequences in other respects of their being admitted.

14. As in some cases it is advisable to give a total exclusion to men not fitly qualified, so in others it is more proper to lay down a general rule of caution, with allowance of some exceptions where men have given such proofs of themselves as create a right for them to be distinguished. Of this nature is that which I shall say concerning lawyers, who, by the same reason that they may be useful, may be also very dangerous.

The negligence and want of application in gentlemen has made them to be thought more necessary than naturally they are in Parliament. They have not only engrossed the chair of the Speaker, but that of a committee is hardly thought to be well filled except it be by a man of the Robe.* This makes it worthy of the more serious reflection of all gentlemen, that it may be an argument to them to qualify themselves in parliamentary learning in such a manner, as that they may rely upon their own abilities in order to the serving their country.

But to come to the point in question, it is not without precedent that practising lawyers have been excluded from serving in Parliament,* and without following those patterns strictly, I cannot but think it reasonable that whilst a Parliament sits no Member should plead at any Bar. The reason of it is in many respects strong in itself, and is grown much stronger by the long sittings of Parliaments of late; but I will not dwell upon this, the matter now in question being concerning lawyers being elected, which I conceive should be done with so much circumspection, that probably it would not often happen.

If lawyers have great practice, that ought to take them up; if they have not, it is no great sign of their ability, and at the same time gives a suspicion that they may be more liable to be tempted. If it should be so in fact, that no king ever wanted judges, to soften the stiffness of the laws that were made, so as to make them suit better with the reason of state and the convenience of the government, it is no injury now to suppose it possible for lawyers in the House of Commons so to behave themselves in the making new laws, as the better to make way for the having their robes lined with fur.*

They are men used to argue on both sides of a question; and if ordinary fees can inspire them with very good reasons in a very ill cause, that faculty exercised in Parliament, where it may be better encouraged, may prove very inconvenient to those that choose them. And therefore, without arraigning a profession that it would be scandalous for a man not to honour, one may, by a suspicion which is the more excusable when it is in behalf of the people, imagine that the habit of taking money for their opinion may create in some such a forgetfulness to distinguish, that they may take it for their vote.

They are generally men who by a laborious study hope to be advanced; they have it in their eye as a reward for the toil they undergo. This makes them very slow and ill disposed (let the occasion never so much require it) to wrestle with the government, which is the only soil where preferment grows. Now, if the supposition is in itself not unreasonable, and that it should happen to be strengthened and confirmed by experience, it will be very unnecessary to say any more upon this article, but leave it to the electors to consider it.

15. I cannot forbear to put in a caveat against men tied to a party.

There must in everybody be a leaning to that sort of men who profess some principles, more than to others who go upon a different foundation; but when a man is drowned in a party, plunged in it beyond his depth, he runs a great hazard of being upon ill terms with good sense or morality, if not with both of them. Such a man can hardly be called a free agent, and for that reason is very unfit to be trusted with the people's liberty, after he has given up his own.

It is said that in some part of the Indies they do so affect little feet that they keep them squeezed whilst they are children, so that they stay at that small size when they are grown men. One may say something like this of men locked up in a party; they put their thoughts into such a narrow mould, that they can never be enlarged, nor released from their first confinement.

Men in a party have liberty only for their motto; in reality, they are greater slaves than anybody else would care to make them. A party, even in times of peace, and though against the original contract and the bill of rights, sets up and continues the exercise of martial law; once enrolled, the man that quits, if they had their will, would be hanged for a deserter.

They communicate anger to one another by contagion; and it may be said that if too much light dazzles the eyesight, too much heat does not less weaken the judgement. Heat reigns in the fancy, and reason, which is a colder faculty of the brain, takes more time to be heard than the other will allow. The heat of a party is like the burning of a fever, not a natural warmth evenly distributed to give life and vigour. There was a time indeed when anger might be a sign of honesty, but that evidence is very much weakened by instances we have seen of late; and the public-spirited choler is grown yet to have less credit with the people, since the government has thought fit to make it a step to preferment.

A strong, blustering wind seldom continues long in one corner. Some men knock loud, only to be let in; the bustle they make is animated by their private interest; the outward blaze only is for religion and liberty; the true lasting fire, like that of the vestals which never went out,* is an eagerness to get somewhat for themselves. A House of Commons composed of such men would be more properly so many merchants incorporated in a regulated company, to make their particular adventures, than men sent from the people to serve and to represent them.

There are some splenetic gentlemen who confine their favourable opinion within so narrow a compass that they will not allow it to any man that was not hanged in the late reigns. Now, by that rule, one might expect they should rescue themselves from the disadvantage of being *now* alive, and by abdicating a world so little worthy of them, get a great name to themselves, with the general satisfaction of all those they would leave behind them.*

Amongst the many other ill consequences of a stated party, it is not the least, that it tempts low and insignificant men to come upon the stage, to expose themselves, and to spoil business. It turns a cypher into a figure, such a one as it is; a man in a party is able to make a noise, let it be never so empty a sound. A weak man is easily blown out of his small senses, by being mustered into a party; he is flattered till he likes himself so well that he takes it extremely ill if he has not an employment. Nothing is more in fashion than for men to desire good places, and I doubt nothing is less so than to deserve them. From nobody to somebody is such a violent stride that Nature, which has the negative voice, will not give its royal assent to it; so that when insufficient men aim at being in business, the worst of their enemies might, out of malice to them, pray for their preferment.

There would be no end, if one did not stop till this theme had no more matter to furnish. I will only say, nothing is more evident than that the good of the nation has been sacrificed to the animosities of the several contending parties, and without entering into the dispute, which of them are more or less in the right, it is pretty sure that whilst these opposite sets of angry men are playing at football, they will break all the windows, and do more hurt than their pretended zeal for the nation will ever make amends for.

In short, a man so engaged is retained before the people take him for their counsel; he has such a reserve for his party, that it is not advisable for those who would choose him to depend upon his professions; all parties assuming such a dispensing power that by their sovereign authority they cancel and dissolve any act or promise that they do not afterwards approve.

These things considered, those who will choose such men deserve whatever follows.

16. Pretenders to exorbitant merit in the late Revolution are not without objections to them when they stand to serve in Parliament.

It would not only be a low but a criminal kind of envy to deny a distinguishing justice to men who have been instrumental and active, when the service of their country required it; but there ought to be moderation in men's claims, or else it is out of the power of our poor island to satisfy them. It is true, service of all kinds is grown much dearer, like labourers' wages, which formerly occasioned several statutes to regulate them; but now the men who only carried mortar to the building, when it is finished, think they are ill dealt with if they are not made master workmen. They presently cry out, the original contract is broken, if their merit is not rewarded, and at their own rate too.

Some will think there never ought to be an end of their reward, when indifferent judges would perhaps be puzzled to find out the beginning of their merit. They bring in such large bills, that they must be examined; some bounds must be put to men's pretensions, else the nation, which is to pay the reckoning, will every way think it a scurvy thing to be undone, whether it be by being over-run by our enemies, or by the being exhausted by our friends.

There ought therefore to be deductions where they are reasonable, the better to justify the paying what remains. For example, if any of these passionate lovers of the Protestant religion should not think fit, in their manner of living, to give the least evidence of their morality, their claims upon that head might sure be struck off without any injustice to them. If there are any who set down great sums as a reward due to their zeal for rescuing property from the jaws of arbitrary power, their pretensions may fairly be rejected, if now they are so far from showing a care and tenderness of the laws, that they look rather like counsel retained on the other side.

It is not less strange than I doubt it is true, that some men should be so in love with their mistress *Old England*, with all her wrinkles, as out of a heroic passion, to swim over to rescue her from being ravished, and when they have done the feat, the first thing after enjoyment is, that they go about to strangle her. For the sake of true love, it is not fit that such ungentle gallants should be too much encouraged; and their arrogance for having done well at first will have no right to be excused, if their so doing ill at last does not make them a little more modest.*

True merit, like a river, the deeper it is, the less noise it makes. These loud proclaimers of their own deserts are not only to be suspected for their truth, but the electors are to consider that such meritorious men lay an assessment upon those that choose them. The public taxes are already heavy enough without the addition of these private reckonings. It is therefore the safer way not to employ men who will expect more for their wages than the mistaken borough that sends them up to Parliament could be sold for.

17. With all due regard to the noblest of callings, military officers are out of their true element when they are misplaced in a House of Commons.

Things in this world ought to be well suited; there are some appearances so unnatural that men are convinced by them, without any other argument. The very habit in some cases recommends or gives offence. If the judges upon the bench should, instead of their furs, which signify gravity and bespeak respect, be clothed like the jockeys at Newmarket,* or wear jackboots and steenkirks,* they would not in reality have less law, but mankind would be so struck with this unusual object, that it would be a great while before they could think it possible to receive justice from men so accoutred. It is to some degree the same thing in this case; such martial habits, blue coats, red stockings, &c. make them look very unlike grave senators. One would almost swear they were creatures apart, and of a differing species from the rest of the body.

In former times, when only the resident shopkeeper was to represent his corporation (which by the way is the law still at this day), the military looks of one of these sons of Mars would have stared the quaking Member down again to his borough. Now the number of them is so increased that the peaceable part of the House may lawfully swear they are in fear of their lives from such an awful appearance of men of war.

It makes the room look like a guardhouse, by such an ill-suited mixture; but this is only the outside, the bark of the argument; the root goes yet deeper against choosing such men, whose talents ought to be otherwise applied. Their two capacities are so inconsistent, that men's undertaking to serve both the cures will be the cause in a little time, that we shall neither have men of war nor men of business good in their several kinds.

An officer is to give up his liberty to obey orders, and it is necessarily incident to his calling that he should do so; a Member of Parliament is originally to be tender of his own liberty, that other men may the better trust him with theirs.

An officer is to enable himself by his courage improved by skill and experience, to support the laws (if invaded) when they are made; but he is not supposed to be at leisure enough to understand and judge how they should be made. A Member of Parliament is to fill his thoughts with what may best conduce to the civil administration, which is enough to take up the whole man, let him be never so much raised above the ordinary level.

These two opposite qualifications, being placed in one man, make him such an ambiguous, divided creature that he does not know how to move. It is best to keep men within their proper sphere. Few men have understanding enough exactly to fill even one narrow circle; fewer are able to fill two, especially when they are both of great compass, and that they are so contrary in their own nature.

The wages he has, as a Member, and those he receives as an officer, are paid for services that are very differing; and in the doubt which of them should be preferably performed it is likely the greater salary may direct him, without the further inducements of complying most where he may expect most advantage by it. In short, if his dependence is not very great, it will make him a scurvy officer; if it is great, it will make him a scurvier Member.

18. Men under the scandal of being thought private pensioners are too fair a mark to escape being considered in reference to the point in question. In case of plain evidence, it is not to be supposed possible that men convicted of such a crime should ever again be elected; the difficulty is in determining what is to be done in case of suspicion.

There are suspicions so well grounded that they may pretend to have the force of proofs, provided the penalty goes only to the forbearing to trust, but not extending it so far as to punish. There must be something plain and express, to justify the latter, but circumstances may be sufficient for the first; as where men have had such sudden cures of their ill humour and opposition to the court, that it is out of the way of the ordinary methods of recovery from such distempers, which have a much slower progress; it must naturally be imputed to some specific that makes such a quick alteration of the whole mass of blood. Where men have raised their way of living, without any visible means to support them in it, a suspicion is justified, even by the example of the law, which in cases of this kind, though of an inferior nature, does upon this foundation not only raise inferences but inflict punishments.

Where men are immoral and scandalous in their lives, and dispense familiarly with the rules by which the world is governed, for the better preserving the bonds of human society, it must be a confidence very ill placed to conclude it impossible for such men to yield to a temptation well offered and pursued, when the truth is, the habit of such *bons vivants*,* which is the fashionable word, makes the suspicion so likely, that it is very hard not to believe it to be true. If there should be nothing but the general report, even that is not to be neglected. Common fame is the only liar that deserves to have some respect still reserved to it; though she tells many an untruth, she often hits right, and most especially when she speaks ill of men. Her credit has sometimes been carried too far when it has gone to the divesting men of anything of which they were possessed, without more express evidence to justify such a proceeding.

If there was a doubt whether there ever was any corruption of this kind, it would alter the question; but sure that will not bear the being controverted. We are told that Charles the Fifth sent over into England 1,200,000 crowns to be distributed amongst the leading men, to encourage them to carry on elections.* Here was the Protestant religion to be bought out for a valuable consideration according to law, though not according to gospel which exalts it above any price that can be set upon it. Now, except we had reason to believe that the virtue of the world is improved since that time, we can as little doubt that such temptations may be offered, as that they may be received.

It will be owned that there is to be a great tenderness in suspecting, but it must be allowed at the same time that there ought not to be less in trusting, where the people are so much concerned; especially when the penalty upon the party suspected goes no further than a suspension of that confidence which it is necessary to have in those who are to represent the nation in Parliament.

19. I cannot omit the giving a caution against admitting men to be chosen who have places of any value.

There needs the less to be said upon this article, the truth of the proposition being supported by such plain arguments. Surely no man has such a plentiful spring of thought, as that all that flows from it is too much to be applied to the business of Parliament. It is not less sure, that a Member of Parliament, of all others, ought least to be exempted from the rule that no man should serve two masters.* It does so split a man's thoughts, that no man can know how to make a fitting distribution of them to two such differing capacities. It exposes men to be suspected and tempted more than is convenient for the public service, or for the mutual good opinion of one another which there ought to be in such an assembly. It either gives a real dependence upon the government, which is inconsistent with the necessity there is, that a Member of Parliament should be disengaged, or at least it has the appearance of it, which makes them not look like freemen, though they should have virtue enough to be so.

More reasons would lessen the weight of this last, which is that a bill to this effect, commonly called the 'Self-denying Bill',* passed even this last House of Commons. A greater demonstration of the irresistible strength of truth cannot possibly be given, so that a copy of that act in every county and borough could hardly fail of discouraging such pretenders from standing, or at least it would prevent their success, if their own modesty should not restrain them from attempting it.

20. If distinctions may be made upon particular men, or remarks fixed upon their votes in Parliament, they must be allowed in relation to those gentlemen who, for reasons best known to themselves, thought fit to be against the Triennial Bill.*

The liberty of opinion is the thing in the world that ought least to be controlled, and especially in Parliament. But as that is an undoubted assertion, it is not less so, that when men sin against their own light, give a vote against their own thought, they must not plead privilege of Parliament against the being arraigned for it by others, after they are convicted of it by themselves.

There cannot be a man who in his definition of a House of Commons will state it to be an assembly, that, for the better redressing the grievances the people feel, and for the better furnishing such supplies as they can bear, is to continue, if the King so pleases, for his whole reign. This could as little be intended, as to throw all into one hand, and to renounce the claim to any liberty but so much as the sovereign authority would allow. It destroys the end of Parliaments; it makes use of the letter of the law to extinguish the life of it. It is in truth some kind of disparagement to so plain a thing, that so much has been said and written upon it; and one may say it is such an affront to these gentlemen's understandings, to censure this vote only as a mistake that, as the age goes, it is less discredit to them to call it by its right name.* And if that is rightly understood by those who are to choose them, I suppose they will let them exercise their liberty of conscience at home, and not make men their trustees who in this solemn instance have shown such unwillingness to surrender.

It must be owned that this bill has met with very hard fortune, and yet that does not in the least diminish the value of it. It has in it such a root of life that it may be said, it is not dead, but sleeps;* it will certainly revive, and be animated by the royal assent, when more fully informed of the consequence as well as of the justice of it.

In the meantime, after having told my opinion who ought not to be chosen, if I should be asked who ought to be? my answer must be, choose Englishmen; and when I have said that, to deal honestly, I will not undertake that they are very easy to be found.

THE GOVERNMENT OF THE WORLD

SIR:

You set me a task* that in this respect is welcome to me, since it shows you have a right belief of my resignation to your commands; but you must allow me to ask you whether you have enough considered what a comprehensive question you have put, and how impossible to be complied with, if taken strictly, &c. All Mr Prynne's volumes* bound in one would not make so great a one, as this must be to give a precise answer to that question. How equal I am, &c.—even your partiality to a friend, which is the only thing that ever misled your judgement, cannot prevail with you to put that upon my shoulders, which would have made the greatest man Nature ever yet produced groan under the weight of it. I take your meaning to be, that you do not so much desire to be informed, which you do not want, as to be entertained, which you do; and concluding that a man wallowing in the idleness of a retreat had the leisure to think extravagantly upon any subject, you would give him a large theme for his thoughts to rove in; 'and to send you a kind of extract, &c.' In this sense therefore only I accept, &c., and for your diversion, I will make no scruple of exposing a rhapsody of thoughts, which may &c., and are only to make you laugh in your closet, not being calculated to bear the examination and censure of an age where malice supplies the want of &c.

1. State your question. How comes it to pass that the world has generally been so ill governed? I will first allow your supposition. My first reason is, because the world was from the beginning such a great blockhead that it could never govern itself; never the wiser for being older, not one jot improved by age. As to its understanding, it will be a minor till the dissolution of the whole frame, whenever it comes. This goes a great way, &c. The bulk of mankind, with all the reverence due to so great a name, confess they are idiots, and as such have chosen their guardians; the rulers of the world in all times have taken it in this sense, therefore do not think they are taken out of kindness, but necessity. Hang them in their own leading strings.* That which is their strength in one kind, *viz.* is their weakness in another; they

cannot agree. So that if the people had that rarity most wrongfully called 'common sense', they are so many, they could not tell what to do with it; but that not being their case, they surrender themselves at discretion, &c., so that the rulers, having the natural insolence of mankind improved by the spirit of government, have ever used them almost as ill as they deserved; not quite, for being such logs, &c.*

2. Another general reason is that there is a mistake passes, as if mankind loved liberty. The contrary is true; they love a stick. Allowing the supposition preceding, it must be true. It is really better suited to them. Where there is not reason, liberty is a grievance. It requires a great deal of thought and application to keep it; now where the rational faculty is wanting, as it is, &c. There is a distinction to be made of a rational faculty, as more comprehensive or more restrained. Men not irrational in their small separate economy, &c., but when it is to go out of that circle, they are at a loss; like some birds that can fly but at such a distance from the ground. If the shortness of their understanding is one reason, their love of sensuality is another. Slavery is fitter for that; taking mankind in the general, they are not troubled with the interruption of thinking, whilst they give themselves up to those subordinate enjoyments, &c. The luxurious climates were those that first were disgusted with liberty; it gave them so much trouble to keep, that it showed it was not a natural thing, &c.

POLITICAL THOUGHTS
AND REFLECTIONS

OF FUNDAMENTALS

EVERY party, when they find a maxim for their turn, they presently call it a Fundamental; they think they nail it with a peg of iron, whereas in truth they only tie it with a wisp of straw.

The word sounds so well that the impropriety of it has been the less observed. But as weighty as the word appears, no feather has been more blown about in the world than this word, 'Fundamental'. It is one of those mistakes that at some times may be of use, but it is a mistake still.

Fundamental is used as men use their friends; commend them when they have need of them, and when they fall out, find a hundred objections to them.

Fundamental is a pedestal that men set everything upon that they would not have broken. It is a nail everybody would use to fix that which is good for them: for all men would have that principle to be immoveable, that serves their use at the time.

Everything that is created is mortal, *ergo* all Fundamentals of human creation will die.

A true Fundamental must be like the foundation of a house; if it is undermined the whole house falls.

The Fundamentals in divinity have been changed in several ages of the world. They have made no difficulty in the several councils,* to destroy and excommunicate men for asserting things that at other times were called Fundamentals.

Philosophy, astronomy, &c. have changed their Fundamentals as the men of art no doubt called them at the time. Motion of the Earth, &c.

Even in morality one may more properly say, There *should be* Fundamentals allowed, than that there *are* any which in strictness can be maintained. However, this is the least uncertain foundation: Fundamental is less improperly applied here than anywhere else.

Wise and good men will in all ages stick to some Fundamentals, look upon them as sacred, and preserve an inviolable respect for them; but mankind in general make morality a more malleable thing than it ought to be.

There is then no certain Fundamental but in nature, and yet there are objections too. It is a Fundamental in nature that the son should not kill the father, and yet the Senate of Venice gave a reward to a son who brought in his father's head, according to a proclamation.*

*Salus Populi** is an unwritten law, yet that does not hinder but that it is sometimes very visible; and as often as it is so, it supersedes all other laws which are subordinate things compared.

The great punishments upon self-murder are arguments that it was rather a tempting sin to be discouraged than an unnatural act.

It is a Fundamental that where a man intends no hurt he should receive none, yet manslaughter, &c. are cases of mercy.

That a boy under 10 shall not suffer death, yet where *malitia supplet ætatem,** otherwise.

That there were witches—much shaken of late.

That the king is not to be deceived in his grant—the practical Fundamental the contrary.

That what is given to God cannot be alienated. Yet in practice it is, by treaties, &c. and even by the Church itself, when they get a better bargain by it.

I can make no other definition of a true Fundamental than this: *viz.* That whatever a man has a desire to do or to hinder, if he has uncontested and irresistible power to effect it, that he will certainly do it. If he thinks he has that power, though he has it not, he will certainly go about it.

Some would define a Fundamental to be the settling the laws of nature and common equity in such a sort as that they may be well administered: even in this case there can be nothing fixed, but it must vary for the good of the whole.

A constitution cannot make itself; somebody made it, not at once but at several times. It is alterable; and by that draws nearer perfection; and without suiting itself to differing times and circumstances, it could not live. Its life is prolonged by changing seasonably the several parts of it at several times.

The reverence that is given to a Fundamental, in a general unintelligible notion, would be much better applied to that supremacy or power which is set up in every nation in differing shapes, that alters the constitution as often as the good of the people requires it.

Neither king nor people would now like just the original constitution, without any varyings.

If kings are only answerable to God, that does not secure them even in this world; since if God upon the appeal thinks fit not to stay, he makes the people his instruments.

I am persuaded that wherever any single man had power to do himself right upon a deceitful trustee, he would do it. That thought well digested would go a great way towards the discouraging invasions upon rights, &c.

I lay down then as a Fundamental, 1st, that in every constitution there is some power which neither will nor ought to be bounded.

2. That the king's prerogative should be as plain a thing as the people's obedience.

3. That a power which may by parity of reason destroy the whole law, can never be reserved by the laws.

4. That in all limited governments it must give the governor power to hurt, but it can never be so interpreted as to give him power to destroy, for then in effect it would cease to be a limited government.

5. That severity be rare and great; for as Tacitus says of Nero, 'Frequent punishments made the people call even his justice cruelty.'*

6. That it is necessary to make the instruments of power easy, for power is hard enough to be digested by those under it at the best.

7. That the people are never so perfectly backed,* but that they will kick and fling if not stroked at seasonable times.

8. That a prince must think if he loses his people he can never regain them. It is both wise and safe to think so.

9. That kings assuming prerogative teach the people to do so too.

10. That prerogative is a trust.

11. That they are not the king's laws, nor the parliament's laws, but the laws of England, in which after they have passed by the legislative power, the people have the property, and the king the executive part.

12. That no abilities should qualify a noted knave to be employed in business. A knave can by none of his dexterities make amends for the scandal he brings upon the Crown.

13. That those who will not be bound by the laws, rely upon crimes: a third way was never found in the world to secure any government.

14. That a seaman be a seaman; a cabinet-counsellor a man of business; an officer, an officer.

15. In corrupted governments the place is given for the sake of the man; in good ones the man is chosen for the sake of the place.

16. That crowds at court are made up of such as would deceive: the real worshippers are few.

17. That *Salus Populi* is the greatest of all Fundamentals, yet not altogether an immoveable one. It is a Fundamental for a ship to ride at anchor when it is in port, but if a storm comes the cable must be cut.

18. Property is not a Fundamental right in one sense, because in the beginning of the world there was none, so that property itself was an innovation introduced by laws.

Property is only secured by trusting it in the best hands, and those are generally chosen who are least likely to deceive; but if they should, they have a legal authority to abuse as well as use the power with which they are trusted, and there is no Fundamental can stand in their way, or be allowed as an exception to the authority that was vested in them.

19. Magna Carta would fain be made to pass for a Fundamental; and Sir Edward Coke would have it, that the Grand Charter was for the most part declaratory of the principal grounds of the fundamental laws of England.* If that refers to the common law, it must be made out that everything in Magna Carta is always and at all times necessary in itself to be kept, or else the denying a subsequent parliament the right of repealing any law does by consequence deny the preceding parliament the right of making it. But they are fain to say it was only a declarative law, which is very hard to be proved. Yet suppose it, you must either make the common law so stated a thing that all men know it beforehand, or else universally acquiesce in it whenever it is alleged, from the affinity it has to the law of nature. Now I would fain know whether the Common Law* is capable of being defined, and whether it does not hover in the clouds like the prerogative, and bolts out like lightning to be made use of for some particular occasion? If so, the government of the world is left to a thing that cannot be defined; and if it cannot be defined, you know not what it is; so that the supreme appeal is, we know not what. We submit to God Almighty though he is incomprehensible, and yet he has set down his methods; but for this world, there can be no government

without a stated rule, and a supreme power not to be controlled neither by the dead nor the living.

The laws under the protection of the king govern in the ordinary administration; the extraordinary power is in acts of Parliament, from whence there can be no appeal but to the same power at another time.

To say a power is supreme, and not arbitrary, is not sense. It is acknowledged supreme, and therefore, &c.

If the common law is supreme, then those are so who judge what is the common law; and if none but the Parliament can judge so, there is an end of the controversy; there is no Fundamental; for the Parliament may judge as they please; that is, they have the authority, but they may judge against right, their power is good, though their act is ill; no good man will outwardly resist the one, or inwardly approve the other.

There is then no other Fundamental, but that every supreme power must be arbitrary.

Fundamental is a word used by the laity, as the word sacred is by the clergy, to fix everything to themselves they have a mind to keep, that nobody else may touch it.

OF PRINCES

A PRINCE who will not undergo the difficulty of understanding must undergo the danger of trusting.

A wise prince may gain such an influence, that his countenance would be the last appeal. Where it is not so in some degree, his authority is precarious. A prince must keep up the power of his countenance, which is not the least of his prerogatives.

The conscience, as well as the prerogative of a king, must be restrained or loosened as is best for his people. It may without scandal be made of stretching leather, but it must be drawn by a steady hand.

A king that lets intercession prevail will not be long worshipped.

A prince used to war gets a military logic that is not very well suited to the civil administration. If he makes war successfully, he grows into a demigod; if without success, the world throws him as much below humanity as they had before set him above it.

A hero must be sometimes allowed to make bold strokes, without being fettered by strict reason. He is to have some generous irregularities in his reasoning, or else he will not be a good thing of his kind.

PRINCES (THEIR REWARDS OF SERVANTS)

WHEN a prince gives any man a very extravagant reward, it looks as if it was rather for an ill thing than a good one. Both the giver and receiver are out of countenance where they are ill-suited, and ill-applied.

Serving princes will make men proud at first, and humble at last.

Resolving to serve well, and at the same time resolving to please, is generally resolving to do what is not to be done. A man that will serve well must often rule the master so hard that it will hurt him.

It is thought an unsociable quality in a court to do one's duty better than other men. Nothing is less forgiven than setting patterns men have no mind to follow.

Men are so unwilling to displease a prince, that it is as dangerous to inform him right, as to serve him wrong. Where men get by pleasing, and lose by serving, the choice is so easy that nobody can miss it.

PRINCES, THEIR SECRETS

MEN are so proud of princes' secrets, that they will not see the danger of them. When a prince trusts a man with a dangerous secret, he would not be sorry to hear the bell toll for him.

LOVE OF THE SUBJECTS TO A PRINCE

THE heart of the subjects yields but a lean crop where it is not cultivated by a wise prince. The goodwill of the governed will be starved, if it is not fed by the good conduct of the governors.

SUFFERING FOR PRINCES

THOSE who merit because they suffered, are so very angry with those that made them suffer, that though their services may deserve employment, their temper renders them unfit for it.

OF MINISTERS

THE world deals with ministers of state as they do with ill fiddlers, ready to kick them downstairs for playing ill, though few of the fault-finders understand their music enough to be good judges.

A minister who undertakes to make his master very great, if he fails, is ruined for his folly; if he succeeds, he is feared for his skill.

A good statesman may sometimes mistake as much by being too humble as by being too proud: he must take upon him in order to do his duty, and not in order to the setting himself out.

A minister is not to plead the king's command for such things as he may in justice be supposed to have directed.

It is dangerous to serve where the master has the privilege not to be blamed.

It is hard for a prince to esteem the parts of a minister without either envying or fearing them; and less dangerous for a minister to show all the weakness than all the strength of his understanding.

There are so many things necessary to make up a good minister, that no wonder there are so few of them in the world. There is hardly a rasher thing, than for a man to venture to be a good minister.

A minister of state must have a spirit of liberal economy, not a restrained frugality. He must enlarge his family soul, and suit it to the bigger compass of a kingdom.

A prince should be asked, why he *will* do a thing, but not why he *has* done it.

If the boys were to choose a schoolmaster, it should be one that would not whip them; the same thing if the courtiers were to choose a minister. They would have a great many play-days, no rods, and leave to rob orchards.—The parallel will hold.

WICKED MINISTERS

A CUNNING minister will engage his master to begin with a small wrong step, which will insensibly engage him in a great one. A man that has the patience to go by steps, may deceive one much wiser than himself.

State business is a cruel trade; good nature is a bungler in it.

INSTRUMENTS OF STATE MINISTERS

MEN in business are in as much danger from those that work under them, as from those that work against them.

When the instruments bend under the weight of their business, it is like a weak-legged horse that brings his rider down with him. As when they are too weak they let a man fall, so when they are too strong they throw him off.

If men of business did not forget how apt their tools are to break or fail, they would shut up shop. They must use things called *men* under them, who will spoil the best scheme that can be drawn by human understanding. Tools that are blunt cannot cut at all, and those that are sharp are apt to cut in the wrong place.

Great difference between a good tool and a good workman. When the tools will be workmen they cut their own fingers, and everybody else's.

OF THE PEOPLE

THERE is more strength in union than in number; witness the people that in all ages have been scurvily used, because they could so seldom agree to do themselves right. 'The more the weaker' may be as good a proverb as 'The more the merrier'.

A people can no more stand without government, than a child can go without leading-strings: as old and as big as a nation is, it can't go by itself, and must be led. The numbers that make its strength are at the same time the cause of its weakness and incapacity of acting.

Men have so discovered themselves to one another that union is become a mere word, in reality impracticable. They trust, or suspect, not upon reason but ill-grounded fame; they would be at ease, saved, protected, &c. and give nothing for it.

The lower sort of men must be indulged the consolation of finding fault with those above them; without that, they would be so melancholy that it would be dangerous, considering their numbers. They are too many to be told of their mistakes, and for that reason they are never to be cured of them.

The body of the people are generally either so dead that they cannot move, or so mad that they cannot be reclaimed: to be neither all in a flame, nor quite cold, requires more reason than great numbers can ever attain.

The people can seldom agree to move together against a government, but they can to sit still and let it be undone.

Those that will be martyrs for the people must expect to be repaid only by their vanity, or their virtue.

A man that will head the mob is like a bull let loose, tied about with squibs and crackers. He must be half mad that goes about it, yet at some times shall be too hard for all the wise men in a kingdom: for though good sense speaks against madness, yet it is out of countenance whenever it meets it.

It would be a greater reproach to the people that their favour is short-lived, if their malice was not so too. The thoughts of the people have no regular motion, they come out by starts.

There is an accumulative cruelty in a number of men, though none in particular are ill-natured. The angry buzz of a multitude is one of the bloodiest noises in the world.

OF GOVERNMENT

AN EXACT administration and good choice of proper instruments does insensibly make the government in a manner absolute without assuming it.

The best definition of the best government is, that it has no inconveniences but such as are supportable; but inconveniences there must be.

The interest of the governors and the governed is in reality the same, but by mistakes on both sides it is generally very differing. He who is a courtier by trade, and the country gentleman who will be popular, right or wrong, help to keep up this unreasonable distinction.

There are as many apt to be angry at being well, as at being ill governed. For most men, to be well governed, must be scurvily used.

As mankind is made, the keeping it in order is an ill-natured office. It is like a great galley where the officers must be whipping with little intermission, if they will do their duty.

It is in a disorderly government as in a river, the lightest things swim at the top.

A nation is best to be judged by the government it is under at the time. Mankind is moulded to good or ill, according as the power over it is well or ill directed. A nation is a mass of dough, it is the government that kneads it into form.

Where learning and trade flourish in a nation, they produce so much knowledge, and that so much equality among men, that the greatness of dependencies is lost, but the nation in general will be the better for it. For if the government be wise, it is the more easily governed; if not, the bad government is the more easily overturned, by men's being more united against it than when they depended upon great men, who might sooner be gained over and weakened by being divided.

There is more reason for allowing luxury in a military government than in another; the perpetual exercise of war not only excuses but recommends the entertainments in the winter. In another it grows into a habit of uninterrupted expenses and idle follies, and the consequences of them to a nation become irrecoverable.

CLERGY

IF the clergy did not live like temporal men, all the power of princes could not bring them under the temporal jurisdiction. They who may be said to be of God Almighty's household should show by their lives that he has a well-disciplined family.

The clergy, in this sense, of divine institution; that God has made mankind so weak that it must be deceived.

RELIGION

IT is a strange thing that the way to save men's souls should be such a cunning trade, as to require a skilful master.

The time spent in praying to God, might be better employed in deserving well from him. Men think praying the easier task of the two, and therefore choose it.

The people would not believe in God at all, if they were not permitted to believe wrong in him.

The several sorts of religion in the world are little more than so many spiritual monopolies. If their interests could be reconciled, their opinions would be so too.

Men pretend to serve God Almighty who does not need it, but make use of him because they need him.

Factions are like pirates that set out false colours; when they come near a booty religion is put under deck.

Most men's anger about religion is as if two men should quarrel for a lady, they neither of them care for.

OF PREROGATIVE, POWER AND LIBERTY

A PREROGATIVE that tends to the dissolution of all laws must be void in itself, *felo de se*;* for a prerogative is a law. The reason of any law is, that no man's will should be a law.

The king is the life of the law, and cannot have a prerogative that is mortal to it.

The law is to have a soul in it, or it is a dead thing. The king is by his sovereign power to add warmth and vigour to the meaning of the law. We are by no means to imagine there is such an antipathy between them, that the prerogative, like a basilisk,* is to kill the law whenever it looks upon it.

The prince has very rarely use of his prerogative, but has constantly a great advantage by the laws.

They attribute to the Pope indeed, that all the laws of the Church are in his breast; but then he has the Holy Ghost for his learned counsel, &c.

The people's obedience must be plain, and without evasions. The prince's prerogative should be so too.

King Charles the First made this answer to the Petition of Right* (to the observation whereof he held himself obliged in conscience, as well as of his prerogative), 'That the People's Liberties strengthen the King's Prerogative, and the King's Prerogative is to defend the People's Liberties.'

That Prince's declarations allow the original of government to come from the people.

Prerogative never yet pretended to repealing.*

The first ground of prerogative was to enable the prince to do *good*, not to do *everything*.

If the ground of a king's desire of power be his assurance of himself that he will do no hurt by it, is it not an argument for subjects to desire to keep that which they will never abuse?

It must not be such a prerogative as gives the government the rickets; all the nourishment to go to the upper part, and the lower starved.

As a prince is in danger who calls a stronger than himself to his assistance; so when prerogative uses necessity for an argument, it calls in a stronger thing than itself. The same reason may overturn it. Necessity too is so plain a thing, that everybody sees it, so that the magistrate has no great privilege in being the judge of it. Necessity therefore is a dangerous argument for princes, since (wherever it is real) it constitutes every man a magistrate, and gives as great a power of dispensing to every private man, as a prince can claim.

It is not so proper to say that prerogative justifies force, as that force supports prerogative. They have not been such constant friends, but that they have had terrible fallings out.

All powers are of God; and between permission and appointment, well considered, there is no real difference.

In a limited monarchy, prerogative and liberty are as jealous of one another as any two neighbouring states can be of their respective encroachments. They ought not to part for small bickerings, and must bear little jealousies without breaking for them.

Power is so apt to be insolent, and liberty to be saucy, that they are very seldom upon good terms. They are both so quarrelsome that they will not easily enter into a fair treaty. For indeed it is hard to bring them together; they ever quarrel at a distance.

Power and liberty are respectively managed in the world in a manner not suitable to their value and dignity. They are both so abused that it justifies the satires that are generally made upon them. And they are so in possession of being misapplied, that instead of censuring their being abused, it is more reasonable to wonder whenever they are not so.

They are perpetually wrestling, and have had their turns when they have been thrown, to have their bones broken by it. If they were not both apt to be out of breath, there would be no living.

If prerogative will urge reason to support it, it must bear reason when it resists it. It is a diminution instead of a glory, to be above treating upon equal terms with reason.

If the people were designed to be the sole property of the supreme magistrate, sure God would have made them of a differing and subordinate species; as he has the beasts, that by the inferiority of their nature they might the better submit to the dominion of mankind.

If none were to have liberty but those who understand what it is, there would not be many freed men in the world.

When the people contend for their liberty, they seldom get anything by their victory but new masters. Liberty can neither be got, nor kept, but by so much care, that mankind generally are unwilling to give the price for it. And therefore, in the contest between ease and liberty, the first has generally prevailed.

OF LAWS

LAWS are generally not understood by three sorts of persons, *viz.* by those that make them, by those that execute them, and by those that suffer if they break them.

Men seldom understand any laws but those they feel. Precepts, like fomentations, must be rubbed into us; and with a rough hand too.

If the laws could speak for themselves, they would complain of the lawyers in the first place.

There is more learning now required to explain a law made, than went to the making it.

The law has so many contradictions, and varyings from itself, that the law may not improperly be called a lawbreaker. It is become too changeable a thing to be defined: it is made little less a mystery than the Gospel. The clergy and the lawyers, like the freemasons, may be supposed to take an oath not to tell the secret.

The men of law have a bias to their calling in the interpretations they make of the law.

OF PARLIAMENTS

THE parliaments are so altered from their original constitution, that between the court and the country, the House, instead of being united, is like troops of a contrary party facing one another, and watching their advantage. Even the well-meaning men who have good sense too, have their difficulties in an assembly; what they offer honestly for a good end, will be skilfully improved for an ill one.

It is strange that a gross mistake should live a minute in an assembly; one would expect that it should be immediately stifled by their discerning faculties. But practice convinces that a mistake is nowhere better entertained.

In parliaments, men wrangle in behalf of liberty, that do as little care for it, as they deserve it.

Where the people in parliament give a good deal of money in exchange for anything from the Crown, a wise prince can hardly have an ill bargain. The present gift begets more; it is a politic kind of generation; and whenever a parliament does not bring forth, it is the unskilfulness of the government that is the cause of the miscarriage.

Parliaments would bind and limit one another, and enact that such and such things shall not be made precedents. There is not a word of sense in this language, which yet is to be understood the sense of the nation, and is printed as solemnly as if it was sense.

OF PARTIES

THE best party is but a kind of a conspiracy against the rest of the nation. They put everybody else out of their protection. Like the Jews to the Gentiles, all others are the offscourings of the world.

Men value themselves upon their principles, so as to neglect practice, abilities, industry, &c.

Party cuts off one half of the world from the other, so that the mutual improvement of men's understanding by conversing, &c. is lost, and men are half undone, when they lose the advantage of knowing what their enemies think of them.

It is like faith without works; they take it for a dispensation from all other duties, which is the worst kind of dispensing power.

It grows to be the master thought; the eagerness against one another at home, being a nearer object, extinguishes that which we ought to have against our foreign enemies; and few men's understandings can get above overvaluing the danger that is nearest, in comparison of that more remote.

It turns all thought into talking instead of doing. Men get a habit of being unuseful to the public by turning in a circle of wrangling and railing, which they cannot get out of. And it may be remarked, that a speculative coxcomb is not only unuseful, but mischievous: a practical coxcomb under discipline may be made use of.

It makes a man thrust his understanding into a corner, and confine it till by degrees he destroys it.

Party is generally an effect of wantonness, peace, and plenty, which beget humour, pride, &c. and that is called zeal and public spirit.

They forget insensibly that there is anybody in the world but themselves, by keeping no other company; so they miscalculate cruelly. And thus parties mistake their strength by the same reason that private men overvalue themselves; for we by finding fault with others, build up a partial esteem of ourselves upon the foundation of their mistakes. So men in parties find faults with those in the administration, not without reason, but forget that they would be exposed to the same objections, and perhaps greater, if it was their adversary's turn to have the fault-finding part.

There are men who shine in a faction, and make a figure by opposition, who would stand in a worse light, if they had the preferments they struggle for.

It looks so like courage (but nothing that is like is the same) to go to the extreme, that men are carried away with it, and blown up out of their senses by the wind of popular applause. That which looks bold is a great object that the people can discern; but that which is wise is not so easily seen. It is one part of it that it is not seen, but at the end of a design. Those who are disposed to be wise too late, are apt to be valiant too early.

Most men enter into a party rashly, and retreat from it as shamefully. As they encourage one another at first, so they betray one another at last; and because every qualification is capable of being corrupted by the excess, they fall upon the extreme, to fix mutual reproaches upon one another.

Party is little less than an inquisition, where men are under such a discipline in carrying on the common cause as leaves no liberty of private opinion.

It is hard to produce an instance where a party did ever succeed against a government, except they had a good handle given them.

No original party ever prevailed in a turn; it brought up something else, but the first projectors were thrown off.

If there are two parties, a man ought to adhere to that which he dislikes least, though in the whole he does not approve it; for whilst he does not list himself in one or the other party, he is looked upon as such a straggler that he is fallen upon by both. Therefore a man under such a misfortune of singularity is neither to provoke the world, nor disquiet himself, by taking any particular station. It becomes him to live in the shade, and keep his mistakes from giving offence; but if they are his opinions, he cannot put them off as he does his clothes. Happy those who are convinced so as to be of the general opinions.

Ignorance makes most men go into a party, and shame keeps them from getting out of it.

More men hurt others, they do not know why, than for any reason.

If there was any party entirely composed of honest men, it would certainly prevail; but both the honest men and the knaves resolve to turn one another off when the business is done. They by turns defame all England, so nobody can be employed that has not been branded: there are few things so criminal as a place.*

OF COURTS

The court may be said to be a company of well-bred fashionable beggars.

At court, if a man has too much pride to be a creature,* he had better stay at home: a man who will rise at court must begin by creeping upon all fours; a place at court, like a place in heaven, is to be got by being much upon one's knees.

There are hardly two creatures of a more differing species than the same man, when he is pretending to a place, and when he is in possession of it.

Men's industry is spent in receiving the rents of a place; there is little left for discharging the duty of it.

Some places have such a corrupting influence upon the man, that it is a supernatural thing to resist it. Some places lie so fair to entertain corruption, that it looks like renouncing a due perquisite not to go into it.

If a getting fool would keep out of business, he would grow richer in a court than a man of sense.

One would wonder that in a court where there is so little kindness, there should be so much whispering.

Men must brag of kind letters from court, at the same time that they do not believe one word of them.

Men at court think so much of their own cunning, that they forget other men's.

After a revolution,* you see the same men in the drawing room, and within a week the same flatterers.

OF PUNISHMENT

WHEREVER a government knows when to show the rod, it will not often be put to use it. But between the want of skill, and the want of honesty, faults generally either escape punishment, or are mended to no purpose.

Men are not hanged for stealing horses, but that horses may not be stolen.

Wherever a knave is not punished, an honest man is laughed at.

A cheat to the public is thought infamous, and yet to accuse him is not thought an honourable part. What a paradox! It is an ill method, to make the aggravation of the crime a security against the punishment; so that the danger is not to rob, but not to rob enough.

Treason must not be inlaid work of several pieces, it must be an entire piece of itself. 'Accumulative' in that case is a murdering word, that carries injustice, and no sense in it.*

An inference, though never so rational, should go no further than to justify a suspicion, not so far as to inflict a punishment. Nothing is so apt to break with stretching as an inference; and nothing so ridiculous, as to see how fools will abuse one.

MORAL THOUGHTS AND REFLECTIONS

OF THE WORLD

IT is from the shortness of thought that men imagine there is any great variety in the world. Time has thrown a veil upon the faults of former ages, or else we should see the same deformities we condemn in the present times.

When a man looks upon the rules that are made, he will think there can be no faults in the world; and when he looks upon the faults, there are so many he will be tempted to think there are no rules. They are not to be reconciled, otherwise than by concluding that which is called frailty is the incurable nature of mankind.

A man that understands the world must be weary of it; and a man who does not, for that reason ought not to be pleased with it. The uncertainty of what is to come is such a dark cloud that neither reason nor religion can quite break through it; and the condition of mankind is to be weary of what we do know, and afraid of what we do not.

The world is beholden to generous mistakes for the greatest part of the good that is done in it. Our vices and virtues couple with one another, and get children that resemble both their parents.

If a man can hardly inquire into a thing he undervalues, how can a man of good sense take pains to understand the world?

To understand the world, and to like it, are two things not easily to be reconciled.

That which is called an able man is a great overvaluer of the world, and all that belongs to it. All that can be said of him is, that he makes the best of the general mistake.

It is the fools and the knaves that make the wheels of the world turn. They *are* the world; those few who have sense or honesty sneak up and down single, but never go in herds.

To be too much troubled is a worse way of overvaluing the world than the being too much pleased.

A man that steps aside from the world, and has leisure to observe it without interest or design, thinks all mankind as mad as they think him, for not agreeing with them in their mistakes.

OF AMBITION

THE serious folly of wise men in overvaluing the world is as contemptible as anything they think fit to censure.

The first mistake belonging to business* is the going into it. Men make it such a point of honour to be fit for business that they forget to examine whether business is fit for a man of sense.

There is reason to think the most celebrated philosophers would have been bunglers at business; but the reason is because they despised it. It is not a reproach but a compliment to learning to say that great scholars are less fit for business; since the truth is, business is so much a lower thing than learning, that a man used to the last cannot easily bring his stomach down to the first. The government of the world is a great thing; but it is a very coarse one too, compared with the fineness of speculative knowledge.

The dependence of a great man upon a greater, is a subjection that lower men cannot easily comprehend. Ambition has no mean, it is either upon all fours or upon tiptoes. Nothing can be humbler than ambition, when it is so disposed.

Popularity is a crime from the moment it is sought; it is only a virtue where men have it whether they will or no. It is generally an appeal to the people from the sentence given by men of sense against them. It is stepping very low to get very high.

Men by habit make irregular stretches of power, without discerning the consequence and extent of them. Eagerness is apt to overlook consequences, it is loth to be stopped in its career; for when men are in great haste, they see only in a straight line.

OF CUNNING AND KNAVERY

CUNNING is so apt to grow into knavery that an honest man will avoid the temptation of it. But men in this age are half bribed by the ambition of circumventing, without any other encouragements. So proud of the character of being able men, that they do not care to have their dexterity confined.

In this age, when it is said of a man, 'He knows how to live', it may be implied he is not very honest. An honest man must lose so many occasions of getting, that the world will hardly allow him the character of an able one. There is however more wit requisite to be an honest man than there is to be a knave.

The most necessary thing in the world, and yet the least usual, is to reflect that those we deal with may know how to be as arrant knaves as ourselves.

The eagerness of a knave makes him often as catchable, as ignorance makes a fool.

No man is so much a fool as not to have wit* enough sometimes to be a knave; nor any so cunning a knave, as not to have the weakness sometimes to play the fool. The mixture of fool and knave makes up the particoloured creatures that make all the bustle in the world.

There is not so pleasant a quarry as a knave taken in a net of his own making. A knave leans sometimes so hard upon his impudence that it breaks and lets him fall. Knavery is in such perpetual motion that it has not always leisure to look to its own steps; it is like sliding upon skates, no motion so smooth or swift, but none gives so terrible a fall.

A knave loves self so heartily that he is apt to overstrain it: by never thinking he can get enough, he gets so much less. His thought is like wine that frets with too much fermenting.

The knaves in every government are a kind of corporation; and though they fall out with one another, like all beasts of prey, yet upon occasion they unite to support the common cause. It cannot be said to be such a corporation as the Bank of England,* but they are a numerous and formidable body, scarce to be resisted; but the point is, they can never rely upon one another.

Knaves go chained to one another like slaves in the galleys, and cannot easily untie themselves from their company. Their promises and honour indeed do not hinder them, but other entangling circumstances keep them from breaking loose.

If knaves had not foolish memories, they would never trust one another so often as they do.

Present interest, like present love, makes all other friendship look cold to it, but it fails in the holding.

When one knave betrays another, the one is not to be blamed, nor the other to be pitied. When they complain of one another as if they were honest men, they ought to be laughed at as if they were fools.

There are some cunning men who yet can scarce be called rational creatures; yet they are often more successful than men of sense, because those they have to deal with are upon a looser guard; and their simplicity makes their knavery unsuspected.

There is no such thing as a venial sin against morality, no such thing as a small knavery. He that carries a small crime easily will carry it on when it grows to be an ox. But the little knaves are the greater of the two, because they have less the excuse of temptation.

Knavery is so humble, and merit so proud, that the latter is thrown down because it cannot stoop.

OF FOLLY AND FOOLS

THERE are five orders of fools, as of building: 1. the blockhead, 2. coxcomb, 3. vain blockhead, 4. grave coxcomb, and 5. the half-witted fellow; this last is of the composite order.*

The follies of grave men have the precedence of all others, a ridiculous dignity, that gives them a right to be laughed at in the first place. As the masculine wit is the strongest, so the masculine impertinence is the greatest.

The consequence of a half-wit is a half-will, there is not strength enough in the thought to carry it to the end.

A fool is naturally recommended to our kindness by setting us off by the comparison. Men are grateful to fools for giving them the pleasure of contemning them.

But folly has a long tail that is not seen at first: for every single folly has a root, out of which more are ready to sprout; and a fool has so unlimited a power of mistaking, that a man of sense can never comprehend to what degree it may extend.

There are some fools so low that they are preferred when they are laughed at. Their being named puts them in the list of men, which is more than belongs to them. One should no more laugh at a contemptible fool than at a dead fly.

The dissimulation of a fool should come within the Statute of Stabbing.* It gives no warning.

A fool will be rude from the moment he is allowed to be familiar; he can make no other use of freedom than to be unmannerly.

Weak men are apt to be cruel, because they stick at nothing that may repair the ill effect of their mistakes. Folly is often more cruel in the consequence than malice can be in the intent.

Many a man is murdered by the well-meant mistakes of his unthinking friends.

A weak friend, if he will be kind, ought to go no further than wishes; if he proffers either to say, or to do, it is dangerous.

A man had as good go to bed to a razor, as to be intimate with a foolish friend.

Mistaken kindness is little less dangerous than premeditated malice.

A man has not the relief of being angry at the blows of a mistaken friend.

A busy fool is fitter to be shut up than a downright madman.

A man that has only wit enough not to do hurt, commits a sin if he aims at doing good. His passive understanding must not pretend to be active. It is a sin against Nature for such a man to be meddling.

It is hard to find a blockhead so wise as to be upon the defensive; he will be sallying, and then he is sure to be ill-used.

If a dull fool can make a vow and keep it, never to speak his own sense or do his own business, he may pass a great while for a rational creature.

A blockhead is as ridiculous when he talks as a goose is when it flies. The grating a gridiron is not a worse noise than the jingling of words is to a man of sense.

It is ill manners to silence a fool, and cruelty to let him go on.

Most men make little other use of their speech than to give evidence against their own understanding.

A great talker may be a man of sense, but he cannot be one, who will venture to rely upon him.

There is so much danger in talking that a man strictly wise can hardly be called a sociable creature.

The great expense of words is laid out in setting ourselves out, or deceiving others; to convince them requires but a few. Many words are always either suspicious or ridiculous.

A fool has no dialogue within himself, the first thought carries him without the reply of a second.

A fool will admire or like nothing that he understands, a man of sense nothing but what he understands.

Wise men gain, and poor men live, by the superfluities of fools. Till follies become ruinous, the world is better with than it would be without them.

A fool is angry that he is the food of a knave, forgetting that it is the end* of his creation.

OF HOPE

HOPE is a kind cheat; in the minute of our disappointment we are angry, but upon the whole matter there is no pleasure without it. It is so much a pleasanter thing than truth to the greatest part of the world, that it has all their kindness, the other only has their respect.

Hope is generally a wrong guide, though it is very good company by the way.* It brushes through hedge and ditch till it comes to a great leap, and there it is apt to fall and break its bones. It would be well if hopes carried men only to the top of the hill, without throwing them afterwards down the precipice.

The hopes of a fool are blind guides,* those of a man of sense doubt often of their way.

Men should do with their hopes as they do with tame fowl, cut their wings that they may not fly over the wall.

A hoping fool has such terrible falls that his brains are turned, though not cured by them. The hopes of a fool are bullets he throws into the air, that fall down again and break his skull.

There can be no entire disappointment to a wise man, because he makes it a cause of succeeding another time. A fool is so unreasonably raised by his hopes, that he is half dead by a disappointment: his mistaken fancy draws him so high, that when he falls he is sure to break his bones.

OF ANGER

ANGER is a better sign of the heart than of the head; it is a breaking out of the disease of honesty. Just anger may be as dangerous as it could be if there was no provocation to it; for a knave is not so nice a casuist but that he will ruin, if he can, any man that blames him.

Where ill-nature is not predominant, anger will be short-breathed, it cannot hold out a long course. Hatred can be tired and cloyed as well as love: for our spirits, like our limbs, are tired with being long in one posture.

There is a dignity in good sense that is offended and defaced by anger.

Anger is never without an argument, but seldom with a good one.

Anger raises invention but it overheats the oven.

Anger, like drink, raises a great deal of unmannerly wit. True wit must come by drops; anger throws it out in a stream, and then it is not likely to be of the best kind.

Ill language punishes anger by drawing a contempt upon it.

OF APOLOGIES

IT is a dangerous task to answer objections, because they are helped by the malice of mankind. A bold accusation does at first draw such a general attention, that it gets the world on its side.

To a man who has a mind to find a fault, an excuse generally gives further hold. Explaining is generally half confessing. Innocence has a very short style.

When a jealousy of any kind is once raised, it is as often provoked as cured by any arguments, let them be never so reasonable. When laziness lets things alone, it is a disease; but when skill does it, it is a virtue.

Malice may help a fool to aggravate, but there must be skill to know how to extenuate. To lessen an object that at the first sight gives offence, requires a dexterous hand: there must be strength as well as skill to take off the weight of the first impression.

When a man is very unfortunate, it looks like a saucy thing in him to justify himself. A man must stoop sometimes to his ill star, but he must never lie down to it.

The vindications men make of themselves to posterity would hardly be supported by good sense, if they were not of some advantage to their own families.

The defending an ill thing is more criminal than the doing it, because it wants the excuse of its not being premeditated. An advocate for injustice is like a bawd that is worse than her client who commits the sin.

There is hardly any man so strict as not to vary a little from truth when he is to make an excuse. Not telling all the truth is hiding it, and that is comforting or abetting a lie.

A long vindication is seldom a skilful one. Long does at least imply doubtful in such a case.

A fool should avoid the making an excuse, as much as the committing a fault; for a fool's excuse is always a second fault: and whenever he will undertake either to hide or mend a thing, he proclaims and spoils it.

OF MALICE AND ENVY

MALICE is a greater magnifying glass than kindness.

Malice is of a low stature, but it has very long arms. It often reaches into the next world, death itself is not a bar to it.

Malice, like lust, when it is at the height, does not know shame. If it did not sometimes cut itself with its own edge, it would destroy the world.

Malice can mistake by being keen as well as by being dull.

When malice grows critical, it loses its credit. It must go under the disguise of plainness, or else it is exposed.

Anger may have some excuse for being blind, but malice none: for malice has time to look before it.

When malice is overgrown, it comes to be the highest degree of impertinence. For that reason, it must not be fed and pampered, which is apt to make it play the fool. But where it is wise and steady there is no precaution that can be quite proof against it.

Ill will is seldom cured on a sudden, it must go off by degrees, by insensible transpiration.

Malice may be sometimes out of breath, envy never. A man may make peace with hatred, but never with envy.

No passion is better heard by our will, than that of envy; no passion is admitted to have audience with less exception.

Envy takes the shape of flattery, and that makes men hug it so close that they cannot part with it.

The sure way to be commended is to get into a condition of being pitied. For envy will not give its leave to commend a man till he is miserable. A man is undone, when envy will not vouchsafe to look upon him.

Yet after all, envy does virtue as much good as hurt, by provoking it to appear. Nay, it forcibly draws out and invites virtue, by giving it a mind to be revenged of it.

OF VANITY

THE world is nothing but vanity cut out into several shapes.

Men often mistake themselves, but they never forget themselves.

A man must not so entirely fall out with vanity, as not to take its assistance in the doing great things. Vanity is like some men who are very useful, if they are kept under; and else not to be endured.

A little vanity may be allowed in a man's train, but it must not sit down at table with him. Without some share of it, men's talents would be buried like ore in a mine unwrought. Men would be less eager to gain knowledge, if they did not hope to set themselves out by it.

It shows the narrowness of our nature, that a man that intends any one thing extremely, has not thought enough left for anything else. Our pride makes us overvalue our stock of thought, so as to trade much beyond what it is able to make good.

Many aspire to learn what they can never comprehend, as others pretend to teach what they themselves do not know. The vanity of teaching often tempts a man to forget he is a blockhead.

Self-conceit drives away the suspecting how scurvily others think of us.

Vanity cannot be a friend to truth, because it is restrained by it; and vanity is so impatiently desirous of showing itself, that it cannot bear the being crossed.

There is a degree of vanity that recommends; if it goes further, it exposes. So much as to stir the blood to do commendable things, but not so much as to possess the brain, and turn it round.

There are as many that are blown up by the wind of vanity as are carried away by the stream of interest. Everybody has not wit enough to act out of interest, but everybody has little enough to do it out of vanity. Some men's heads are as easily blown away as their hats.

If the commending others well did not recommend ourselves, there would be few panegyrics.

Men's vanity will often dispose them to be commended into very troublesome employments.

The desiring to be remembered when we are dead is to so little purpose that it is fit men should, as they generally are, be disappointed in it. Nevertheless, the desire of leaving a good name behind us is so honourable to ourselves, and so useful to the world, that good sense must not be heard against it.

Heraldry is one of those foolish things that may yet be too much despised. The contempt of escutcheons is as much a disease in this age as the overvaluing them was in former times. There is a good use to be made of the most contemptible things, and an ill one of those that are the most valuable.

OF MONEY

IF men considered how many things there are that riches cannot buy, they would not be so fond of them.

The things to be bought with money are such as least deserve the giving a price for them.

Wit and money are so apt to be abused that men generally make a shift to be the worse for them. Money in a fool's hand exposes him worse than a pied coat.*

Money has too great a preference given to it by states, as well as by particular men.

Men are more the sinews of war than money.

The third part of an army must be destroyed, before a good one can be made out of it.

They who are of opinion that money will do everything, may very well be suspected to do everything for money.

FALSE LEARNING

A LITTLE learning misleads, and a great deal often stupifies the understanding.

Great reading without applying it is like corn heaped that is not stirred, it grows musty.

A learned coxcomb dyes his mistakes in so much a deeper colour; a wrong kind of learning serves only to embroider his errors.

A man that has read without judgement is like a gun charged with goose-shot, let loose upon the company. He is only well furnished with materials to expose himself, and to mortify those he lives with.

The reading of the greatest scholars, if put into a limbeck,* might be distilled into a small quantity of essence.

The reading of most men is like a wardrobe of old clothes that are seldom used.

Weak men are the worse for the good sense they read in books, because it furnishes them only with more matter to mistake.

OF COMPANY

MEN that cannot entertain themselves want somebody, though they care for nobody. An impertinent fellow is never in the right, but in his being weary of himself.

By the time that men are fit for company, they see the objections to it.

The company of a fool is dangerous as well as tedious.

It is flattering some men to endure them. Present* punishment attends the fault.

A following wit will be welcome in most companies; a leading one lies too heavy for envy to bear.

Outdoing is so near reproaching that it will generally be thought very ill company. Anything that shines does in some measure tarnish everything that stands next to it.

Keeping much company generally ends in playing the fool or the knave with them.

OF FRIENDSHIP

FRIENDSHIP comes oftener by chance than by choice, which makes it generally so uncertain.

It is a mistake to say a friend can be bought. A man may buy a good turn, but he cannot buy the heart that does it.

Friendship cannot live with ceremony, nor without civility.

There must be a nice diet observed to keep friendship from falling sick; nay, there is more skill necessary to keep a friend than there is to reclaim an enemy.

Those friends who are above interest are seldom above jealousy.

It is a misfortune for a man not to have a friend in the world, but for that reason he shall have no enemy.

In the commerce of the world, men struggle little less with their friends than they do with their enemies.

Esteem ought to be the ground of kindness, and yet there are no friends that seldomer meet. Kindness is apt to be as afraid of esteem, as that is to be ashamed of kindness. Our kindness is greatest to those that will do what we would have them, in which our esteem cannot always go along.

MISCELLANEOUS THOUGHTS
AND REFLECTIONS

OF ADVICE AND CORRECTION

THE rule of doing as we would be done by* is never less observed than it is in telling others their faults. But men intend more to show others that they are free from the fault, than to dissuade them from committing it. They are so pleased with the prudent shape of an adviser, that it raises the value they have of themselves, whilst they are about it. Certainly, to give advice to a friend, either asked or unasked, is so far from a fault that it is a duty; but if a man loves to give advice, it is a sure sign that he himself wants it.

A man whilst he is advising puts his understanding upon tiptoes, and is unwilling to bring it down again.

A weak man had rather *be thought* to know than *know*, and that makes him so impatient to be told of a mistake.

He who will not be the better for other men's faults has no cure left for his own. But he that can probe himself to cure his own faults will seldom need either the surgery of his friends or of his enemies.

OF ALTERATIONS

IN a corrupted age the putting the world in order would breed confusion.

A rooted disease must be stroked away, rather than kicked away.

As soon as men have understanding enough to find a fault, they have enough to see the danger of mending it.

Desiring to have anything mended is venturing to have it spoiled: to know when to let things alone is a high pitch of good sense. But a fool has an eagerness, like a monkey in a glass shop, to break everything in the handling.

Curing and mending are generally mere words of art not to be relied upon. They are set out in bills, but the mountebanks only get by them.

BASHFULNESS

GREAT bashfulness is oftener an effect of pride than of modesty. Modesty is oftener mistaken than any other virtue.

BOLDNESS

WISE venturing is the most commendable part of human prudence. It is the upper storey of prudence, whereas perpetual caution is a kind of underground wisdom that does not care to see the light. It is best for great men to shoot over, and for lesser men to shoot short.

BORROWERS OF OPINIONS

MEN who borrow their opinions can never repay their debts. They are beggars by nature, and can therefore never get a stock to grow rich upon.

A man who has not a distinguishing head is safest by not minding what anybody says. He had better trust to his own opinion, than spoil another man's for want of apprehending it.

CANDOUR

IT is some kind of scandal not to bear with the faults of an honest man. It is not loving honesty enough to allow it distinguishing privileges. There are some decent faults which may pretend to be in the lower rank of virtues; and surely where honour or gratitude are the motives, censure must be a good deal silenced.

OF CAUTION AND SUSPICION

MEN must be saved in this world by their want of faith.

A man that gets care into his thoughts cannot properly be said to trade without a stock. Care and right thought will produce crops all the year without staying for the seasons.

A man is to go about his own business as if he had not a friend in the world to help him in it.

He that relies upon himself will be oppressed by others with offers of their service. All are apt to shrink from those that lean upon them.

If men would think how often their own words are thrown at their heads, they would less often let them go out of their mouths. Men's words are bullets that their enemies take up and make use of against them.

A man watches himself best when others watch him too.

It is as necessary for us to suppress our reason when it offends, as our mistakes when they expose us. In an unreasonable age, a man's reason let loose would undo him. A wise man will do with his reason as a miser does with his money, hoard it, but be very sparing in the expense of it.

A man that should call everything by its right name would hardly pass the streets without being knocked down as a common enemy. A man cannot be more in the wrong than to own without distinction the being in the right.

When a man is very kind or very angry, there is no sure guard but silence upon that subject. A man's understanding is easily shoved out of its place by warm thoughts of any kind. We are not so much masters of our heat as to have enough to warm our thoughts, and not so much as to set them on fire.

A great enemy is a great object that invites precaution, which makes him less dangerous than a mean one.

An old man concludes from his knowing mankind that they know him too, and that makes him very wary. On the other hand, it must be allowed, that a man's being deceived by knaves has often this ill effect, that it makes him too jealous of honest men. The mind, like the body, is subject to be hurt by everything it takes for a remedy.

There are some such very great foreseers, that they grow into the vanity of pretending to see where nothing is to be seen. He that will see at too great a distance, will sometimes mistake a bush for a horse. The prospect of a wise man will be bounded. A man may so overdo it in looking too far before him, that he may stumble the more for it.

And, to conclude, he that leaves nothing to chance will do few things ill, but he will do very few things.

Suspicion is rather a virtue than a fault, as long as it does like a dog that watches, and does not bite.

A wise man, in trusting another, must not rely upon his promise against his nature.

Early suspicion is often an injury, and late suspicion is always a folly.

A wise man will keep his suspicions muzzled, but he will keep them awake.

There can no rules be given to suspicion, no more than to love.

Suspicion takes root, and bears fruit, from the moment it is planted.

Suspicion seldom wants food to keep it up in health and vigour. It feeds upon everything it sees, and is not curious in its diet.

Suspicion does not grow up to an injury till it breaks out.

When our suspicion of another man is once discovered by him, there ought to be an end of all further commerce.

He that is never suspected is either very much esteemed, or very much despised.

A man's interest is not a sufficient ground to suspect him, if his nature does not concur in it.

A weak man has less suspicion than a wise one, but when he has it, he is less easily cured. The remedies as often increase the disease as they do allay it; and a fool values himself upon suspecting at a venture.

CHEATS

MANY men swallow the being cheated, but no man could ever endure to chew it.

Few men would be deceived, if their conceit of themselves did not help the skill of those that go about it.

COMPLAINT

COMPLAINT is a contempt upon oneself. It is an ill sign both of a man's head and of his heart.

A man throws himself down whilst he complains; and when a man throws himself down, nobody cares to take him up again.

CONTENT

CONTENT lays pleasure, nay virtue, in a slumber, with few and faint intermissions. It is to the mind like moss to a tree, it binds it up so as to stop its growth.

CONVERTS

THE impudence of a bawd is modesty compared with that of a convert.

A convert has so much to do to gain credit that a man is to think well before he changes.

DESIRES

MEN generally state their wants by their fancy, and not by their reason. The poor young children are whipped and beaten by the old ones, who are much more inexcusably impertinent.

Not having things is a more proper expression for a man of sense than his wanting them. Where sense is wanting, everything is wanting. A man of sense can hardly want, but for his friends and children that have none.

Most men let their wishes run away with them. They have no mind to stop them in their career, the motion is so pleasing.

To desire what belongs to another man is misprision of robbery. Men are commanded not to covet,* because when they do they are very apt to take.

DIFFICULTY

A DIFFICULTY raises the spirits of a great man, he has a mind to wrestle with it, and give it a fall.

A man's mind must be very low, if the difficulty does not make a part of his pleasure. The pride of compassing may more than compare with the pleasure of enjoying.

DISSEMBLING

NOTHING so ridiculous as a false philosopher, and nothing so rare as a true one.

Men take more pains to hide than to mend themselves.

DREAMS

MEN'S pride, as well as their weakness, disposes them to rely upon dreams, from their thinking themselves of such importance as to have warning of what is to befall them.

The enquiry into a dream is another dream.

DRUNKENNESS

IT is a piece of arrogance to dare to be drunk, because a man shows himself without a veil.

EXPERIENCE

THE best way to suppose what may come is to remember what is past. The best qualification of a prophet is to have a good memory. Experience makes more prophets than revelation.

The knowledge that is got without pains is kept without pleasure. The struggling for knowledge has a pleasure in it like that of wrestling with a fine woman.

EXTREMES

EXTREMITY is always ill, that which is good cannot live a moment with it.

Anybody that is fool enough will be safe in the world, and anybody that can be knave enough will be rich in it. The generality of the world falls into an insufficient mean that exposes them more than an extreme on either side.

FACULTIES OF THE MIND

THOUGH memory and invention are not upon good terms, yet when the first is loaded, the other is stifled. The memory has claws by which it holds fast; but it has no wings, like the invention, to enable it to fly.

Some men's memory is like a box, where a man should mingle his jewels with his old shoes.

There ought to be a great difference between the memory and the stomach; the last is to admit everything, the former should have the faculty of rejecting.

It is a nice mean between letting the thought languish for want of exercise, and tiring it by giving it too much.

A man may dwell so long upon a thought that it may take him prisoner.

The hardest thing in the world is to give the thoughts due liberty, and yet retain them in due discipline. They are libertines that are apt to abuse freedom, and do not well know how to bear restraint.

A man that excels in any one thing has a kind of arbitrary power over all that hear him upon that subject, and no man's life is too short to know any one thing perfectly.

The modern wit is rather to set men out, than to make them of any use.

Some men have acted courage who had it not; but no man can act wit, if Nature does not teach him his part. True wit is always revenged upon any false pretender that meddles with it.

Wit is the only thing that men are willing to think they can ever have enough of.

There is a happy pitch of ignorance that a man of sense might pray for.

A man that has true wit will have honour too, not only to adorn, but to support it.

FAMILIES

THE building up a family is a manufacture very little above the building a house of cards. Time and accidents are sure to furnish a blast to blow it down. No house wants new tiling so often as a family wants repairing.

The desire of having children is as much the effect of vanity as of good nature. We think our children a part of ourselves, though as they grow up they might very well undeceive us.

Men love their children, not because they are promising plants, but because they are theirs. They cannot discredit the plant, without disparaging the soil out of which it came. Pride in this, as in many other things, is often mistaken for love.

As children make a man poor in one sense, so in another they enforce care, and that begets riches.

Love is presently out of breath when it is to go up hill, from the children to the parents.

FEAR

IT is good to have men in awe, but dangerous to have them afraid of us. The mean is so nice that the hitting upon it is oftener the effect of chance than of skill. A degree of fear sharpens, the excess of it stupifies.

It is as scandalous not to fear at some times, as it can be to be afraid at others.

FLATTERY

FOLLY begets want, and want flattery; so that flattery, with all its wit, is the grandchild of folly.

Were it not for bunglers in the manner of doing it, hardly any man would ever find out he was laughed at. And yet, generally speaking, a trowel is a more effectual instrument than a pencil for flattery. Men generally do so love the taste of flattery, their stomach can never be overcharged with it.

There is a right reverend flattery that has the precedence of all other kinds of it. This mitred flattery is of all others the most exalted. It ever grows in proportion, and keeps pace with power. There is a noble stroke of it in the articles sent to Princess Mary from Henry VIII: 'Such is his Majesty's Gracious and Divine Nature—showing mercy to such as repentantly cry and call for the same.'*

FORGETFULNESS

FORGETTING is oftener an aggravation than an excuse. The memory will seldom be unmannerly but where it is unkind.

GOOD MANNERS

THERE needs little care to polish the understanding; if true means were used to strengthen it, it will polish itself.

Good manners is such a part of good sense that they cannot be divided; but that which a fool calls good breeding is the most unmannerly thing in the world. Right good manners require so much sense that there is hardly any such thing in the world.

GOOD NATURE

GOOD nature is rather acted than practised in the world.

Good nature to others is an inseparable part of justice.

GOODWILL

GOODWILL, like grace, flows where it lists.

Men mean so very well to themselves, that they forget to mean well to anybody else.

HEAT

GOOD sense will allow of some intermitting fevers, but then the fit must be short.

HONESTY

HE that can be quite indifferent when he sees another man injured, has a lukewarm honesty that a wise man will not depend upon.

He that is not concerned when he sees an ill thing done to another, will not be very eager to do a good one himself.

HYPOCRISY

THERE is so much wit necessary to make a skilful hypocrite that the faculty is fallen amongst bunglers, who make it ridiculous.

INJURIES

AN INJURY may more properly be said to be postponed, than to be forgiven. The memory of it is never so subdued, but that it has always life in it.

The memory of an enemy admits no decay but age. Could we know what men are most apt to remember, we might know what they are most apt to do.

It is a general fault that we dislike men only for the injuries they do to us, and not for those they do to mankind. Yet it will be hard to give a good reason why a man who has done a deliberate injury to one, will not do it to another.

The memory and the conscience never did, nor never will agree about forgiving injuries. Nature is second* to the memory, and religion to the conscience. When the seconds fight, the latter is generally disarmed.

INTEGRITY

A MAN in a corrupted age must make a secret of his integrity, or else he will be looked upon as a common enemy. He must engage his friends not to speak of it, for he sets himself for a mark to be ill used.

JUSTICE

As far as keeping distance is a sign of respect, mankind has a great deal for justice. They make up in ceremony what they want in goodwill to it.

Where the generality are offenders, justice comes to be cruelty.

TO LOVE AND BE IN LOVE DIFFERENT

To love, and to be in love with anything, are things as differing as good sense and impertinence. When we once go beyond bare liking, we are in danger of parting with good sense; and it is not easy for good sense to get so far as liking.

LUCRE

WHEN by habit a man comes to have a bargaining soul, its wings are cut, so that it can never soar. It binds reason an apprentice to gain, and instead of a director, makes it a drudge.

LYING

THE being kind to a liar is abetting a treason against mankind. A man is to inform the first magistrate, that he may be clapped up.

Lies are embroidered with promises and excuses.

A known liar should be outlawed in a well-ordered government.

A man that renounces truth runs away from his trial in the world.

The use of talking is almost lost in the world by the habit of lying.

A man that does not tell all the truth, ought to be hanged for a clipper.* Half the truth is often as arrant a lie as can be made. It is the more dexterous, but not the less criminal kind of lying.

NAMES

NAMES to men of sense are no more than fig leaves; to the generality they are thick coverings that hide the nature of things from them. Fools turn good sense upon its head, they take names for things, and things only for names.

PARTIALITY

IT is a general mistake to think the men we like are good for everything, and those we do not, good for nothing.

PATIENCE

A MAN who is master of patience is master of everything else. He that can tell how to bear in the right place is master of everybody he deals with.

POSITIVENESS

POSITIVE is the perfection of coxcomb, he is then come to his full growth.

PROSPERITY

IT shows men's nature, that when they are pampered in any kind, they are very apt to play jadish tricks. One of the tricks of any creature that is wanton, is to kick what is next them.

QUIET

EVERYTHING that does us good is so apt to do us hurt too, that it is a strong argument for men to be quiet.

If men would think more, they would act less. The greatest part of the business of the world is the effect of not thinking.

REASON AND PASSION

MOST men put their reason out to service to their will. The master and the man are perpetually falling out. A third man will hazard a beating, if he goes about to part them.

Nothing has an uglier look to us than reason, when it is not of our side. We quarrel so often with it, that it makes us afraid to come near it.

A man that does not use his reason is a tame beast; a man that abuses it is a wild one.

REPUTATION

IT is a self-flattering contradiction, that wise men despise the opinion of fools, and yet are proud of having their esteem.

SELF-LOVE

SELF-LOVE rightly defined is far from being a fault. A man that loves himself right will do everything else right.

SHAME

A MAN who does not think he is punished when he is blamed, is too much hardened to be ever reformed.

The court of shame has of late lost much of its jurisdiction. It ought by right both to judge in the first instance, and to exclude all appeals from it.

Shame is a disease of the last age; this seems to be cured of it.

SINGULARITY

SINGULARITY may be good sense at home, but it must not go much abroad.

It is a commendation to be that which a crowd of mistaken fools call singular. There can hardly be a severer thing said to a man in this age, than that he is like the rest of the world.

SLANDER

SLANDER would not stick if it had not always something to lay hold of.

A man who can allow himself the liberty to slander has the world too much at his mercy. But the man that despises slander deserves it.

SPEAKERS IN PUBLIC

SPEAKERS in public should take more pains to hold in their invention than to raise it. Invention is apt to make such sallies that it cannot secure its retreat.

He that will not make a blot, will be pretty sure in his time to give a stroke.

A patient hearer is a sure speaker.

Men are angry when others do not hear them, yet they have more reason to be afraid when they do.

TIME THE LOSS OF IT

MISSPENDING a man's time is a kind of self-homicide, it is making life to be of no use.

TRUTH

TRUTH is not only stifled by ignorance, but concealed out of caution or interest; so if it had not a root of immortality, it must have been long since extinguished.

WISDOM

THE most useful part of wisdom is for a man to give a good guess, what others think of him. It is a dangerous thing to guess partially, and a melancholy thing to guess right.

Nothing would more contribute to make a man wise than to have always an enemy in his view.

A wise man may have more enemies than a weak one, but he will not so much feel the weight of them. Indeed, the being wise does either make men our friends, or discourage them from being our enemies.

Wisdom is only a comparative quality, it will not bear a single definition.

YOUTH

A MAN has too little heat, or wit, or courage, if he has not sometimes more than he should. Just enough of a good thing is always too little.

Long life gives more marks to shoot at, and therefore old men are less well thought of, than those who have not been so long upon the stage. Other men's memories retain the ill, whilst the good things done by an old man easily slip out of them. Old men have in some degree their reprisals upon younger, by making nicer observations upon them, by virtue of their experience.

SELECTIONS FROM THE *MISCELLANYS* AND *MISCELLANEOUS MAXIMS*

THE definition of a philosopher is, a man that is ever thinking of something that is not his present business. He sends his understanding so far from him, in the search of what ought to be done in cases that have not happened, that he has it not about him in those that do. His knowledge is such as makes him ignorant in all the ordinary duties of life; he thinks them too coarse for him. No creature might be better spared from the world than a knowing coxcomb.

His thoughts dwell in the empty regions of the air and he would look upon them as degraded from their dignity if they stooped to anything that is practical. He despises those who have not his kind of knowledge, which is to little purpose, whilst he is proud of being ignorant of those things every man ought to know. His thoughts feed upon precepts, sentences, and problems, which rather swell than nourish them.

It may be said of knowledge as it is of hunting; the entertainment is more valuable than the quarry. That which is generally called knowledge, might more properly be termed a rational guessing. There is hardly a right name given to any one thing in the world.

Men are to dig deeper for knowledge than they do for gold, or else they will not get so much as will be worth their pains. Knowledge lies at the bottom of the mine, it is only some loose ore which can be got at the surface. When laziness keeps the accounts, it concludes the trouble of getting it is more than it is worth.

Knowing is so bold a word that wise men will not often use it.

The more men know, the less they will care to do. Knowledge raises so many objections, that it makes a man less active.

If men would consider the consequences of altering, before they went about it, there would be few revolutions in the world.

A man that should put the true value upon the state of human life would for that reason acquit himself worse of the duties that belong to it. It fits a man more for retiring from the world than for acting a good part in it. A man's industry is kept up by the mistake of thinking most things of more importance than they are.

There are very few things in the world that can in truth excuse men's being busy about them.

Men used to live in storms are sick of a calm; the best definition of men's nature, is not that which is born with them, but that which they are used to.

One reason, and not the least, why elder men mistake less than younger, is that they do less. The lively spirits of young men put them upon perpetual action, and consequently upon frequent mistakes. Every action requires more thought, than the heat of young men will allow them to bestow upon it.

A question that elder men ask themselves, what then? If the young ones asked it too, the world would be very quiet and inactive.

A man that has lived long in the world, treads tenderly; suspects the ground he goes upon, because it has so often failed him.

Young men are not apt to think of doing wise things, and old men are so long before they can resolve them, that no wonder there are so few done in the world. Hard to pitch upon the space, between the ebbings and overflowings of age.

The reason why mending generally makes things worse, is that most men have only a desire to alter, the skill how to do it is wanting. There is plenty of ill men to spoil things and scarcity of good ones to mend them.

Menders are very apt to pull the faults down upon their heads, which they go about to reform. They have generally such a rough hand at pulling down, that they are not apt to look about them. Mankind in general is divided between the sleepiness of those who would let everything alone, and the activity of such as spoil everything in the mending it.

The people is a slow heavy beast; a great while before it can get up, and a great while too before it can lie down again.

The people are either a dead water or a rough sea, they have no mean. It is so little to them to distinguish, that they cannot imagine there is anything between the two extremes.

The best definition of the people is, a certain thing, that is either dead or mad; no mean.

From the moment the people cease to be afraid, they begin to be terrible: that beast knows no mean.

Man is still a beast of prey: he is only brought out of the woods, and ranges in towns.

The laws necessary to preserve society are so many and so mysterious that mankind was at more quiet whilst they lived in the woods. If they could have foreseen the trouble of being civilized, they would probably have spared their pains in it. Men have paid such fees for being civilized, that they have but a very indifferent bargain of it.

The laws are so many libels against mankind, by showing they have need of them, to keep them within the bounds of common justice. The multiplication of laws is an undesirable evidence of the world's growing worse. New chains are made in every age to tie up the beast mankind, and yet they must still be mended and renewed.

In former times hunting was not the entertainment so properly as the business of life, as it is still among the savage Indians. A man is naturally so wild a creature, that he is easily reduced again to it, and is by nothing more so, than by continual hunting. The being civilized is a forced thing upon our nature. The least thing brings us back to the original beast again.

We are sure men will not hurt us, when they cannot; a wise man will not easily go much further in his belief.

Liberty is a comprehensive word, and not enough understood. To be at liberty to do what one will, is desirable only by those who know what they should do; a weak man is by that liberty, only more let loose to do himself hurt.

It is impudence in a fool to pretend to talk of liberty, when he so little knows how to make use of it. As an idiot is not capable in law of enjoying an estate, an unthinking fool should as little pretend to lay in his claim for liberty. It is fit a man should know what he does, before he is allowed to do what he will.

Complaining of an injustice serves only to make it lie heavier, &c. A man must be very sure he does not deserve to be ill-used, before he complains of it. Men that take pleasure in bemoaning themselves have less right to expect others should pity them.

Mankind have the less reason to complain, since it is hard for them to be worse governed than they deserve.

The world hates quiet, though it hardly knows what it is. The ends of government scarce deserve the pains that belong to it.

Complaint for pain or misery comes from the mistaken thought, at that time, that somebody will give remedy. Men in pain complain less when alone than when there is somebody in the room.

It always lessens a man to complain.

It was some respect to that age, that Diogenes* carried a lantern in the daytime to find out a *man*; in this age, he would not so much as have looked for one. It may be said that most men are apparitions, they are not really *men*. There were not stranger beasts in the Ark, than those that are in human shape.

Men flatter themselves extravagantly with the dignity of their species, and at the same time let the beast predominate.

Mankind keep such a stir about themselves, that one would swear they were something.

The herd of mankind are all of one religion and do not know it; that is, they understand nothing, and are therefore ready to submit to whatever is told them. They are children as long as they live, and therefore age will not undeceive them from the fables they learnt in the nursery. They are such scurvy things in this world, that they have a temptation to believe those who tell them they may be better in the next.

There is not so much difference in men's opinions in the world as is imagined; since not one man in twenty has any opinion, but follows other men without inquiring.

Being alone gives a man time to think, and the more one thinks, the less one likes mankind.

It is an unmannerly thing to think of most men as they deserve.

A man cannot be the better for reading history, except it makes him melancholy, by seeing so many instances of the villainy of mankind.

To think well of mankind, or to speak ill of it, are two mistakes men of sense will avoid. The first is against good sense, the second against common prudence.

A man that will keep up his zeal for the liberty of mankind, must forget how little it deserves it. Without deceiving oneself with the hopes that the next generation will grow better, the present mankind will give little encouragement to be zealous for them.

There is a greater evidence of having a soul in vegetables, than there is in most men: smell, taste, growth, medicinal virtue, fruit, &c.

Speaking before thinking is a kind of vomiting before digesting. A loud wind in a window, a better noise, than most men's discourse.

Some chattering women would do well to be planted in a cherry tree, to fright away the birds. There are chattering men too, that might keep them company. All chatterers are but another kind of monkeys, with this difference only, that they have less wit.

The tongue is the pulse of the mind. Like a wild beast, it ought to be kept in chains.

It is a great mercy to mankind, that God Almighty does not allow them to think so ill of themselves as they deserve; if they did, it would make a melancholy world.

It is well for our quiet, that our thoughts cannot endure to dwell upon the faulty side of ourselves.

A man's memory is like a flattering looking glass; it is too partial to be honest.

The memory naturally retains whatever makes for our interest, and as easily lets everything slip out of it, that is not welcome to us.

It were well if we divided our suspicions, and had at least as many of ourselves as of others.

Men in the list of their enemies, forget to set down themselves.

Passions to the mind are like factions to a government: the last disturb the peace of a nation, the first of a man's life.

The greatest slaves are those that are tied by invisible chains. No stronger fetters than our own passions.

A man should do with his passions as he does with his horse; check them so as that they may not run away with him; but not tame them into such a dullness that they can never gallop.

That war which never yet had a truce, between our reason and our passions, will be eternal.* And from the moment we let our reason sleep we are surprised.

Mankind has not yet deserved to have right reason discovered to it. Some dawnings, small glimmerings, a light that does not stay with us, but leaves in the dark, groveling to seek it.

Our reasoning faculty seems to be a thing so abstracted from all matter, that it must flow entirely from the soul, and has no other dependance upon the body, than by the consequence of being lodged, or rather imprisoned in it.

Few men have that strength of reason, as to hinder the affections of the mind from having an influence upon their health. It must be so strong a head to make that resistance, that there are very few of them in the world. The mind and the body are so near akin, that it raises reflections of several kinds.

The heart has thoughts, that differ from those of the mind. They have frequent and warm disputes, and let a man's arguing faculty be never so strong, the heart generally gets the better of it.*

Though princes are glad of a good reason to justify a war against their neighbours, yet the not having it will not hinder the war, where other circumstances invite to it. Reasons are less necessary than is generally thought; they are oftener mustered to make a show, than for anything else. Men's resolutions are generally formed by their appetite or their interest. Reason is afterwards called in for company, but it has no vote.

Well examined, the greater part of our desires are no better than longings. They are really diseases. Desire is in truth an incurable disease, a devouring beast, that when it has swallowed one kingdom will grumble till it has another.

Hoping must be a greater pleasure than having, because there is no bounds to fancy, but there are such to sense and to enjoyments, that for the time, at least, the pleasure is extinguished by the being enjoyed.

It is a question whether exile without confiscation be a punishment, since the hopes of returning entertain a man with more pleasure than he would have had at home.

There is an end of the romance, when the lovers are married.

A man who is cured of the mistake of hoping, is at the same time robbed of the pleasure of living.

It is a clear proof that nothing has any real value in it, that nobody cares for what they have long enjoyed.

He that would never be deceived, shall very seldom be pleased.

The most disappointing thing that can befall us, is to have what we pretend to, for then there is an end of the pleasure of hoping, and a shame as well as a surfeit of what we sought with so childish an earnestness.

If the true motives that persuade us in most things were laid open, there would be no man so wise as not to have his turn of blushing for it. It is a spiteful piece of injustice, to discourage a good end, by disparaging the cause of it.

It is too spiteful a thing to inquire into the causes of good actions. He that asks why a good thing was done does not much oblige him that did it. A fault may sometimes have a good effect; as the ostentation of virtue may incite others to it, whilst he who uses it deserves nothing but reproach.

If all the motives to good actions were seen, it would direct us better to know when and when not to commend them. The effect of things is plain, but the cause is so often mistaken, that it is a rare thing to guess right. Compassion of a man oppressed, is often no more than a disguise for the hatred men have to those that oppress him, &c.

There is hardly a virtue that is not mixed with a vice, nor a vice that has not the tincture of a virtue. They are twisted, &c.*

There is generally more pride than kindness in giving advice. A man takes himself to stand upon the higher ground, when he gives advice to another. It is standing upon stilts, when we dictate to an humble hearkener to our wisdom.

There is a superiority in the man that pities, which makes as many do it out of pride, as out of good nature.

There are several causes of pity more frequent than that of good nature. Turning the thought towards ourselves, by imagining we might be in the same condition. We seem to be in a state of superiority, whilst we commiserate others.

Men are more restrained by outward good manners than by inward morality. Shame is the more immediate penalty; besides that it cannot be hidden. Shame is oftener the effect of our pride, than of our morality.

Shame is a quality lost in the world; men of sense will not incur it; fools do not see it; and knaves are hardened against it.

We seldom commend heartily any but those we think are like us; so that generally, when men speak well of others, they are making their own panegyric. If it was not for this, men would hardly speak a good word of one another. The surest way to have another man kind to us, is to be like him.

If men would put what they say together, they would often find contradictions, of which they would not imagine they could be guilty. It is a spiteful thing in others, and a melancholy thing for ourselves to remember all we say at differing times upon the same subject. The same man may in those cases, truly say, it was *another man* that said it; our thoughts change our inward shape every day, though our outward features remain.

It is not in strictness a proper expression to say a man changes his opinion, since it is another man. Every man's name is legion.* Every differing humor and interest creates at the time a differing man.

The greatest objection to monastical vows is a natural argument, *viz.* that it is binding another man; self being made up of several distinct creatures, as accidents, nourishment, circumstances, &c. It is an arrogance from what we are, to presume too resolutely, what we shall be. The mind alters more than the outward features.

We shrink at the anatomy of this life, when we let it be exposed to us.

A reasonable man must be miserable, if he has no prospect beyond this life.

A reasonable man must conclude there is no true happiness in our present nature, so he must seek it in something that is more exalted, which can be nothing but a belief and prospect of a future and better being.

There is a scurvy side of every kind of life to which a man can apply himself. We must take all together, and make the best of it.

That equality of long life to mankind who are so unequal amongst themselves seems to be an objection to the frame of the world, but that we go beyond our tether when we undertake to make any. May not another life, and the immortality of the soul, be an answer to this objection? It shows that the whole frame was not thought of so much consequence by him that made it, as our partiality to the dignity of our being would make us believe.

The shortness of life makes the distinction between a wise man and a fool to be ridiculous. Whence one would think that wise men, of all others, should entertain the thoughts of the immortality of the soul, and of another state.

Men are loth to look back to the time when they were nothing. An unwelcome prospect.

If death without pain was in our choice there are many times of one's life a man would be ashamed not to have made use of such a privilege. If death would come whenever we desire it, we might the better forgive its coming when it is not invited.

There are so many things worse than death and yet there are so few who choose death, that it shows the weakness of our nature is too hard for the strength of our reason.

The grave is a kinder thing than men are generally willing to think it. One may say, we are afraid of our best friend.

If old age did not steal upon us insensibly, men would be tempted not to stay for it.

There is no sure way of avoiding the anguish of death, but the being surprised by it. Thinking is of use only when it is of such things as we can compass; but when it is to get the better of death, the less we think of it, the less we suffer. Thinking against death, is like pushing against a wall with our head, to throw it down.

The loss of an old acquaintance has often the consolation of being rid of an evidence against us.

Time is less to be thrown away than money, because the last may be recovered, the first not.

If men would employ that time for their instruction that their vanity makes them spend to set themselves out, a reasonable term of life would bring a great improvement.

The spilling of time is a degree of self-murder. It is the business of mankind to push on that which of itself runs swiftly away from them.

A man that would value every minute as much as a thrifty man does a shilling, would be very wary in laying it out.

Nothing so rapid as time; and yet we are so void of reflection, that we scarce perceive it moves. It is like the motion of the spheres, swift yet undiscernible, &c. It takes its revenge of us, for endeavoring to murder it; it kills us without remorse or remission.

If a man should think of the time that is gone, as much as a miser does of the money that is spent, he would destroy himself out of despair. Money may be recovered, time cannot, and yet is less considered by us; and with all this we, &c.

He that will believe nothing but what he understands, will not believe much; and he that believes what he does not understand, may as well believe one thing as another. Faith is rather a submitting for a good reason, to think such a thing may be, than a believing that really it is.

When we do not comprehend a thing, the best is to let it alone, for else we shall play the fool about it.

A melancholy brain will breed a miracle. As corruption breeds flies, a crazed fancy breeds miracles. It may be strange that a miracle should be done, but it is not strange that it should be believed, considering the ignorance of mankind.

As good go preach to the children in the nursery the vanity of rattles and hobby-horses, as persuade mankind of the emptiness of ceremonies and mysteries. Instead of bawling they will beat out brains; they never were, nor never will be without them. Nothing can be built upon a surer foundation than the follies of mankind.

Superstition being built upon such a lasting foundation as the folly of mankind, it will live as long as the world, let good sense say the worst it can against it.

Nothing so ill joined as a fool and a stratagem. A child and a razor are not worse coupled. They should never be left alone in a room.

Some men's eloquence is like a woman, so painted, that nothing is seen of her natural complexion. Neither flesh nor sinews; nothing but colour. A painted sound, a shining nothing, an empty abundance.

The easiness of printing has brought swarms of ill books into the world.

If no books were written but for the sake of truth, the leanest trade in a town would be that of a printer.

The world is so old that it is hard for a man to have any new thoughts.

A new thing is an old mistake; there is nothing new. The world has lived too long to admit anything that is really new; it looks new because it is either forgotten or not enough considered.

We must take the world as it is, and not be angry with God Almighty for not making it as we would have it.

To a man of sense the whole world is such a comedy, that he needs not to seek one at the playhouse. A wise man who sees so many scurvy actors, must needs incline to be as much a spectator as the circumstances of life will admit. The playhouse is but a copy of the original coxcombs that swarm in all companies.

He that has wit enough must despise the world; he that has not enough does not know how to live in it. How shall that be reconciled?

A wise man will not be discouraged by the shortness of life from pleasing himself; he looks upon life as a scurvy business, and he will slide as easily through it as he can.

APPENDIX
NOTABLE HISTORICAL JUDGEMENTS
ON HALIFAX

THE four selections in the Appendix, drawn from writers of the seventeenth, eighteenth, nineteenth, and twentieth centuries respectively, illustrate Halifax's distinctive and enigmatic character, and the central role he played in the political life of his time.

Gilbert Burnet

[Gilbert Burnet (1643–1715) was a Scottish historian and prominent Whig who became Bishop of Salisbury in 1689. A confidant of William III, Burnet also knew Halifax well. The account of Halifax's character included here is drawn from *Bishop Burnet's History of His Own Time*, the first volume of which was published, posthumously, in 1724.]

I name Sir George Saville last, because he deserves a more copious character. He rose afterwards to be Viscount, Earl, and Marquis of Halifax. He was a man of great and ready wit; full of life, and very pleasant; much turned to satire. He let his wit run much on matters of religion: so that he passed for a bold and determined atheist; though he often protested to me, he was not one; and said, he believed there was not one in the world: he confessed, he could not swallow down every thing that divines imposed on the world: he was a Christian in submission: he believed as much as he could, and he hoped that God would not lay it to his charge, if he could not digest iron, as an ostrich did, nor take into his belief things that burst him: if he had any scruples, they were not sought for, nor cherished by him; for he never read an atheistical book. These were his excuses, but I could not quite believe him, yet. In a fit of sickness, I knew him very much touched with a sense of religion. I was then often with him. He seemed full of good purposes: but they went off with his sickness. He was always talking of morality and friendship. He was punctual in all payments, and just in all his private dealings. But, with relation to the public, he went backwards and forwards, and changed sides so often, that in conclusion no side trusted him. He seemed full of commonwealth notions: yet he went into the worst part of King Charles's reign. He was out of measure vain and ambitious. The liveliness of his imagination was always too hard for his judgement. A severe jest was preferred by him to all arguments whatsoever. And he was endless in consultations: for when after much discourse a point was settled, if he could find a new jest, to make even that which was suggested by himself seem ridiculous, he could not hold, but would study to raise the credit of his wit, though it made others call his judgement in question. When he talked to me, as a philosopher, of his contempt of the world, I asked him what he meant by getting so many new titles, which I called the hanging himself about with bells and tinsel. He had no other excuse for it, but this, that, since the world were such fools as to value those matters, a man must be a fool for company: he considered them but as rattles: yet rattles please children: so these might be of use to his family. His heart was much set on raising his family. But, though he made a vast estate for them, he buried two of his sons himself, and almost all his grandchildren. The son that survived was an honest man, but far inferior to him, which appeared the more sensibly, because he affected to imitate him; but the distance was too wide.

David Hume

[The great Scottish philosopher and historian David Hume (1711–76) provides this brief and rather caustic assessment of Halifax in his celebrated *History of England*. In the first edition of the *History* (1754–7), Hume had simply noted that Halifax 'was always regarded as an intriguer rather than a patriot'; Horace Walpole pressed Hume on this matter, and the critical judgement of Halifax's contemporaries was in subsequent editions underscored by the addition of the two words, 'with reason'.]

The king [Charles II]..., who loved to maintain a balance in his councils, still supported Halifax, whom he created a marquess, and made privy seal; though ever in opposition to the Duke [of York, later James II]. This man, who possessed the finest genius and most extensive capacity, of all employed in public affairs during the present reign, affected a species of neutrality between the parties, and was esteemed the head of that small body, known by the denomination of *Trimmers*. This conduct, which is more natural to men of integrity than of ambition, could not however procure him the former character; and he was always, with reason, regarded as an intriguer rather than a patriot.

Thomas Babington Macaulay

[The historian and Whig politician Thomas Babington Macaulay (1800–59) wrote perhaps the most famous of tributes to Halifax. What follows is drawn from his multi-volume *History of England*, first published in 1848. The principal focus of the *History* is the Revolution of 1688, and in Macaulay's account, Halifax emerges as a vital and laudable figure, whose spirit helped to mould the revolution and its subsequent settlement.]

Among the statesmen of those times Halifax was, in genius, the first. His intellect was fertile, subtle, and capacious. His polished, luminous, and animated eloquence, set off by the silver tones of his voice, was the delight of the House of Lords. His conversation overflowed with thought, fancy, and wit. His political tracts well deserve to be studied for their literary merit, and fully entitle him to a place among English classics. To the weight derived from talents so great and various he united all the influence which belongs to rank and ample possessions. Yet he was less successful in politics than many who enjoyed smaller advantages. Indeed, those intellectual peculiarities which make his writings valuable frequently impeded him in the contests of active life. For he always saw passing events, not in the point of view in which they commonly appear to one who bears a part in them, but in the point of view in which, after the lapse of many years, they appear to the philosophic historian. With such a turn of mind he could not long continue to act cordially with any body of men. All the prejudices, all the exaggerations, of both the great parties in the state moved his scorn. He despised the mean arts and unreasonable clamours of demagogues. He despised still more the doctrines of divine right and passive obedience. He sneered impartially at the bigotry of the Churchman and at the bigotry of the Puritan. He was equally unable to comprehend how any man should object to Saints' days and surplices, and how any man should persecute any other man for objecting to them. In temper he was what, in our time, is called a Conservative: in theory he was a Republican. Even when his dread of anarchy and his disdain for vulgar delusions led him to side for a time with the defenders of arbitrary power, his intellect was always with Locke and Milton. Indeed, his jests upon hereditary monarchy were sometimes such as would have better become a member of the Calf's Head Club than a Privy Councillor of the Stuarts. In religion he was so far from being a zealot that he was called by the uncharitable an atheist: but this imputation he vehemently repelled; and in truth, though he sometimes gave scandal by the way in which he exerted his rare powers both of reasoning and of ridicule on serious subjects, he seems to have been by no means unsusceptible of religious impressions.

He was the chief of those politicians whom the two great parties contemptuously called Trimmers. Instead of quarrelling with this nickname, he assumed it as a title of honour, and vindicated, with great vivacity, the dignity of the appellation. Everything good, he said, trims between extremes. The temperate zone trims between the climate in which men are roasted and the climate in which they are frozen. The English Church trims between the Anabaptist madness and the Papist lethargy. The English constitution trims between Turkish despotism and Polish anarchy. Virtue is nothing but a just temper between propensities any one of which, if indulged to excess, becomes vice. Nay, the perfection of the Supreme Being himself consists in the exact equilibrium of attributes, none of which could preponderate without disturbing the whole moral and physical order of the world. Thus, Halifax was a Trimmer on principle. He was also a Trimmer by the constitution both of his head and of his heart. His understanding was keen, sceptical, inexhaustibly fertile in distinctions and objections; his taste refined; his sense of the ludicrous exquisite; his temper placid and forgiving, but fastidious, and by no means prone either to malevolence or to enthusiastic admiration. Such a man could not long be constant to any band of political allies. He must not, however, be confounded with the vulgar crowd of renegades. For though, like them, he passed from side to side, his transition was always in the direction opposite to theirs. He had nothing in common with those who fly from extreme to extreme, and who regard the party which they have deserted with an animosity far exceeding that of consistent enemies. His place was on the debatable ground between the hostile divisions of the community, and he never wandered far beyond the frontier of either. The party to which he at any moment belonged was the party which, at that moment, he liked least, because it was the party of which at that moment he had the nearest view. He was therefore always severe upon his violent associates, and was always in friendly relations with his moderate opponents. Every faction in the day of its insolent and vindictive triumph incurred his censure; and every faction, when vanquished and persecuted, found in him a protector. To his lasting honour it must be mentioned that he attempted to save those victims whose fate has left the deepest stain both on the Whig and on the Tory name.

He had greatly distinguished himself in opposition, and had thus drawn on himself the royal displeasure, which was indeed so strong that he was not admitted into the Council of Thirty without much difficulty and long altercation. As soon, however, as he had obtained a footing at court, the charms of his manner and of his conversation made him a favourite. He was seriously alarmed by the violence of the public discontent. He thought that liberty was for the present safe, and that order and legitimate authority were in danger. He therefore, as was his fashion, joined himself to the weaker side. Perhaps his conversion was not wholly disinterested. For study and reflection, though they had emancipated him from many vulgar prejudices, had left him a slave to vulgar desires. Money he did not want; and there is no evidence that he ever obtained it by any means which, in that age, even severe censors considered as dishonourable; but rank and power had strong attractions for him. He pretended, indeed, that he considered titles and great offices as baits which could allure none but fools, that he hated business, pomp, and pageantry, and that his dearest wish was to escape from the bustle and glitter of Whitehall to the quiet woods which surrounded his ancient mansion in Nottinghamshire; but his conduct was not a little at variance with his professions. In truth he wished to command the respect at once of courtiers and of philosophers, to be admired for attaining high dignities, and to be at the same time admired for despising them.

Winston Churchill

[Sir Winston Churchill (1874–1965) twice served as British prime minister (1940–5 and 1951–5). In his biography of John Churchill, 1st Duke of Marlborough—*Marlborough: His Life and Times*, published in 1933—Churchill penned a fulsome portrait of Halifax's moderate character, including the memorable line that the great Trimmer 'could strike as hard for compromise as most leaders for victory'.]

At the end of the reign we see Charles working with several representatives of this moderate Tory view. Among these, opposed to Popery, opposed to France, mildly adverse to Dissent, content with peace, and respecting the government of King *and* Parliament, the famous Halifax was pre-eminent. His nature led him to turn against excess in any quarter; he swam instinctively against the stream. The taunt of 'Trimmer' levelled at him by disappointed partisans has been accepted by history as the proof of his uprightness and sagacity. He compared himself with justice to the temperate zone which lies between 'the regions in which men are frozen and the regions in which they are roasted.' He was the foremost statesman of these times; a love of moderation and sense of the practical seemed in him to emerge in bold rather than tepid courses. He could strike as hard for compromise as most leaders for victory. Memorable were the services which Halifax had rendered to the Crown and the Duke of York. His reasoned oratory, his biting sarcasm, his personal force and proud independence, had turned the scale against the first Exclusion Bill. His wise counsels had aided the King at crucial moments, and he himself often formed the rallying-point for men of goodwill. His greatest work for the nation and for modern times was yet to be done. Meanwhile he stood, a trusted Minister, at King Charles's side in the evening of a stormy day.

EXPLANATORY NOTES

THE CHARACTER OF A TRIMMER

First circulated in manuscript in 1685, *The Character of a Trimmer* was published in 1688 and was attributed to Halifax's uncle, Sir William Coventry, but by the 1690s Halifax's authorship was realized. It was included in the posthumous *Miscellanies by the Right Noble Lord, the Late Lord Marquess of Halifax*, first published in 1700. For more on the context in which this text was written, see the Introduction, pp. xii–xv.

3 *overrun...as Egypt was with flies and locusts*: a reference to two of the plagues inflicted by God on Egypt, as described in Exodus 8:20–4 and 10:12–15.

6 *the Bench...the Bar*: the Bench refers to the judges, the Bar to the lawyers.

Westminster Hall: centre of the law courts in the seventeenth century.

7 *the ill example...provoked by their desire of revenge:* a reference to Sir Thomas Armstrong, a Rye House Plotter in 1683 who was tried in his absence and when returned to England was summarily executed.

commonwealth: a republic.

8 *Lycurgus*: the mythical lawmaker of Sparta.

9 *Nero...Vespasian*: Nero, Roman emperor from 54 to 68 CE, known for his debauched and tyrannical rule; and Vespasian, emperor from 69 to 79 CE, credited with restoring stability to Rome.

10 *'take up your bed and walk'*: Mark 2:9; John 5:8 (Jesus's words to the man sick of the palsy).

flesh of his flesh, and bone of his bone: Genesis 2:23.

11 *quod principi placuit lex esto*: (Lat.) what pleases the prince is the law.

Praetorian bands: bodyguards of the Roman emperor, instituted by Augustus.

13 *The two Czars are an example that...the world will not be proud to follow*: Czars Ivan and Peter (the Great) who ruled Russia jointly until 1696 when Peter assumed sole rule.

14 *the old one may be left to look a little out of countenance*: a reference to James, Duke of York.

15 *And as of all the orders of building the composite is the best, so ours by a wise mixture...is...the envy of our neighbours who cannot imitate it*: in architecture, the composite order of building combined Ionic and Corinthian elements; Halifax's appeal to this idea illustrates his characteristic preference for a happy mean between extremes.

18 *Triennial Act*: the law requiring elections to Parliament to be held every three years, which Charles II ignored after 1681.

any other country: almost certainly a reference to France.

a prince who could so forgive his people...in the right: a reference to the Act of Oblivion which pardoned most offences committed during the Commonwealth period.

20 *The late conspiracy*: the Rye House Plot of 1683 to assassinate Charles II and James, Duke of York, and install the Duke of Monmouth as king.

21 *prerogative declarations...to such an end*: Charles II's 1672 Declaration of Indulgence permitted Dissenters, briefly, to exercise their religion freely, until Parliament outlawed the provision.

23 *calenture*: a feverish delirium, said to affect sailors in the tropics, in which the sufferer imagines the sea to be green fields and desires to leap into them.

24 *Scotch apostles*: Covenanters.

25 *to make the better legs at court*: to make a deep bow, drawing the right leg back in the process.

26 *what has passed at other times in the world*: the Gunpowder Plot of 1605 had been the work of Catholics.

28 *those princely liberties she was sometimes disposed to*: a hint at Christina's lesbianism.

a popish Queen: Queen Mary, who reigned from 1553 to 1558.

revenge for '88: the defeat of the Spanish Armada in 1588.

the Queen of Scots: Mary Stuart, also known as Mary, Queen of Scots.

the late King: Charles I, reigned 1625–49.

29 *The Queen Mother*: Henrietta Maria of France, widow of Charles I.

the Duke of Gloucester: Henry, Duke of Gloucester, younger brother of Charles II and James II, d. 1660.

another of her sons: James, Duke of York, later James II.

30 *the indulgence promised to Dissenters at Breda*: the Declaration of Breda made before the Restoration in 1660 when Charles announced his support for religious toleration.

31 *the breach of the Triple League*: Charles broke a treaty to declare war on Holland in concert with France in 1672.

the Test to all in office: the Test Act of 1673, requiring office holders to swear an oath to the King and the Protestant Church and to deny the doctrine of transubstantiation.

it is to be hoped, in our age nothing like it will be reattempted: a reference to the Popish Plot of 1678–81.

32 *St Omers*: Jesuit seminary and college in Saint-Omer, France.

sub annulo Piscatoris: (Lat.) from the ring of the fisherman; an official part of the regalia worn by the Pope.

33 *abbey lands*: the lands sold by Henry VIII at the dissolution of the monasteries.

35 *the Gunpowder treason*: the Gunpowder Plot of 1605.

37 *Gondomar*: Diego Sarmiento de Acuña, Count of Gondomar, a Spanish diplomat who advised on relations with England.

Cromwell: Oliver Cromwell (1599–1658), Lord Protector of the Commonwealth from 1653 until 1658.

Flanders being a perpetual object in their eye: the French desire to obtain Flanders from Spain remained a goal throughout the seventeenth century.

Amboyna and the Fishery: Halifax is alluding to two sources of tension between the English and the Dutch. The Dutch massacre of English merchants on Ambon Island ('Amboyna') in 1623 was never forgotten by anti-Dutch writers; the 'Fishery' refers to disputes over herring fisheries in the North Sea.

38 *peace between the two Crowns*: the Triple Alliance of 1668.

the peace of Aix-la-Chapelle was a little after concluded: the Treaty (or 'Peace') of Aix-la-Chapelle was negotiated in May 1668.

a forced put: an action made unavoidable by circumstances.

the Duchess of Orleans: Henrietta, Charles II's sister, wife of the Duke of Orléans, brother of Louis XIV, known as Madame.

40 *what passed afterwards at Nijmegen*: the peace treaty between France and Holland.

Alost: the Belgian city of Aalst.

42 *vizard*: mask.

persecution of the poor Protestants in France: the Huguenots ejected from France following the Revocation of the Edict of Nantes in 1685.

Ratisbon: seat of the Diet of the Holy Roman Empire.

44 *kitchen yacht*: a naval provision ship, serving a grander vessel.

45 *to go out of the world like a Roman philosopher*: in other words, by taking his own life, as Seneca did.

47 *'A Trimmer is worse than a rebel'*: see the Introduction, pp. xiii–xiv, for details of Tory attacks upon the Trimmer.

48 *Leviathan*: name of a great sea monster mentioned several times in the Bible (Job 3:8 and 40:25–41:26; Psalms 74:14 and 104:26; Isaiah 27:1); also the name of Thomas Hobbes's major work of political philosophy, where Leviathan is a metaphor for the state.

Machiavelli: Niccolò Machiavelli (1469–1527), Florentine philosopher and diplomat; the term 'Machiavellian' came to signify realpolitik and political deceit.

A CHARACTER OF KING CHARLES II

First published in 1750, this account of Charles II (1630–85) was probably composed at various times during Charles's life, though it seems that it was finished after his brother's overthrow in 1688.

50 *The ill-bred familiarity . . . veneration for it*: references to Charles's time in Scotland in 1650 and in exile in France until 1654.

51 *Cardinal de Retz*: Jean François Paul de Gondi (1613–79), French churchman and an agitator against Louis XIV in the French Wars of Religion.

I conclude . . . he was as certainly a Roman Catholic: Halifax confidently states this, though it is generally accepted that Charles was formally received into the Catholic Church on his deathbed.

52 *Roman Catholics complained of his breach of promise to them very early*: Charles's Declaration of Breda in 1660 had promised religious toleration.

53 *As to his writing those papers, he might do it*: James II after Charles's death claimed to have found papers which explained his brother's conversion.

he was in a school: Halifax's attack on Charles's dissimulation was written in the knowledge that the King had signed a secret Treaty of Dover in 1670 in which Charles supported French policy in Europe and promised to convert to Catholicism in exchange for a pension from France.

54 *rooks at play*: rooks were those who cheated at card games.

56 *The last especially was quite out of the definition of an ordinary mistress*: Louise de Kéroualle, Duchess of Portsmouth.

a powerful second: Louis XIV.

57 *stans pede in uno*: (Lat.) standing on one foot; i.e. effortlessly and perhaps with too little care.

His brother: James, Duke of York.

58 *ruelle*: the space between the bed and the wall but usually referring to a lady's salon.

61 *tiendro cuydado*: a corruption of *tendre cuidado* ('I will be careful').

62 *beauté journaliere*: (Fr.) an unreliable beauty.

63 *side with the farmers against the improvement of the revenue*: Halifax had wanted Charles to reallocate the Farm of the Excise.

Plate Fleet: the annual bullion shipment from Mexico to Spain.

66 *further overturnings*: a reference to his brother's failure in 1688.

67 *Should nobody throw a stone . . . a slender shower*: an allusion to John 8:7.

THE LADY'S NEW YEAR'S GIFT:
OR, ADVICE TO A DAUGHTER

This was addressed to Lady Elizabeth Savile, Halifax's daughter, and published in January 1688 when she was 12. It was frequently reprinted. Elizabeth's husband, 3rd Earl of Chesterfield, was said to have scribbled in her copy 'wasted effort'.

68 *present growth of your understanding*: a reference to Elizabeth's young age (12).

69 *show*: probably a misprint for 'share'.

　　hanging sleeves: baby clothes.

　　babies: dolls.

70 *vizard*: mask.

71 *signposts*: inn signs.

72 *like a loose garment*: this image appears also in Halifax's 'Character of Lady Pakington', in which he wrote that 'The world hung about her like a loose garment; she truly kept herself unspotted from it' (*Works of George Savile, Marquis of Halifax* (Oxford: Clarendon Press, 1989), ed. Brown, ii. 471). Lady Dorothy Pakington (née Coventry) was Halifax's maternal aunt, and he clearly saw her as a role model for his own daughter.

76 *your husband may love wine more than is convenient*: it may be related that Elizabeth ultimately had to struggle with this problem, for her husband, Lord Stanhope, became a heavy drinker.

87 *the Line*: the equator.

89 *ruelle*: see note to p. 58.

91 *complaisance*: a word indicating compliance, graciousness, and a willingness to please, hence the ambiguity noted by Halifax.

92 *chirurgery*: surgery.

　　brokerage: the act of mediating between a buyer and a seller; in the context of this passage there are implications here of pimping.

　　admiral: flagship.

　　beat their drums for volunteers: recruit for an army.

94 *she-numps*: she-fool.

　　Bartholomew Fair: a charter fair in London, originating in 1133 and occurring yearly until 1855, after which it was banned for causing public disturbances.

95 *croupière*: feminine form of *croupier*, a person in charge of a gambling table.

99 *privateer*: a privately owned armed ship authorized for use in war, especially for the capture and pillage of commercial vessels.

104 *as Bessus was for duels*: in the Jacobean stage play *A King and No King*, by Francis Beaumont and John Fletcher, Bessus is a cowardly character who pretends to have fought many duels.

A LETTER TO A DISSENTER, UPON OCCASION OF HIS MAJESTY'S LATE GRACIOUS DECLARATION OF INDULGENCE

Written in response to James II's Declaration of Indulgence in April 1687, this pamphlet was published secretly in August 1687 and circulated among

Anglicans and Dissenters alike with the intention of warning them not to trust James's promise of toleration.

106 *exclusion and rebellion*: the Exclusion Crisis of 1679–81 and the Monmouth Rebellion of 1685 in which Protestant Dissenters were thought to have been prominent.

107 *your new friends*: the King's Catholic allies who promoted religious toleration as a feint to introduce Catholicism.

Mr Coleman's Letters: letters claimed to be written by Edward Coleman during the Popish Plot.

108 *non obstante*: shortened from *non obstante veredicto* (Lat.: 'notwithstanding the verdict'), something notwithstanding (or despite) a law or the verdict of a court.

Taunton and Tiverton: towns in Somerset and Devon that supplied the Monmouth rebels and were bywords for Dissenting communities.

a man of that persuasion... master of the ceremonies: a reference to William Penn, a Quaker close to James II.

109 *sprinkled money amongst the Dissenting ministers*: a reference to Charles II's practice of giving money to Dissenters in 1672.

If there should be men... such men are to be lamented, but not to be believed: Halifax is referring to Dissenters implicated in the Rye House Plot of 1683 and the Monmouth Rebellion of 1685 who were not punished in the hope that they would persuade other Dissenters to support James II.

110 *the addresses that fly... Another to the same*: Halifax is here alluding to the extent of the addresses written 'To the King's most excellent majesty' in the pages of the *Gazette*.

112 *This is so far... no thing could possibly be intended*: this is a reference to Halifax's sarcastic thanks in the House of Lords in November 1685 for James II's openly proposing the commissioning of Catholic officers; it was misunderstood to be a genuine proposal of thanks.

114 *to picqueer*: variant spelling of 'pickeer', meaning 'to skirmish' (compare the Italian verb *picchiare*, 'to hit').

a fray: an affray.

congé d'elire: (Fr.) the writ used to elect a bishop.

Roman consistory: formal meeting of cardinals called by the pope.

Lords of the Articles: committee carrying out much of the legislative business of the Scottish Parliament.

115 *You have formerly blamed the Church of England... for going so far as they did in their compliance*: Anglicans in the Parliaments of the 1660s, supported by the Church of England, introduced measures to try to ensure that former Anglicans who had become Dissenters were not allowed to lead public worship. These included penalties for going within 5 miles of their

former parishes and failure to use the Book of Common Prayer. These laws, which resulted in the imprisonment of Dissenting ministers, were called the 'Clarendon Code' after Lord Clarendon who proposed them.

115 *'It is impossible for a Dissenter not to be a rebel'*: because of the Civil War, the Rye House Plot, and the Monmouth Rebellion.

116 *the next heir bred…pattern of indulgence*: Princess Mary was James's daughter by his first wife and had been raised as an Anglican. She married the Protestant William of Orange (who was also James's nephew) in 1677 and lived in Holland. Until the birth of Prince James Edward to Queen Mary of Modena, it was assumed that she would eventually succeed to the throne.

receipt: recipe.

Legend: the *Golden Legend*, a collection of lives of the saints, written in the thirteenth century.

THE ANATOMY OF AN EQUIVALENT

This pamphlet was probably written in 1687 and published in 1688. The 'Equivalent' was offered by James II as legal protection for the Church of England in exchange for repeal of the Test Act which excluded all except Anglicans from holding public office.

117 *coffee-houses*: coffee-houses proliferated in London after the Restoration, and became fashionable places in which to discuss politics and current events; by twinning coffee-houses with pamphlets, Halifax is here depicting the politically excitable atmosphere of the time.

Oaths and Tests: the Test Act of 1673 required all those holding public office to take the oaths of supremacy and allegiance (declaring the King to be the only supreme governor of the land), and to declare against transubstantiation.

118 *melior conditio possidentis*: (Lat.) the onus of a claim lies on the party making it.

119 *chaffering*: haggling.

volenti non fit injuria: (Lat.) to the willing, it is not wrong.

120 *chapman*: peddler.

121 *Peter Pence*: or Peter's Pence, donations made directly to the papal treasury, a form of tax.

the value of a bodkin in Lombard Street: a bodkin is a pin; Lombard Street was the centre of banking in London.

122 *de Haeretico Comburendo*: a writ condemning heretics to burn.

126 *basilisk*: mythical reptile with a lethal gaze.

carted: paraded in a cart, the standard punishment for a prostitute.

127 *Adamite*: a medieval sect, members of which imitated Adam by going naked (hence Halifax's use of the words 'naked truth'); by Halifax's time it was a term of abuse for any enthusiastic Protestant sect, the Quakers included.

134 *a King's brother of England*: Richard, 1st Earl of Cornwall, brother of King Henry III.

distrain: confiscate or sequester.

It is the only exception to his omnipotence, that…he is incapacitated to do wrong: Halifax is here referring to one of the great puzzles of philosophical theism, namely the (perceived or real) incompatibility of divine goodness with divine omnipotence.

135 *suppose a prince…should…promise marriage to one of his subjects, and… press to take possession before the necessary forms could be complied with*: this would appear to refer to the case James II's first wife, Anne Hyde, who was pregnant when he married her in 1661.

136 *Interest is an uncertain thing…excess of zeal*: the themes contained in this paragraph are explored also in Halifax's reflections on the maxim that 'Interest will not lie' (see p. 144), and in his more general thoughts on the instability of human nature found in the selections from the *Miscellanys* and *Miscellaneous Maxims* (see pp. 222–3).

MAXIMS OF THE GREAT ALMANSOR

These maxims were sent by Halifax to friends in manuscript form in 1692 and published a year later as a broadsheet entitled *Maxims found among the Papers of the Great Almansor*. From 1700, when they appeared in the *Miscellanies*, they were usually titled *Maxims of State*.

137 *the Great Almansor*: Abu ʿĀmir Muḥammad ibn ʿAbdullāh ibn Abi ʿĀmir al-Maʿafiri (938–1002), a military leader in the Muslim conquest of Spain. The figure of Almansor captured the imagination of a number of other writers of Halifax's time, including John Dryden and Sir William Temple.

138 *That it is a gross mistake…by anybody else*: maxims 14 and 15 may refer to Lord Sunderland who was minister under James II and returned to favour under William III.

freebooters: pirates.

A ROUGH DRAUGHT OF A NEW MODEL AT SEA

Published anonymously in May 1694, and subsequently included in the *Miscellanies* of 1700, this work ostensibly treats of the social composition of the naval officer class, though that question operates largely as a pretext for Halifax to explicate one of his core themes, namely the desirability of a mixed monarchy as a mean between an absolute monarchy and a commonwealth. Having teased the reader with the promise of offering suitable probationary qualifications for naval officers, Halifax at the very end of *Rough Draught* suddenly withdraws, citing as reasons for his retraction his non-parliamentary standing (as a 'man without doors') and the unacceptable presumption of setting his 'slender stock of reason' against 'the supreme wisdom of the nation'.

140 *'Martha, Martha...one thing is necessary'*: Luke 10:41–2.

141 *tarpaulins*: officers drawn from the ranks of enlisted sailors, whose experience and skill had resulted in promotion to a commanding position; tensions existed between the 'gentlemen officers' and these men of the lower classes.

generals: generalizations.

142 *positive*: theoretical, not subject to conditions.

144 *'Interest will not lie'*: seventeenth-century maxim, proclaiming the centrality of human designs and concerns in the understanding of social and political conduct. Halifax's doubts concerning the truth of this maxim are consistent with his scepticism towards the transparency of human motivation. Human beings are not the best experts on their own interests or their own reasons, and so the maxim about interest could only be applicable to creatures made of 'new clay', not to human beings as they actually are.

147 *the men of Wapping*: working sailors; Wapping was the principal dock area of London.

149 *man without doors*: not a Member of Parliament (MP).

SOME CAUTIONS OFFERED TO THE CONSIDERATION
OF THOSE WHO ARE TO CHOOSE MEMBERS
TO SERVE IN THE NEXT PARLIAMENT

This pamphlet was first circulated, anonymously, in 1694, and was ascribed to Halifax when it appeared in the *Miscellanies* of 1700. The motivation for its composition was the prospect of a general election in the autumn of 1695, and in its sharply worded twenty sections Halifax describes a range of types unsuitable to be elected to the House of Commons. There are a number of significant differences between the original circulated manuscript and later editions; where useful, details from the later editions have here been incorporated.

150 *their picture*: i.e. their representatives.

151 *Muscovites have...to St Nicholas*: a reference to a Russian burial custom, in which something akin to a letter of recommendation was placed in the hand of the corpse; this would be addressed to St Nicholas, as chief mediator.

152 *in a house where there were so many officers*: there were so many army officers in the Parliament of 1690–5 that it became known as the Officers' Parliament.

ride the wooden horse for it: 'to ride the wooden horse' was a method of torture in which the victim was made to straddle the sharp cross plank of a triangular 'horse', weights added to the victim's legs so as to increase the downward pressure and accordingly the agony. The imagery of torture is removed in later versions of *Some Cautions*, and replaced with a less physical form of punishment: 'the penalty had not been improper to have cashiered them for not appearing at the general muster'.

154 *like paying great fines…the constant rent*: the cost of leased land was divided between an entry 'fine' and annual rent.

Solon: Athenian statesman and lawmaker (*c.*630–*c.*560 BCE).

lawful to kill a magistrate if he was found drunk: see Jean Bodin, *Six Books of the Commonwealth* (1576), bk. iii, ch. 5: 'By a provision in his laws Solon allowed the magistrate who was drunk in the exercise of his duties to be put to death.'

Wanting: needy.

155 *There is a subordinate wit…sound of an organ*: a variant version of this sentence appears in later editions: 'There is a subordinate wit, as much inferior to a wit of business as a fiddler at a wake is to the lofty sound of an organ.'

156 *quoad hoc*: (Lat.) with respect to this matter.

quoad hanc: (Lat.) with respect to this woman.

157 *age of 21*: Sir Edward Coke, in the *Institutes of the Laws of England* (1628–44) (pt. IV, ch. i, p. 47), declared that no one under the age of 21 should be eligible for election to Parliament.

severity of wardships: Halifax's own childhood experience at the hands of Lord Wharton may have contributed to this judgement.

triers: a trier is one who examines judicially; also a Dissenter who listened to sermons to see if the preacher was good enough to be invited to come to their meeting house.

leading strings: narrow pieces of fabric used to support a child learning to walk.

the best school for young men: a reference to William Prynne's 1646 pamphlet *Minors No Senators*, in which Prynne criticized the opinion that young gentleman from eminent families should be MPs, 'it being the best School of Experience'.

158 *green geese that are said to have saved the Capitol*: see Livy, *The History of Rome*, bk. v, chs. 47–9.

long continued parliaments: Charles II's Long Parliament lasted from May 1661 to January 1679.

carpet-knights: a carpet-knight was one who had never known the battlefield, distinguishing himself only at table or in the boudoir; an idler.

159 *falling out about privilege*: parliamentary privilege protected members against prosecution for debt.

159 *the 4th of Ed. 3*: the fourth year of the reign of Edward III.

maintenance: unauthorized interference in a legal action.

as if the benches in Westminster Hall…out of Newgate: once the most notorious of London's prisons, Newgate was commissioned during the reign of Henry II in the twelfth century and remained in use until 1902. Halifax's point is that if breakers of the law were in Parliament, it would be as though the country's lawmakers were convicted criminals.

160 *ex vicineto*: (Lat.) of the neighbourhood.

161 *choosing valentines*: valentines were chosen by lot.

a man of the Robe: a barrister.

practising lawyers have been excluded from serving in Parliament: this was the case under the reign of Edward III.

162 *having their robes lined with fur*: i.e. becoming judges.

163 *the true lasting fire, like that of the vestals which never went out*: the sacred eternal flame at the Temple of Vesta in Rome, tended by vestal virgins.

There are some splenetic gentlemen…would leave behind them: Halifax is here mocking those who had sought to incriminate him in the executions of the Whig leaders of the Rye House Plot. The sarcastic reference to 'the disadvantage of being *now* alive' would seem to be directed against John Hampden the Younger (1656–96), who had declared to a special committee of the House of Lords that he had himself been murdered as much as those executed. Of this testimony, Halifax wrote: 'His next business was to give evidence that he was dead; and really he had almost persuaded me into it, for from a living man I never heard such evidence' (see *Works*, ed. Brown, i. 333).

165 *It is not less strange…a little more modest*: in this paragraph, the words 'with all her wrinkles' appeared in later editions, though not in the original pamphlet.

166 *Newmarket*: racecourse, founded in 1636.

steenkirks: fashionable cravats named after the Battle of Steenkirk, August 1692.

167 *bons vivants*: (Fr.) individuals fond of good living.

168 *We are told…to carry on elections*: this occurred in 1554.

no man should serve two masters: Matthew 6:24; Luke 16:13.

'Self-denying Bill': this bill, the aim of which was to exclude office holders from Parliament, was passed by the Commons in December 1692 but rejected by the Lords in January 1693. It was reintroduced and passed in both Houses in November 1693.

169 *Triennial Bill*: a bill requiring elections every three years passed both Houses in January 1693, but was vetoed by William III.

call it by its right name: i.e. bribery or corruption.

it is not dead, but sleeps: Matthew 9:24; Mark 5:39; Luke 8:52.

THE GOVERNMENT OF THE WORLD

This short piece, probably written sometime between 1690 and 1695, remained unpublished until 1989, when it appeared in Mark N. Brown's three-volume edition of Halifax's complete works.

170 *You set me a task*: the essay is a response to a question, from an unnamed correspondent, as to why the world has generally been so badly governed.

All Mr Prynne's volumes: William Prynne (1600–69), Puritan lawyer and highly prolific pamphleteer.

leading strings: see note to p. 157.

171 *so that the rulers . . . for being such logs, &c.*: this sentiment is worth comparing with Halifax's maxim in *Political Thoughts and Reflections*: 'For most men, to be well governed, must be scurvily used' (p. 180). See also *A Character of King Charles II*: 'If princes are under the misfortune of being accused to govern ill, their subjects have the less right to fall hard upon them, since they generally so little deserve to be governed well' (p. 67).

POLITICAL THOUGHTS AND REFLECTIONS

This set of *Political Thoughts and Reflections* (along with two others: *Moral* and *Miscellaneous*) was first published, together with *A Character of King Charles II*, in 1750. Halifax's granddaughter, the Countess of Burlington, oversaw their publication, and the selection was drawn and ordered by Alexander Pope. It is possible that Lady Burlington made further adjustments after Pope's death in 1744.

172 *councils*: Councils of the Church.

173 *the Senate of Venice . . . according to a proclamation*: see Jean Bodin, *Six Books of the Commonwealth* (1576), bk. i, ch. 4.

Salus Populi: Salus populi suprema lex: (Lat.) the health (or welfare, safety) of the people should be the supreme law. This principle, stated in Cicero's *De Legibus* (bk. iii, sect. 8), was used by John Locke as the epigraph for his *Two Treatises of Government* (1689).

malitia supplet ætatem: (Lat.) malice makes up for want of age.

174 *Frequent punishments made the people call even his justice cruelty*: a paraphrase of Tacitus' *Annals*, bk. xv, ch. 44.

backed: mounted, as a horse is mounted.

175 *Magna Carta would fain . . . fundamental laws of England*: the jurist Sir Edward Coke (1552–1634) held that the Magna Carta ('Great Charter') of 1215 was 'for the most part declaratory of the principal grounds of the fundamental Laws of England' (*Institutes of the Laws of England* (1628–44), pt. II, proem).

175 *Common Law*: the body of law created by judicial ruling and precedent rather than statute.

182 *felo de se*: suicide.

   basilisk: see note to p. 126.

   Petition of Right: the Petition of Right of 1628 sought recognition of four principles: no taxation without the consent of Parliament, no imprisonment without cause, no billeting of troops on civilian households, and no martial law in peacetime.

   Prerogative never yet pretended to repealing: this would appear be directed against James II, whose claimed powers of suspending laws approximated to repealing.

187 *a place*: public office or employment.

   a creature: i.e. one created, a person dependent upon a patron.

188 *a revolution*: Halifax may mean here the Revolution of 1688 or simply any changed political situation.

   'Accumulative' in that case...no sense in it: an allusion to the Earl of Strafford's defence in his impeachment trial. Strafford argued against the doctrine of accumulation, whereby a large number of actions, none of which were individually treasonable, might—by accumulation—amount to treason.

MORAL THOUGHTS AND REFLECTIONS

Like the *Political Thoughts and Reflections*, and under the same publication conditions, this set of remarks first appeared in 1750.

190 *business*: politics (public business).

191 *wit*: intelligence.

   Bank of England: the Bank of England was established in July 1694. Halifax strongly opposed its creation.

192 *There are five orders...the composite order*: the five classical orders of architecture ('building') were the Doric, Ionic, Corinthian, Tuscan, and Composite.

   Statute of Stabbing: parliamentary Act introduced during the reign of James I (1 Jac 1 c 8). Under its terms, stabbing became a capital offence if the person stabbed had not drawn any weapon and died within six months of their injury. It was repealed in 1828.

194 *end*: purpose.

   Hope is generally...by the way: compare La Rochefoucauld: 'Hope, utterly deceptive though she is, at least leads us to life's end by an attractive route' (*Maxims*, no. 168).

The hopes of a fool are blind guides: Matthew 23:16, 24.

198 *a pied coat*: a coat that is variegated or covered with patches.

   a limbeck: a still.

199 *Present*: immediate.

MISCELLANEOUS THOUGHTS AND REFLECTIONS

This was the third of the three sets of *Thoughts and Reflections* first published in 1750 alongside *A Character of King Charles II*.

201 *rule of doing as we would be done by*: Matthew 7:12; Luke 6:31.

205 *commanded not to covet*: Exodus 20:17.

208 '*Such is his Majesty's . . . call for the same*': a quotation from 'Certain Articles and Injunctions given by the Kings Highness to his right Trusty and right entirely beloved Cousen and Counsellor, the Duke of Norfolk, whom with certain others in his company, His Majesty sendeth to the Lady Mary his Daughter, for the Purposes ensuing' (1536).

210 *second*: the second in a duel, one who supported the duellist.

211 *clipper*: one who debases coin by cutting (definition from Samuel Johnson's 1755 *Dictionary of the English Language*).

SELECTIONS FROM THE *MISCELLANYS* AND *MISCELLANEOUS MAXIMS*

The three sets of Thoughts and Reflections (*Political*, *Moral*, and *Miscellaneous*) that first appeared in 1750 represented only a very small sampling of Halifax's voluminous maxims. The complete extant maxims were first published in the 1989 edition of Halifax's *Works*. Presented here is a new selection which reveals the depth and distinctiveness of Halifax's thought, particularly as it pertains to such philosophical questions as the continued identity of the human person, the relation of virtue and vice, the frailty of human nature, the battle between reason and passion, and humanity's preoccupation with death and time. Fragmentary in their original form, this selection, from the *Miscellanys* and *Miscellaneous Maxims* of volume iii of the Brown edition, has been ordered and arranged by the present editors.

219 *Diogenes*: Greek philosopher (d. 323 BCE), one of the founders of Cynicism; the allusion is to Diogenes' act of carrying a lantern during the day, claiming to be looking for an honest man.

220 *That war which never yet had a truce . . . will be eternal*: compare Pascal in *Pensées* (no. 412): 'There is internal war in man between reason and the passions. If he had only reason without passions . . . If he had only passions

without reason…But having both he cannot be without strife, being unable to be at peace with the one without being at war with the other. Thus he is always divided against and opposed to himself.'

221 *The heart has thoughts…gets the better of it*: compare La Rochefoucauld, *Maxims*, no. 102: 'The mind is always deceived by the heart.'

222 *There is hardly a virtue… They are twisted, &c.*: compare La Rochefoucauld, *Maxims*, no. 182: 'Vices have a place in the composition of virtues, as poisons have a place in the compositions of medicines. Prudence gathers them and tempers them, and puts them to good use against the ills of life.'

223 *Every man's name is legion*: Mark 5:9; Luke 8:30.